Bradley Nathanson

AMERICAN

DEPARTURES

THE CURIOUS PLIGHT OF A UNIQUELY PRIVILEGED QUIETLY DESPERATE BABY BOOMER

Published in the United States by Fineline Publishing,
An imprint of Airtime Entertainment Corp, New York
www.finelinepublishing.com

Library of Congress Cataloging-in-Publication Data

Nathanson, Bradley
American Departures: The Curious Plight of a Uniquely
Privileged, Quietly Desperate Baby Boomer
[B} LCCN: 2007903483

ISBN-13: 978-0-9794031-7-0
ISBN-10: 0-9794031-7-0

PRINTED IN THE UNITED STATES OF AMERICA
FIRST EDITION

For John and Virginia,
Valerie, John and Emily

A jumbo cats-eye marble
Blue
Speeds across the kitchen floor
Under the refrigerator monster
Clumps of dust and darkness
The jumbo marble is no more.

LOST

FOR THE RECORD, I am not a miserable person. Nor did I plan, scheme, wish, or hope ever to be one in my lifetime – ever. Yet somehow, this afternoon, as I sit in my tastefully decorated living room, gazing through my bay window at the whimsical dance of light on falling snow, I am miserable.

My son is in the basement taking a guitar lesson. The muffled rumble of some newly acquired riff rises through the floorboards like a bird taking flight. It sounds surprisingly good. I am proud of my son, and I am still miserable. Curious, because I have been living with this feeling for a long time, and I can't remember how it first began.

My daughter ambles through the living room. She looks lovely. Wearing a bright smile, she plies me sweetly with a delicious kiss before skipping upstairs to her bedroom. Why do I feel miserable? What is wrong with me?!

My beautiful wife is still at work. She will remain there long after dinner has been prepared, the dishes have been cleared, the kids are snug in my bed for an hour or so of reading, the dog arrives, and we finally fall asleep in a generous pile of down pillows and blankets, and fur. When my wife arrives she rouses me and we steer our sleeping kids to their own beds - something they will have no recollection of in the morning. After this, my wife slips into her pajamas. She is asleep in less than five minutes.

At this moment in time, I am happy. I have made it through another day. Everyone I love is under one roof again, safe. But I know, after a few restless hours, I will be fully awake, feeling my way downstairs in the dark, rummaging through the fridge for something comforting to eat, and flipping through a plethora of bad television programming with the sound barely audible. This is my nightly ritual. It has been this way for so long, I am not sure whether I hate it, or have grown to love it.

The dog will join me for awhile, on the lookout for a generous handout, no doubt, (I rarely disappoint him), but, in time, even he will head back to bed, where any sane human being (or dog, for that matter) should be at three or four in the morning. With any luck, I will join him before sunrise, and sleep for two or three hours when the house begins to stir; the kids pack off to school, my wife leaves for work, and I am alone to live yet another day of misery. I wonder why I am so miserable, and I realize it's because I feel lost. I desperately need to find myself; and it's getting late.

To make matters worse, I have recently been diagnosed with a disease called Avascular Necrosis. It is a rare degenerative bone disease which afflicts about ten thousand people, between the ages of 30 and 50, each year. It strikes for unknown reasons, although some doctors have their own theories. My theory is that it is a result of running. I have always had a passion for running, and have been running four to five miles almost every day for the past thirty years. Suddenly, I can barely walk and need a total hip replacement. I am scheduled to have surgery in about six weeks.

A total hip replacement is no small matter. Regardless of how many times the doctor has told me not to worry, that "the procedure is performed thousands of times a day in this country," I do not feel any greater relief about my fate. The doctor reassures me he has patients who ski following this type of surgery (although not black diamonds), and yet this does little to assuage my increasing fear and reluctance.

I show my wife a document I recently received in the mail. It is a cautionary note from the surgeon's office containing a list of activities which, following the installation of my porcelain and titanium hip, would be "off limits" for the *rest of my life*. This does not sit well with me. I am too young to be told what I can or cannot do for "the rest of my life." I am repulsed by the permanence of this language. I remember, several years ago, when I created a scene in the office of my primary care physician when he advised me to take Lipitor to lower my cholesterol. He pushed the prescription for a three-month supply across his desk and casually instructed me to take one pill every morning.

"How long do I need to take this stuff?" I protested.

"Forever," he replied, nonchalantly.

"Forever…? What do you mean, forever?" I heard my voice rising. "Are you telling me I have to take a pill for the rest of my life?" I sounded almost hysterical.

"Is there a problem?" asked my doctor, brightly.

"I can't take a pill every day for the rest of my life!"

"Why?" he said, calmly. "How long are you going to live?"

My doctor had a point. The rest of my life, in the grand scheme of things, is not very long. Taking a pill every day for, say, 40 years, may be a lot of pills (14,600 to be exact), but it's not a lot of years.

Because I am a reasonable person, I have surrendered to swallowing that tiny pill every day, forever, to reduce my odds of an untimely death. I owe it, at least, to my family. But this business with the hip is considerably more difficult to swallow.

I reviewed the list of restrictions for patients with artificial hips (and what I think of them). It says:

DO NOT:
- Lift anything over thirty pounds. *(Ridiculous. My toothbrush weighs more than that fully loaded. Can I negotiate this up to fifty pounds?)*
- Play singles tennis. *(I can't play singles tennis anyway. Difference is, now I can't play singles tennis off the court.)*
- Jump, skip or run. *(So I guess hopscotch is out. Anyone for a game of Jacks?)*
- Walk more than three miles a day. *(Then, when my new digital pedometer reads 2.9 miles, I suppose I'll just stop what I'm doing and hail a cab.)*

It is not my intention to whine, but I cannot be happy living a life in which I am anything other than completely self-sufficient. I like to do things myself, and am too young to be soliciting help when buying, for example, a forty-pound bag of dog kibble at the local pet store. I can also say, positively, that if I had been hampered with the above mentioned physical limitations at any time in my life prior to today, I most certainly would have ended up prematurely dead for lack of exercise, with or without the added life saving benefit of Lipitor.

I have my own questions for the hip surgeon, and arrange to meet him in his office, one last time prior to my surgery. My wife accompanies me to the appointment.

"What about running? It's always been my favorite aerobic activity." I say, pointing to item number one his list of "no, no's."

"No running," the doctor says, as if I were blind. Already he seems annoyed with me since "no running" is clearly first on the list.

"I can't run, ever?" I cringe.

"No running. What is not clear? You simply CAN NOT run anymore, ever."

"Not even a little? That's impossible," I protest, "I'm too young."

"Not even a little, unless you want to end up back in the hospital." Now the surgeon is obviously perturbed.

"I have a problem with this," I protest again, more passionately this time.

My wife, clearly worried that if I piss-off the doctor any more, he might throw me out of his office, or worse, vindictively sew a sponge into my pelvis during the operation, resolves to silence me.

"Why is running so important to you all of a sudden?" she blurts out, siding with the doctor. "You're being ridiculous."

Feeling attacked from both sides, I am now the one losing patience. Still, I remain calm and try a different approach.

"What if I'm late and need to catch a train?" I ask, triumphantly.

"You catch the next one," the doctor suggests, fielding my clever question.

I try a different tack. "What if I'm being chased?" I ask. My wife jumps in. "What's wrong with you?" she says. "No one is going to chase you. You've never been chased in your life!" she adds, with great satisfaction. But she is wrong. In fact, I had been chased, many times throughout my life. And I will probably be chased again.

I was through arguing. It was pointless telling a guy like me I can't run again for the rest of my life; not while I still have a leg to stand on, anyway. Running has always been a part of me. I run to keep fit and strengthen my heart. I dash for baseballs and footballs and Frisbees. I sprint for the thrill of the wind in my face. I race against the swiftly rolling surf at the beach. I run for the rush of it. I run to live.

So, you see, it's not that simple. Yet, it appears I won't be running anytime soon. This is sad. And yet, pain and time, it seems, are two big motivators; particularly when you have too much pain, and too little time. Either one will do the trick. This is why I am, at once, miserable and happy. It's an odd combination, but it works; that is, if trying to understand where you got lost, and writing a book about it in an attempt to find yourself again, is how you want to spend the next several years of your life. And so, rather than stagnate around the house, steeped in self pity for a life unlived, and languishing in squalor, I have set out to write this book. I have come to regard it as my destiny. And so, for the next few years, I will stop running and write.

In six weeks I will be splayed nude across an operating table at the mercy of a knife-wielding surgeon. My left hip will be replaced with a new type of prosthetic device made of titanium and porcelain, used extensively in Europe. My porcelain hip is designed to last fifteen, possibly even twenty years, but since the materials are so new, and research goes back only so far, I will have to wait and see about the ultimate lifespan of my new hip. Who knows? It may outlive me.

There are several complications associated with the prosthesis. There is a tendency for the hip to become dislocated, and there have been cases where the porcelain surfaces have cracked. A crack requires emergency surgery, but I dread either of these things happening to me. I do, however, enjoy the idea of having a European hip. Presumably, this means my hip can drink plenty of wine, smoke, and eat a lot of cheese and pate (two personal favorites), without my suffering any ill effects. I could paint a thin mustache on my hip, throw on a beret, and, voila, it's a very hip, hip.

Writing "American Departures" is my attempt to revisit some of the most emotional and memorable moments of my life – the life of someone born in the stormy eye of the baby boom generation, where childhood came easy, and growing up was hard to do. Baby boomers share a singular window in history. Although there are some variations in our collective experience – namely, when we were dropped on the planet, whoever dropped us, and where we were dropped - we are all essentially the same.

If you read on, (and I hope you do), you will learn about some of the really dumb things I have done in the past, most of which I am not proud of. While I have approached the task of writing this manuscript with honesty and humility, I would be remiss if I did not at least question whether this endeavor was not the most recent of those dumb things. Odds are it will never attract the interest of a publisher. So, if you are reading this now, odds are that I have printed, autographed, and shipped you a complimentary hardcover copy, at my own expense, because you are either extremely intelligent, or a friend, or a friend of a friend, or some combination of each. If this is the case, I ask nothing in return except your reading pleasure, although any honest reaction would be greatly appreciated.

I don't know why things turned out the way they did, but I can tell you what happened. There's a story inside these pages, and a boarding pass with your name on it. The sky is clear. There's a good tail wind. It's time to fly.

BOOK ONE

Innocence

LIFE AND DEATH

I HAD ASKED my mother for an open casket. This is not traditionally something that happens at a Jewish funeral, but my mother, being born Episcopalian, agreed without hesitation. At the moment, religious customs hardly seemed very important. All I knew was I needed to say goodbye to my father, and this meant seeing him one last time.

As I peer down at him I'm thinking how magnificent he looks, even in death. His suit is immaculately crisp and tidy, his hair neatly combed back (not a strand out of place), and his smooth receding hairline (the one resembling mine today) shines. I notice a hint of clear polish on his fingernails; it is as if he had told the mortician exactly what to do. My father is lying on his back with his hands folded across his chest. I want to touch him. His thick Russian eyebrows, white like his hair, had not lost their spring or resilience. But there is no life, no animation, no sign of the charismatic twinkle in his eye, no sight of the shiny gold molar he revealed whenever his half-smile would bloom into a full blown grin. This is not my father, I thought. *This is not my father.*

I search his sleeping eyes, hoping to see even the slightest movement behind the lids, so that I might, in the next moment, mount a chair and announce to everyone present that this is all a terrible mistake; that everyone should go home and resume their normal lives – most would do that, anyway. For me (and I was too young to realize it at the time), life would never be normal again. I took my cue from my mother, and thought I would be okay. She was wired for survival. Even though she loved my father with all her heart, her overriding signal to me and my brother was: life goes on.

* * *

WHEN I WAS BORN, my mother was 42, and my father was 54. Those were unlikely childrearing ages in 1955, and my father, whose hair had been snow white since his early twenties, was oftentimes mistaken for someone else. My mother tells the story of how on Sunday mornings, as spring approached, and if the weather was good, my father would bundle me up in my blue baby blanket, strap me in my carriage, and we'd stroll up and down Broadway for hours. Passersby would often pause to admire my angelic features, and my father would invariably hear the same remark: "What a beautiful *grandson* you have." He always got a big kick out of this, but never revealed the truth. He'd simply smile and say, "Thank you."

But our fun in the city was short-lived. I was barely two months old when my parents joined the great exodus to the suburbs. We settled on the north shore of Long Island in the town of Great Neck, seventeen miles east of Manhattan. My father had to adjust to a new way of commuting to work. He no longer taxied fifty city blocks to his showroom each morning. Instead, he took a bus to the Great Neck station, and the Long Island Railroad took care of the rest. The express train was nineteen minutes to Penn Station, which gave my father just enough time to read the New York Times cover to cover. His return commute was somewhat different; he read the Daily News, and my mother would meet him at the station to drive him home. He always caught the same train; the 4:22, which arrived in Great Neck at 4:41.

If my father was running late in the morning and didn't have time to wait for the bus, my mother would drive him to the station. Oftentimes, I would go along for the ride. Every time my father was about to exit the car, my parents exchanged three short kisses. It was their little ritual. One morning, as I watched my father walk down the stairs leading to the platform for the train, I asked my mother "Why?" She said the three kisses meant this: "Goodbye, God bless you, I love you." I smiled; glad my parents were deeply in love. And as my mother drove away, she hummed a breezy tune all the way home.

Happiness in our household was the norm. My parents rarely disagreed, and when they did there were never any displays of hysterics. As I recall, my parents created an atmosphere which was virtually without stress, and I grew up surrounded by unconditional love. Everything felt safe and in good order. It never occurred to me that my parents didn't participate in many of the family activities my friends enjoyed with their parents: we didn't ski, golf, play tennis, or go hiking in the woods together. I think I played catch with my father only a handful of times, and remember him coming to just one of my Little League games. My first trip to Yankee Stadium – a game I will always remember (the Yankees beat the Cleveland Indians 10 to 6) – I was the guest of my neighbor's father; my father was not present. But I rarely gave much thought to these things, or the fact that my parents were roughly the same age as my friend's grandparents. In almost every respect life felt good, either in spite of the unorthodox circumstances into which I was born, or because of them.

GIBSON GIRL

AT THE TURN of the 20ᵀᴴ century, the American public was displaying a robust appetite for coffee, tea, and spices. Frank Gibson, a Nebraska farmer hoping to start a family with his wife Dora, decided to capitalize on the trend and established the Gibson Tea & Spice Company in the town of Omaha where they lived. Both the family and the business thrived, even through the Great Depression. "When it hit," Frank often asserted, "we barely felt it."

Born May 17ᵀᴴ, 1913, Virginia was Frank and Dora's second youngest of four children. The eldest sibling, Irene, was thirteen years her senior. Her brother Howard was a professional aviator; pilot, flight instructor, and occasional barnstormer. Once, on a perfect day for flying, Howard sat in the cockpit beside a new student, buzzing along at five-thousand feet above the ground. The student was soloing nicely, but then something went wrong. Perhaps the student panicked and froze at the control stick, and Howard was unable to wrestle it away. We'll never know for sure, but the biplane spiraled to earth, exploding in a cornfield as Virginia watched from the ground. The two perished. Howard was only 34.

Virginia also had a baby sister. Picnicking one summer afternoon, the Gibson family suddenly found themselves caught in the vortex of a violent thunderstorm. There was a blinding flash, and the huge oak tree under which they were huddled cracked wide open. The tree fell on Dora as she clung to her baby, pinning them both to the ground. Dora suffered several broken bones. The baby did not survive.

Virginia continued to thrive despite these family tragedies. As a child, Virginia demonstrated a remarkable talent for dance, and her parents treated her to ballet lessons. By the time she reached junior high, she had added singing to her passions. Before graduating high school, she began teaching ballet, giving voice lessons, and dreaming of a life in show business.

Frank roasted his own coffee beans; something he did twice a week. He fired up huge copper roasters which infused the entire town with the smell of fresh coffee. Virginia's schoolmates would often tease her as the aroma wafted through the open classroom windows, "Your dad's roasting again, Ginny," and they'd all laugh as though intoxicated from the air they were breathing.

On the day Virginia turned 19, she announced to her parents that she was moving to New York to follow her passion for performing. Dora supported the move. Frank adamantly objected. Ultimately, Virginia and Dora moved to New York together, leaving the rest of the family behind. It wasn't long before Virginia's talents were discovered. She found a manager whom she admired. His name was George Libby. George helped her develop an act, and then entrenched her in the frenetic ranks of the vaudeville circuit. She was always in demand and doing what she loved most. Virginia shared the stage with legends such as Jack Benny, Bud Abbott, Lou Costello, and Milton Berle. She played every Big House in every major city in the country. She traveled by train, bus, and automobile. She traveled with her own orchestra. She had an ardent admirer who often appeared at her Chicago engagements. His name was Al Capone.

JOHN

JOHN, SON OF OSIAS, grew up in New York City. Following the Great Depression, and seeking to capitalize on a growing trend in fashion, Osias established the Nathanson Dress Company. He designed and manufactured elegant beaded evening gowns and sequined cocktail dresses. John grew up in his father's business, assuming a major role with the company after returning from active duty in World War II where he served as a gunner in Europe.

The Nathanson Dress Company enjoyed considerable success at a time when the cocktail dress was the customary means for a sophisticated woman to accessorize her dry martini. When John "worked" the showroom, he was in his element. He presented himself in refined custom suits, always with a pressed linen handkerchief tucked into his breast pocket. His shirts were made of select cotton, and monogrammed at the cuff. He smoked unfiltered Pall Malls in the soft, dark burgundy pack. His coif of hair, elegantly white and combed back, was carefully groomed, yet long enough to form a stylish wave above his ears. He liked his fingernails professionally manicured, finished off with a layer of clear polish.

Literally and figuratively, John was perfectly suited to the dress business. He excelled at it, and enjoyed the interaction. He was also charming and gregarious by nature; his personality tended to exert a gravitational pull on those who entered his orbit. Oftentimes his professional relationships with importers, wholesalers, manufacturers, and buyers evolved into personal friendships. And he was always surrounded by beautiful women who worked as models in his showroom.

Probably the most *famous* of John's creations was the evening gown Bess Meyerson wore on stage in the 1945 Miss America Pageant. Meyerson captured the title that night, and it's likely the gown had something to do with it. But the most *significant* of John's creations was the evening gown Virginia Gibson wore on stage in 1945, the night she appeared at the Copacabana in New York City. That evening, the dressmaker captured the heart of the singer, and it's likely the gown had something to do with it. The incident played like a scene from a classic Hollywood movie:

* * *

FADE IN:

EXT. ESTABLISHING SHOT - COPACABANA – NIGHT
Super TITLE: "New York City, 1945"

The War is over. No one can escape the heightened energy that pervades the streets of Manhattan. Sailors making a scheduled stop on their return to the States, take advantage of an overnight lay-over. The streets are jammed with taxis. Sidewalks undulate with waves of jubilant city goers. Everyone, it seems, is in the mood to celebrate New York City nightlife.

CUT TO:

INT. COPACABANA – NIGHT

The club is filled to capacity. On stage, a BIG BAND delivers lively music as an army of waiters in white coats serve martinis on SILVER TRAYS. Men and women in fancy attire fill the room with copious amounts of conversation, laughter, and tobacco smoke.

JOHN NATHANSON and ARTHUR SMALL sit at a table near the stage. A WAITER arrives holding a TELEPHONE.

WAITER
Mr. Nathanson, Sir?

JOHN
I'll take that. Thanks.

John looks immaculate in his white dinner jacket, monogrammed shirt, and black bow tie; a look heightened by his shock of snow-white hair, each strand perfectly in place.

> JOHN
> (into the phone)
> Yeah. Listen, Susie, I'm with Arthur and I can't see any buyers tonight. I'll start as early as they want Monday. Okay? You're a sweetheart.

John returns the phone to the waiter.

> ARTHUR
> She wants to meet you... after the show.

> JOHN
> What? Who wants to meet me?

> ARTHUR
> Miss Gibson. She was quite insistent that I introduce her to the man who designed her gown.

> JOHN
> Is that so? Alright... ask her to join us for cocktails. But I don't want to talk business. Tonight we relax and have fun. That was our agreement.

> ARTHUR
> You have my word on it.

A hush fills the room as the EMCEE steps up to a large, round, MICROPHONE.

> EMCEE
> Ladies and Gentlemen... It is with great pleasure

that I introduce to you tonight our featured performer. She has played every BigTime theater, and
shared the vaudeville stage with Burns & Allen,
Jack Benny, Eddie Cantor, and Abbot & Costello.
We're delighted to have her here tonight for the
second time... Please give a warm New York City
welcome to Miss Virginia Gibson.

Radiant and smiling, VIRGINIA approaches the microphone to the
cheers and applause of the eager crowd. She wears a stunning, tailored
satin EVENING GOWN adorned with gold and blue sequins. She
seems to embody the very definition of glamour. Her hair is golden;
wavy, a single curl over her forehead. She is radiant, magical. Already
this is more than the audience expected, and the room goes still.

ARTHUR
(whispering)
It's her last night in New York, then...

John lifts his hand to block the sound of Arthur's voice.

JOHN
Shh...

Virginia signals her CONDUCTOR, who leads the orchestra in a
mellifluous rendition of "Smoke Gets in Your Eyes." She sings in a
voice as smooth as her fine satin dress.

VIRGINIA
(singing)
They asked me how I knew,
My true love was true,
I of course replied, something here inside,
Cannot be denied...

At the moment John is elsewhere, transported by the hypnotic beauty on stage and the soothing tone of her voice, the likes of which he has never heard before.

JOHN
I could design a world of dresses for her.

In the spotlight, Virginia appears to be singing only to him. Perhaps she is...

SMASH CUT TO:

* * *

WHEN MY PARENTS MET, my mother was married to the spotlight and looked after her mother, Dora. My father was married to another woman, and looked after a teenage daughter. But John and Virginia quickly developed a fierce attraction, and romance would not be denied. My mother left show business, my father left his wife, and the couple took off for exotic places around the globe, sharing a magic known only to those who have been deeply in love.

I recently discovered a shoebox at the bottom of a cabinet in my mother's apartment. It contained several reels of home movies taken by my father. They were neatly tucked into small Kodak boxes, faded yellow and fragile over time, and labeled with dates penned on strips of scotch tape. The tape had become brittle, like delicate fragments of glass, yet the dates were still mostly legible; South America 1946, Puerto Rico 1947, Florida 1948. I carefully laid out the reels, set up our old Bell & Howell projector, and drew the shades. I began with the earliest film:

The celluloid is scratched. The colors are faded. The camera is unsteady. But the images are unmistakable. A young version of my mother is stretched across a padded lounge chair outside a cabana. She is wearing a one piece bathing suit and brushing her golden hair in the sun. The camera zooms in, caressing her smiling face; an intimate portrait by an artist in love with his subject. The image draws me in. It is not my mother I am seeing. It is a desirable woman of thirty-three; beautiful, sophisticated, feminine.

I stare at these movies for hours until the shoebox is finally empty, and realize the discovery of this shoebox has raised more questions about my parents than it has answered. I have only a vague notion of their life. In fact, I have just revealed, in these few pages, almost everything I know about my parents before I came into this world. Dates, especially, elude me: When did they meet? When were they engaged? When were they married? (I don't recall them ever celebrating their wedding anniversary.)

What I do know for sure is this: when my mother was ready to start a family of her own, my father concurred. My brother Rex came first, in 1952. The three of them lived in one of two penthouse apartments atop 545 West End Avenue, at 86th street in New York City. The other penthouse apartment was occupied by two successful music producers, Ethel Gabriel and her husband Gus. They grew to become the closest of friends. Two years after my brother descended upon that New York rooftop, I arrived.

SIGNS OF CONSCIOUSNESS

I AM IN THE KITCHEN, scurrying on my hands and knees trying to intercept a jumbo, cats-eye marble rolling toward the Hotpoint refrigerator. My skin is clammy, and my palms stick to the scuffed yellow linoleum floor. My knees screech as I pull them along behind me. The jumbo marble is beautiful: there's blue fire inside. I want to taste its cool, smooth surface. I want to hold it, squeeze it. But it is swifter than me. The marble disappears under the refrigerator, swallowed up by a vast black hole, and vanishing from the universe. It happened so quickly. I feel like crying. The refrigerator towers over me, humming with life. Warm air seeps from the dark space below the unit. I slide my arm under, reaching for the lost marble, and touch things that are hard, rough, and gooey. I am afraid and pull back. My forearm emerges covered in dust and crumbs. There is nothing more I can do. I feel small and helpless, but I'm reassured by the cheerful melody my mother is humming nearby.

Three years later, I am playing unsupervised in the living room. The house is unusually quiet; my mother's whereabouts are unknown to me. I realize the luxury of infancy is coming to an end (I will soon be faced with the rigorous demands of nursery school), and decide to practice my new, self-taught gymnastic skill, the somersault. I steady myself then tumble forward perfectly, experiencing only mild dizziness at the finish. But as I sit up, I am unexpectedly seized by a vision. It is the silhouetted image of a tall, gaunt, powerful gentleman with a beard. He wears a stovepipe hat and a long, silken coat. I feel a strong connection to this imposing figure and think to myself, "That's me," but I am too young to draw any further conclusions about the incident.

This vision haunted me for years. Then one day in elementary school, someone handed me a picture book of American history. I was surprised to discover within its pages the precise image I had been carrying around in my head. It was an image, in silhouette, of Abraham Lincoln. Printed below his name was his date of birth, February 12TH. Like an apparition winking at me, I suddenly sensed the presence of some otherworldly spirit imploring a connection between us. Then I remembered the date of my own birth, February 11TH, and it sent a chill down my spine.

SADDLE ROCK

The town of Great Neck is subdivided into smaller communities: Harbor Hills, Strathmore, Kensington, Great Neck Estates, Kings Point, etc. I grew up in the incorporated village of Saddle Rock: a village. What is a village, anyway? Is it bigger than a breadbox? Technically (I did some research), it is smaller than a town but larger than a hamlet. Wasn't Camelot a hamlet? Our village borders a picturesque stretch of beachfront on the Long Island Sound. A small floating dock available to resident boaters offers a majestic view of the Throgs Neck Bridge. Beyond that, on a clear day, a sharp eye can detect the atmospheric dome of New York City in the distance.

The Village of Saddle Rock is an enchanting place where the tap water flows clear, and sweet; the sky is a deep shade of blue; and every tree is more perfect than the next for climbing. The streets are named after the great poets: Cooper, Byron, Keats, and Longfellow. When we moved there in 1955, Saddle Rock was a new development and ours was the model house; the one the builder showed to potential buyers of the remaining available lots. One of my father's two younger brothers already owned a house in Saddle Rock, just a block away from ours. I enjoyed growing up within close proximity to my older cousins Barry and Linda. Among other things, Barry would be instrumental in weaning me off my training wheels, and Linda often supplied me with valuable insight regarding the opposite sex.

My grandmother, who we called Nana, lived with us in the middle bedroom that separated mine from my brother's. She was old and weak, and she rarely left her room without my mother's assistance. But her mind was active. From her bedside, she taught me how to tell time by manipulating the hands on a plastic clock until I could recognize and name any configuration. Then she would hand *me* the clock, announce a time of day, and I'd arrange the hands accordingly. The system worked beautifully and helped me earn the distinction of being precocious based solely on my demonstrated ability to accurately interpret a clock. At other times, I'd play with toy soldiers at the foot of her bed. It was reassuring for me to pass many of my preschool days in her company. I suspect she felt the same. On my Nana's dresser was a stainless tin for sterilizing glass syringes. Around the same time everyday my mother would twist a needle onto the end of a steaming hot syringe, fill it with medicine, and inject my grandmother in the fleshy part of her bottom while I watched, fascinated, clutching my plastic clock fast to my chest.

Saddle Rock had a working grist mill built in 1702. The mill was open to the public and offered free daily tours from May to September. A visitor could leave with a small sack of cornmeal as a souvenir. Sometimes I'd hide a few extras in the waistband of my shorts, (if I could without getting caught), so my mother would have enough to bake fresh corn muffins. Adjacent to the Grist Mill was the site of the Saddle Rock Park. There was an Olympic-sized pool with two diving boards, a separate kiddie pool, a playground with swings and a sliding pond, a little league field, and two clay tennis courts, all fenced inside of several picturesque acres of manicured property at the edge of the Long Island Sound.

Crashing like a giant wave, me and a hundred other kids from Saddle Rock would flood the shallow kiddie pool all summer long, our frenetic bodies sparing little room for much water. Eventually we graduated en masse to the main pool where the water was four and one-half feet deep at the shallow end – still over my head at first. The main pool was huge and the water was much colder than in the kiddie pool. The reason for the vast difference in temperature was clear: when nature called, the kiddies were inclined to relieve themselves in the pool, covertly, beneath the sprawling sur-face of the water. Everyone knew this, and measures were taken to minimize the problem. Chlorine levels were checked hourly, and plentiful amounts of chemicals were added to combat bacteria; this was the best defense. Much less effective (but far more amus-ing) was a small sign posted in front of the lifeguard station which separated the men's and woman's locker rooms. It read: "We don't swim in your toilet. Please don't pee in our pool."

Kiki Kutner was in charge of all pool activities. She approved overtime for the lifeguards on hot summer nights; staged spectacu-lar fireworks displays on the fourth of July; held races on Labor Day, awarding magnificent trophies to the fastest swimmers in each stroke (and crisp blue ribbons to the slower ones); and hosted a poolside dance party in late August to ease the disappointment everyone felt as another season came to an end.

Saddle Rock was a safe place to live. In the latter part of the 1950's and early '60's, typically little was ever reported in the local police blotter. The only real danger, it seemed, came from somewhere cold and dark, half a world away.

Prior to entering the first grade, my primary responsibility was to accompany my mother on her daily rounds. This included regular trips to the A&P, the bank, the post office, and the cleaners. I derived great pleasure from this duty; I was not only helping my mother, but learning about the world as well. Once, while waiting in line at the drive-thru teller, I was startled by the overwhelming blast of a siren.

"What's that?" I screamed, trying to yell over the ear-splitting shrill.

"It must be noon," my mother yelled. I assumed she didn't hear me correctly because her answer made no sense.

"What?" I said, but the din made communication impossible. I had heard this noise before, but only as a faint sound in the distance, and never paid it much attention. Now, it was way too loud for me to ignore.

My mother drove up to the teller window while I pressed my palms firmly against my ears. Finally, the whirring stopped. When my mother completed her transaction with the bank, we sped off for the post office.

"What was that noise?" I asked again, after the ringing in my ears had subsided.

"That was the air raid siren," my mother replied cheerfully. "They test it every day, precisely at noon. You can set your watch by it." She glanced at her watch, smiled. "It's right on."

"Can everyone hear it?" I asked.

"Just about," she said. "From now on, you'll always know when it's noon."

I remember thinking Great Neck must be very special to have its own air raid siren to tell time, even if I had no idea what "air raid" actually meant.

* * *

ALTHOUGH MY BROTHER AND I were close in age, we were very different. Rex had the physical characteristics of my mother: fair skin, long legs, lean. I more closely resembled my father. I was stocky, and my skin turned brown easily in the summer sun. The same applied to our personalities. Like my father, I was gregarious, and often boisterous. Rex was more reserved. He cried when trying on new shoes. I cried when getting a haircut. Surprisingly, neither of us cried at the dentist, despite the fact the doctor had a moral imperative against using any type of anesthesia.

I was a physical creature; bold and daring. I believed I was indestructible. I was stoic, with a high tolerance for pain. My muscles revealed themselves very early on. I had stamina, and could hold my breath underwater for an inhumanly long period of time. Rex's physicality was at least partially predetermined by several medical issues which plagued him from birth. Rex had a bad kidney which had to be removed when he was three. He could live normally with the one that remained, but the doctors cautioned him about the inherent dangers of participating in contact sports. Naturally, with this concern in mind, my parents encouraged him to engage in other activities. Rex was also afflicted with a left eye that turned inward, and had to wear corrective lenses as a child. He was rarely seen without his thick, horn-rimmed glasses perched atop the bridge of his nose. When he turned five, my parents found a specialist who said the eye could be permanently repaired with surgery. His name was Dr. Wrinkleheim. I remember numerous times when we would head off to his office in Brooklyn on Saturday mornings in the fall. The drive seemed endless. Then we'd arrive outside of a residential brownstone, open a wrought iron gate, and descend a few steps to the doctor's basement-level office. My parents always let me ring the buzzer. That was my reward for accompanying them on the long journey. It delighted me, but the distraction was soon overshadowed by long stretches in the doctor's waiting room. I couldn't wait to turn around and go home. My one consolation was the thought that Rex might someday be able to go around without his glasses. I'd keep this in mind as I watched the minute hand on the clock creep slowly forward; sometimes even in reverse.

Just prior to Rex's sixth birthday, Dr. Wrinkleheim performed surgery on his crossed left eye. For months Rex wore a black pirate's eye patch. It made him look really cool, though I privately cringed at what possibly lay underneath. When the patch was finally removed, my brother's eye was completely normal, and his glasses were ceremoniously tossed away.

Rex was cerebral and analytical. He sought deeper explanations for things. I was content asking questions which didn't require answers. When I was outside playing some kind of sport, Rex was inside tinkering. He was fascinated with the inner workings of things, particularly things powered by electricity. When Rex was only nine, he built a crystal radio set consisting of a small piece of wood and a copper coil. He handed me the tiny earpiece and I could hear the broadcast of a Yankee game in progress. I was amazed, but puzzled. "Where are the batteries?" I asked. Rex explained that it operated off invisible waves sent from radio transmitters. "The waves are all around us, in the air," Rex said proudly.

As he got older, Rex began to tackle more sophisticated projects. He built short wave radios and CB's from a mail-order company called Heathkit. (Coincidently, it was on his CB radio that Rex later met his wife, Judy). As Rex approached driving age, he spent an entire summer building a mini-bike from scratch. Rex and I may have been different, but in many ways we were as complementary as tea and honey. I broke things; Rex fixed them. I had questions; Rex had answers. Wherever we appeared together in photographs, Rex smiled normally, and I made the silly face. He was Abbott, and I was Costello; possibly a genetic vestige from my mother's years in vaudeville.

Once, my mother took me and Rex to visit my father's showroom in the heart of New York City's garment district. While it was impressive and exciting, I only wanted to play with the company's adding machine. My father's sister, Aunt Susie, ran the accounting department from a small, cluttered office without windows. The advance of the digital calculator was still years off, but Susie's machine was no less of a wonder. It was a heavy steel contraption with large numbered buttons in three columns. The columns were color-coded, representing hundreds, tens and ones. The operator would simply depress a combination of numbers on the keyboard, and register them by pulling on the handle of a large lever attached to the side. At my age, this took a great deal of effort. When the lever was released, the buttons popped up and the total was miraculously computed and printed in thick black ink on a roll of paper that advanced through the top of the machine.

When my arm got tired from pulling the lever, and I wandered out of Aunt Susie's office, my father would hand me a giant box full of sequins; colorful reams of lightweight metallic disks on delicate bands of elastic. I would pull them apart, (releasing thousands of loose sequins), throw handfuls in the air, and marvel at the flickering light reflected from the blinding pin spots on the ceiling. The effect was mesmerizing. It was like watching fireworks close-up on the Fourth of July.

Another time, on a cloudless Sunday morning in September, my father and I set out in our '58 Oldsmobile. We were headed for a warehouse owned by an importer named Mr. Callas. He supplied my father with the beads and sequins for his dresses. As it turned out, Mr. Callas was also the chief importer for the FAO Schwarz toy company. When we arrived, he led me to a dimly-lit storage area containing hundreds of large, corrugated boxes. Many were open and overflowing with an assortment of plush stuffed animals: brown bears, black bears, unicorns, toucans, rainbow fish, squirrel monkeys, gorillas. They came in all sizes. Some were several times larger than me. It was a wondrous thing to behold.

Mr. Callas smiled, encouraging me to "go on safari" while he and my father discussed business. I plowed through the boxes like a kid, well, on safari, and discovered that sewed inside each toy was a tiny, wind-up music box.

When my father came to collect me several hours later, Mr. Callas praised me for being such a well-behaved boy, and insisted I leave with a souvenir. I chose a small Panda I had admired but which was beyond my reach. He instantly retrieved it for me, wound the copper crank protruding from its back, and out poured a hauntingly beautiful melody, one which seemed to please my father as well. Throughout the car ride home, my father kept urging me to play it again. I did so until my thumb and forefinger throbbed from repeatedly turning the crank. I watched my father as he listened to that melody, and saw in his eyes a dreamy, faraway look. At the time I didn't understand, but now I do. The tune was, "Smoke Gets in Your Eyes"... the very song my mother sang on the night my parents met.

GREAT INVENTIONS

IN 1899, the Commissioner of the U.S. Patent Office is reported to have said, "Everything that can be invented has been invented." It makes me think about all the great inventions that have kept the patent office buzzing in the short span of my lifetime alone.

I experienced the early 60's as a time of wonder, Wonder Bread, and Wonderama. Technology seemed to be advancing at the speed of light. I was witness to the historic birth of the electric can opener, with the little magnet which retained the lid after the machine had successfully completed its task. Unfortunately, (and I'm not sure why), the electric can opener usually failed to perform as advertised, especially with regard to its ability to puncture the top of the can cleanly and grab the edge, effectively allowing it to rotate smoothly. I wasn't sure if this was due to poor can design, poor can opener design or operator error – although I hate to think I was that dumb. In any event, whenever I was in control of the device, the can would wobble as it began to rotate, the paper label got pulled into the gear mechanism, and the entire procedure failed miserably. The resulting damage to the rim of the can rarely afforded me a second attempt, and I was forced to search for another can of Bumble Bee tuna or Underwood Deviled Ham.

The other type of can opener, the one all but replaced by the invention of the flip-top, takes me back to a summer day in the early 1960's. Our neighbor, Mrs. Harriett Goldstein, is reclining on a chaise lounge smack in the middle of her backyard. There wasn't much to separate the third-acre lots where I lived - no solid fences, high or dense hedges, or any sort of landscape screening whatsoever. We all basically shared one common lawn. By today's standards, this configuration would be regarded as an unacceptable and obscene lack of privacy. But in 1962, it was cool. Overt barriers were considered "un-neighborly." There was no other way. And that is why Mrs. Goldstein was always clearly visible, wearing her gold lame, one-piece swim suit, lazily clinging to another great invention of all time: the three-panel sun reflector. One could drench their face in baby oil and, finding just the right angle of reflection, burn the top layer of skin right off in just a few short minutes. Mrs. Goldstein is presently doing exactly that on this hot summer day.

Mrs. Goldstein was a dog person. She loved them and they loved her. I had a dog named Fritz, a dachshund. He was a gift, given to my mother by a friend when I was an infant. It is impossible for me to imagine a friend surprising me with a puppy while I was in the midst of parenting both a newborn and a two year old son (my brother). I mean, really, what kind of a friend is that? In any event, Fritz always ran away. Whenever he saw a crack of daylight in any of the doors leading outside, he would push his way through and be gone. Fritz was especially adept at pushing past me. Though small, he was extremely powerful - all muscle. I was no match for him. He bolted like a suckling pig fleeing a bacon factory. Since I was the one who fed him and kept him with a fresh supply of drinking water, his disappearing act was an insult to me. Still he persisted. Once free, I was unable to catch him, and he never came when I called. But when Mrs. Goldstein called, "Fritzie!" he always ran full bore into her outstretched arms. I would grab his collar and drag him back inside the house. I never could figure out what it was, but Fritz never failed to race toward the sound of Mrs. Goldstein's voice.

She had a dog of her own. It was a white toy poodle named Peppy. Presently, Peppy was curled up at the foot of the chaise lounge, while Mrs. Goldstein angled her reflector with astronomical precision.

Mr. Goldstein – Hy, as everyone affectionately called him, (I suppose because he preferred it to "Hyman," the legal name on his driver's license), stepped through the sliding glass doors onto his patio. In one hand was a frosty can of Schaefer beer. In the other, his trusty, oft-deployed, rust-stained can opener. This was simply the only patented household device capable of puncturing a beer can, thus releasing the prized, thirst-quenching liquid contained within. One needed to make two holes. The first was a full-sized cut, making use of leverage to create a triangular opening equal in size and shape to the head of the appliance. He would then rotate the can 180 degrees and make a smaller puncture. The smaller opening was not used for drinking, but facilitated proper air flow, allowing the beer to pour freely out the other side. I watched as Hy, showing clear determination, proceeded to dig in. "Psssst." I swear I could hear the sound from across the yard, as a wisp of golden smoke curled around his meaty thumb.

While Hy pounded down beers, and his wife fried the epidermal cells on her face, their son Ira peddled about the driveway on his tricycle. On his head was a bright red football helmet with a white stripe running down its center. The tricycle was a great invention. It was stable and could therefore be ridden by most small kids without posing significant danger - except in Ira's case. Ira loved his trike, but he had the uncanny habit of falling on his head whenever he rode it. After suffering several violent concussions on concrete, Mrs. Goldstein decided the only way she would permit Ira to ride his tricycle was with a football helmet strapped to his cranium. This was not meant as a punishment, but rather as a convenient solution that would allow Ira to enjoy all the glories of childhood without spilling all his brains onto the driveway.

"How's your head?" I ask.

"Okay," he replies.

"Is it hard? I mean, having to wear that helmet all the time?" I felt sorry for him, imprisoned behind that face mask. It seemed the helmet inhibited the delightful sensation of the wind rushing through your hair.

"You get used to it," he assures me.

A delivery truck stops at the curb in front of the house; pneumatic brakes screeching and huffing.

"It's here!" Ira shouts, eyes bulging.

He spins his cycle around and peddles feverishly toward the house. Seconds later, I hear the "swack-thunk" of Ira's helmet bouncing off the concrete driveway. It's a striking blow. Because the football helmet was securely strapped to his chin, Ira is spared the inconvenience of another trip to the North Shore Hospital Emergency Room. Instead, he brushes himself off and scurries into his house.

Two large men with thick necks drag a large wooden crate into the Goldstein's backyard. A few minutes later, Ira reemerges from the house and waves me inside.

"You gotta see this," he yells. "It's a HUMDINGER!"

I show Ira two thumbs up. He disappears back inside, and I follow, hurrying to catch the screen door before it latches shut.

"Hi, Hy!" I gasp, as I breathlessly enter the den. I loved the resonant quality of this greeting; "Hi, Hy." It easily rolled off the tongue. And Hy didn't seem to mind being addressed this way; at least he never indicated the slightest hint of annoyance when I uttered it. I was conscious, however, to use it sparingly, lest he interpret the salutation as one of disrespect.

Hy does not seem to notice me enter the room. He is too busy unpacking a carton full of individually-boxed paper scrolls, each about the size of a roll of aluminum foil. Each box is labeled with the name of a song and its composer.

A rear door is removed from its hinge, and the crate is successfully wheeled into the den on a dolly. Huge hammers appear and the crate is pried open. Inside is a player piano, an impressive contraption that looks like an ordinary upright, but has the addition of two large foot-pedals at the base, and a front panel that slides open to accommodate the song scrolls. The pedals are pumped in opposition; this powers the gears that turn the wheel that pushes the air through tiny chit holes in the song scrolls that unravel vertically onto a catch roller. The truly amazing thing is that the ivories on the keyboard actually move as if being depressed by some unseen virtuoso, and the song flawlessly, magically, and organically resonates throughout the room.

With Hy at the controls, the player piano rolled out several pitch-perfect tunes that afternoon; tunes like, "Bicycle Built for Two," "Yellow Rose of Texas," and "Adeline." Finally, "When the Saints Come Marching In" started playing: that's when I lost interest and marched out. Mrs. Goldstein continued to enjoy Hy's newly acquired musical talent from her chaise lounge out back, as the innocent-looking, three-panel reflector continued to compromise her good health. As I headed home, I recall she looked rather crispy.

Later that day, I watched my father empty a bag of charcoal briquettes in the bottom of his barbeque grill, then plunge his new electric starter-iron into the center of the pile. The device (probably now gone the way of Schaefer beer and the player piano) had no on/off switch. One end plugged into a wall outlet, and within minutes the coil at the other end was glowing bright orange, igniting the mound of coals surrounding it. This space age device was reportedly cleaner and more efficient than lighter fluid, which some claimed tainted the taste of the food.

Dinner that evening consisted of hot dogs and hamburgers, B&M baked beans, potato salad, and my mother's homemade apple pie topped with vanilla ice cream. When twilight set in, around nine o'clock, a few of the neighborhood kids stopped by and we roasted marshmallows over the last viable charcoal embers. Some preferred their marshmallows lightly toasted while others preferred them charred. Traditionally, we would let our marshmallows catch fire and then race around the yard, circling my house, our Olympic torches punching orange holes in the star-soaked sky. We'd arrive back at the barbeque grill out of breath, and our marshmallows would be ready to eat.

All summer long, the kids in my neighborhood would routinely wander from one house to the next, unceremoniously claiming space and snacks in the unconditional spirit of communal living. Boundaries were nonexistent. Time flowed like a meandering stream. Nothing was planned, and there were no schedules to follow. All daily activities sprung from an endless well of spontaneity. I was like a rowboat without oars, drifting with the tide, and wherever it happened to take me, it felt right.

The next morning, my mother summoned me to the phone. It was Rona. "You wanna come over and hear our new player piano?" she asked.

"Ahh… sure," I said, but having already suffered through the most popular titles a day earlier, I was being polite. No big deal, I thought.

When I arrive, Rona and the rest of the family are gathered around the player piano singing, "Bicycle Built for Two." Another endless, lazy summer day had begun.

SELF-RELIANCE

WHEN I WAS GROWING UP, we did everything ourselves. While my father brought home the money, my mother and I painted bedroom walls, laid carpet tiles in the kitchen, decorated the house for the holidays, and sometimes folded laundry together. My brother, Rex, specialized in everything electrical or mechanical. He changed the oil in our cars and tuned the engines, resurfaced the driveway, repaired broken appliances, wired the house for sound, and installed telephone jacks and TV antennas. We took turns mowing the lawn.

On weekends in summer, my father often relaxed by tending to his vegetable garden; a prolific 8 by 12 foot patch of dirt he carved out in a corner of the backyard. I used to watch him pour measured spoonfuls of toxic white powder in circles around the base of the tomato plants, and he would warn me not to breathe the dust. The stuff must have worked, because his tomatoes were always plump, bright red, and flavorful. He also cultivated radishes, cucumbers, scallions, squash, and carrots, all looking as if they had come straight off the farm. As the garden grew, so did my father's love for it. Then summer would turn to fall, and my father would eventually pull the stakes from the ground; a somber act of recognition that nothing more would emerge from this vital patch of earth until another winter had come and gone. I'd help my father with his ritual, and then watch him turn toward the house and slowly walk away, his shoulders slumped forward, and his head heavy with resignation. My father's beloved garden, bursting with life the previous month, had turned skeletal, and faded into the earth tones of autumn.

When the house was new, my father had planted five trees in a straight line across our narrow backyard: three peach, a pear, and a green apple. After several years, they were all bearing luscious fruit. He seemed to know just when the fruit was at its peak of ripeness; usually when the branches bent and the stems were about to break. If the fruit hit the ground, it meant it was too ripe, and already belonged to the worms and the bees. Each season, my father removed several large bushel baskets from a corner of the garage. We would fill each one, a dozen times throughout the summer, with fruit from our trees, and my mother would bake fresh apple pies loaded with heaps of brown sugar and cinnamon. I'd help make the crust (always from scratch): rolling dough until it was flat, draping it over mounds of sliced apples in pie tins, then poking holes on top with a fork to let out the steam as it baked. It was a veritable assembly line, and there was always apple pie in the house. After dinner she would heat one up and serve it piping hot with a generous scoop of vanilla ice cream on top. It was essential to eat quickly, before the ice cream had a chance to melt. This sometimes led to a medical condition commonly known as "pizza palate," but it was worth it.

The peach trees were more finicky than the apple trees, and the fruit was less abundant, but we were still treated to an occasional cobbler or shortcake to break up the deluge of apples (although I never really tired of them). I'd have cold apple pie with a tall glass of milk for breakfast. I'd dig in with a fork or spoon if I grew hungry between meals. I also found my mother's apple pie appealing, hot or cold, as a late night snack.

Notwithstanding my mother's fantastic homemade pies, her homemade meals were often less appealing. I was raised, primarily, on food that came out of cans and boxes. Canned fruits and vegetables were especially prevalent in our household. In fact, I was an adult out of college before I realized that asparagus was available outside of a can, and didn't have to smell like dirty socks. It was an epiphany. For dessert (when her supply of apple pie was nearly exhausted), my mother was often fond of serving canned fruit cocktail in heavy syrup. And if she thought of it soon enough, she would jazz it up by suspending it in lemon-lime JELLO and top it off with a generous dollop of Cool Whip. I particularly remember consuming massive quantities of Hamburger Helper, Sloppy Joes (on Wonder Bread), Potato Buds, Underwood Deviled Ham (on Wonder Bread), spinach Wagon Wheels laced with ketchup, and creamed chipped beef (on toasted Wonder Bread). At the time, I found these foods to be magnificently enduring, though hardly fare to be found anywhere on the nutritional food pyramid chart – which didn't seem to matter: I was strong and healthy throughout my formative years, despite the government's scientifically derived recommendations – after all Wonder Bread helps build strong bodies twelve ways (though they never did tell us what those twelve ways were) – although I've always suspected that the food I ate profoundly influenced the content and quality of my nocturnal impulses.

DREAMS

My MOTHER HAS ALWAYS maintained it was rare for a night to pass in which I wasn't found conversing with some imaginary friend, usually at around two in the morning. Certain times, she would discover me roaming the dark house, my eyes wide open, climbing or descending stairs, nimbly negotiating my way around furniture and the dog, all while I was sound asleep. I vividly recall a dream I once had when Ira, my humdinger of a friend and neighbor, slept over. In the dream, we were playing a game in which we took turns trying to guess what the other person had hidden under the blanket. The blanket was then lifted and the object was revealed. When it came my turn, I ripped the blanket away and was shocked to have uncovered the presence of the most horrific, growling, spitting, slimy, hairy, eighty-legged spider the size of a large dog. I was terrified beyond belief and screamed with the full force of my lungs; only the scream was not part of the dream. I really did let out the most bloodcurdling scream imaginable, waking the entire household, myself included. Both my parents raced down the hall expecting to discover someone had died, but by the time they arrived I had stopped screaming and was sitting up in bed clutching my pillow. Ira was sitting up in bed too, crying.

"What is it? What happened?" my father asked.

I knew what had happened but was too embarrassed to speak. My overactive brain had conjured up the monstrous spider in a dream and I had been awakened by the sound of my own screams. They accepted my silence as an explanation, and calmly coaxed me and Ira back to sleep. We slept soundly and without further incident for the remainder of the night. The next day my parents drew little attention to the incident, which was a great relief, saving me further embarrassment. Everything returned to normal – as I recall, dinner that evening consisted of creamed chipped beef on toast, followed by canned fruit cocktail in heavy syrup – but it was not the last of my nocturnal antics.

Another night, my mother was in the kitchen having a late night cup of tea with her friend and neighbor, Jeanette Lipmann. Jeanette lived down the block, but for some reason – perhaps she was escaping a domestic quarrel – she was sleeping in our guest room that evening. It was close to midnight, and I had been asleep upstairs in my room for several hours. The way my mother tells it, Jeanette was sitting at the kitchen table with her back to the door when I entered, crept up behind her, gripped her neck with both hands, and began to strangle her with a force befitting of someone three times my age. With her air supply all but cut off, Jeanette began to turn blue. This concerned my mother who, up to this point, was quite amused, and she realized I must be sleepwalking.

As Jeanette struggled to breathe, my mother cautioned her against gasping too loudly. "Hush…," she said. "You're not supposed to wake a sleepwalker."

Apparently, the more Jeanette squirmed, the more I tightened my grip. And by the time my mother had pried off the last of my fingers, Jeanette was an unearthly shade of purple. While Jeanette caught her breath, my mother gently guided me back to bed.

When I awoke the next morning, my mother and Jeanette were at the breakfast table. I had a fuzzy recollection of the night before but, out of embarrassment, decided to play dumb. Jeanette recoiled when she saw me enter the room. She had wrapped a silk scarf around her neck to disguise the bruising, but I could still see vague impressions of my small fingers in places the scarf could not conceal. Poor Jeanette may have avoided a fight with her husband that night, but had to suffer at the hands of a nine-year-old version of the Boston Strangler.

Although my mother continued to maintain a close friendship with Jeanette until her death more than twenty years later, I don't think Jeanette ever looked at me the same way again. Not that I blame her. My behavior that night remains a mystery to me (perhaps an explanation of sorts will unfold in a later chapter), but I am happy to report I have not strangled anyone since, consciously or unconsciously, nor have I even contemplated such action against any other of my mother's subsequent houseguests.

BOOK TWO

THE ATOMIC AGE

RECESS

MOST OF MY FELLOW baby boomers can attest that, throughout our youth, there were always scores of other kids around to start a game of SPUD, Ringo-Levio, Capture the Flag, running bases, football, or any other seasonally appropriate activity. Saddle Rock, where I grew up, was no exception; it was always teeming with kids. The village elementary school was practically brand new in 1960, the year I matriculated into kindergarten. Each morning, swarms of children, grades K thru six, would converge upon Saddle Rock School - a massive red brick edifice housing a sparkling cafeteria, a theater-like auditorium with a proscenium stage, and an Olympic-grade gymnasium. We called our school, "The pride of Great Neck." The nurses' office was replete with enough apparatus to qualify as a small hospital, equipped to treat most types of emergencies, even those requiring surgery. (I can attest from personal experience, however, that the nurse generally limited her use of needle and thread to repairing split seams in clothing, which plagued growing boys at recess, and almost always occurred in the seat of their pants.)

Her name was Nurse Avery; an attractive blond with an inviting smile. I split my pants more often than I care to remember, but the frequency of my visits helped diminish the anxiety I felt when stripping down to my Fruit-of-the-Looms in the presence of a pretty woman. I was reasonably comfortable removing my slacks to her repair, and equally at home if my visit called for the less pleasant task of regurgitating a partially digested breakfast (usually eggs or blueberry Pop Tarts), into her sterile chrome basin, as was sometimes the case. Getting sick to my stomach was not the result of some unresolved gastrointestinal issue; as a child I was the picture of health. Rather, my visits to Miss Avery's office were often the result of daily harassment on the playground. Recess was always the time I fell prey to a frenzied pack of ravenous females. I called them the Evil Empire of Girls. Every day, they chased me. Every day, I ran for my life. I couldn't understand why I was the one being singled out, while all my other friends, treacherously oblivious to my plight, played unhindered in the wide open spaces. I hated recess: I did not have the experience or the tools to exorcize my stalkers; I was ill-equipped to diffuse the situation; and I was not clever enough to devise an effective distraction, so recess was a time of day that brought me nothing but shame and embarrassment. The EEoG (Evil Empire of Girls) hunted me with a relentless single-mindedness. What did they want? What unimaginable thing would they do to me if I was caught? Whatever it was, I was too terrified to find out. Allowing them to capture me was simply not an option. But evasion was not easy. Although I was significantly motivated by intense fear, with ten or twelve girls in pursuit it took more than a young boy's determination, stamina, and agility to escape; it took reckless abandon. I twisted and turned from the threat of their eager, groping fingers, throwing myself into uncharted bogs and thickets, sloshing through puddles of rain, slipping in gooey mud, thrashing through painful prickle-berries and thorns. I barreled down rocky slopes, sometimes gathering surprising speed, which invariably resulted in me splitting the seat of my pants. This was good. For some reason, when this occurred, the girls backed off and permitted me to proceed unimpeded to the nurse's office. Maybe they felt sorry for me. Nevertheless, I would arrive there winded, scratched, muddy and holding back tears, but at least I was safe. Realizing that the nurse's office was my only refuge during recess, I would strategically try to split my pants as quickly and as often as possible. When my pants refused to split in spite of my wild gyrations, I could still get to Nurse Avery's office by making myself throw up. This was a less desirable but no less effective alternative, especially when I came dressed for school in Levis, which were double stitched in the seams and significantly more durable than regular chinos.

Don't get me wrong; I like girls, even desired them at times. Nurse Avery (though more woman than girl), was particularly kind and approachable. If it weren't for the irreconcilable age difference between us, I believe I could have married her. On the other hand, the girls in my peer group terrified me. They were intimidating. I didn't trust them or understand them. And I was always outnumbered. What was I to do as they chased me around the playground? I was only six, and not equipped to stand my ground and challenge their act of intimidation. But I still had my pride to consider. Would I cower behind the teacher's skirt like a crybaby? Not a chance. As long as the girls resolved to play cat and mouse with me, I was destined to embody the scampering rodent.

* * *

ON SCHOOLDAYS, unless the weather was inclement, everyone walked to school. This was rarely a hardship because no one lived more than a few blocks away. One morning, with just an hour to go before we were released to the playground, someone from the audio visual department wheeled a movie projector into the room.

Our teacher addressed the class with an uncharacteristic edge of formality: "Many students have been asking about the yellow and black signs posted around the building." She pointed to a small, yellow sign with the words *fallout shelter* surrounded by black triangles. "It means that this facility is an official public bomb shelter. In the event of an attack, we initiate *duck and cover* protocol. We are also capable of providing emergency medical treatment, if necessary."

I am suddenly aglow with deep respect and affection for Nurse Avery. More significantly, however, I am gravely curious about the teacher's use of the word, "attack."

I raise my hand. "What kind of attack?"

"An air raid, of course," the teacher replies. Her words hit me like a ton of crumbling cinderblocks: AIR RAID. The movie rolls. The title appears as simple white letters on a black background: "Duck and Cover." For the next ten minutes, I sit quietly staring at the movie screen. My mind goes numb.

Recess began early that day. Our teacher must have noticed that the grayish pallor on our faces, reflected from the light of the movie, remained, even after the film had ended and the lights in the room were restored. I felt queasy and feverish, and the fresh air on the playground offered scant relief. Outside, in fact, my level of discomfort actually increased. I dropped supine on the cold paved fringe of the basketball court and stared at a cloud formation in the sky: it resembled a mushroom. Then, at noon, I heard the familiar drone of the air raid siren. Just twenty four hours earlier, the same siren was a wonderful service provided by our town, a convenient reminder, an indication to the citizens of Great Neck that midday had begun - lunch, recess, permission to indulge in a leisurely nap. Now, the sound was an abhorrence - thirty seconds of dread in which to contemplate annihilation; to experience the unbridled fear of impending doom. I studied the mushroom cloud in the sky (it seemed to expand), and covered my ears until the wailing finally abated. I thought about the world we live in, how truly dangerous it is, and it scared the living daylights out of me.

My prior notion of security had been permanently altered. The air raid siren continued to sound everyday at noon; and everyday at noon I was shaken by a daunting fear of the end. Armageddon... would today be the day? And then those irritating girls would be stalking me again. Frankly, I was not sure what frightened me most. I realized I had little control over my fate at recess; I could only hope for the best. Perhaps, one day, the air raid would come - and blow the Evil Empire of Girls off the face of the earth.

OCCULT BOOK CLUB

IN 1963, I was eight years old and hooked on monster movies. I raised the subject in every conversation, regardless of how the conversation began. The notion of movie monsters pervaded my life like a Gothic religion. To help satisfy my hunger (or maybe to shut me up), my mother bought me a subscription to "Famous Monsters of Filmland," the premiere magazine for creeps like me, filled with haunting black and white images of Boris Karloff's Frankenstein, Bela Lugosi's Dracula, the Wolf Man, the Mummy, and the Creature from the Black Lagoon. One issue featured photos of Karloff in various stages of makeup. I was fascinated to learn it took eight grueling hours to transform Karloff into the Frankenstein monster. I often wondered what he was thinking while he was being slowly buried alive under all those thick slabs of rubber, foam and latex. Was he transforming his inner self, actually becoming the monster he portrayed on film? I'd gaze at Karloff's face and see a man cloaked in mystery. It drew me in. There was something lovely and approachable about Karloff. On the other hand, I never saw a shot of Bela Lugosi, either in or out of character, that didn't give me nightmares and make me want to run in the opposite direction. The monsters mesmerized me, but the actors who brought them to life were my real obsession. How did they do it? They were either brilliant magicians, or their monsters actually lived inside them to be summoned at will. It was a mystery I was compelled to unveil, and at the age of eight, my natural curiosity for all the hidden and mysterious forces in the universe was beckoning as never before.

I still have my copy of "Famous Monsters of Filmland" from December, 1965. It featured *The Mummy* on the cover, and I can sell it on eBay® for eight bucks, but I wouldn't dream of it. That was the issue that led to my membership in the Occult Book Club. An ad in the magazine urged me to return a postage-paid coupon entitling me to four free books of my own choosing. If I decided to keep them, I would receive a new Book Club selection each month which I would be required to purchase at the regular low membership rate. I could cancel my membership at any time. It sounded too good to be true, but I signed my name to the bottom of the enrollment postcard and dropped it in the mail. I supposed they assumed most people would get hooked after reading the free books, and begin purchasing additional books each month after that. But I was only ten. I had no money. Nevertheless, I was fortunate to receive a brand new hardcover title from the Occult Book Club delivered to my door the first week of every month: "Hidden Channels of the Mind," "Numerology Simplified,"

"Reincarnation," "ESP: A Personal Memoir," "I-Ch'ing," and "A Treasury of Kahlil Gibran." My search for the truth had evolved beyond the world of classic Hollywood movie monsters into the realm of all things mystical. It became my latest obsession. For Christmas, I asked for a Ouija Board, Tarot Cards, and magic tricks. I collected rabbit-foot key chains in every imaginable size and color. I would spend hours searching my front lawn for four-leaf clovers. I performed mind-reading experiments on my brother, and practiced auto-suggestion techniques on my neighbor, Ira. I made predictions about the future and wrote them down. I practiced ancient healing arts on wounded insects, and sacred restoration rituals on assorted roadkill. And I continued to immerse myself in a steady stream of free books from the Occult Book Club.

Sadly, after about two years, the books stopped arriving. The postman assured me there was no mistake. Someone at the book club must have discovered that no payment had ever been recorded for the books they had dispatched to my address. Fortunately for me, the books were no longer part of my plan. My education in the occult, I believed, was firmly established, and I understood that there was more to life than what meets the naked eye. Life was swarming with things unseen.

IRENE AND ED

FOR TWO WEEKS every August, my Aunt Irene and Uncle Edgar would fly in from Omaha, Nebraska for a visit. My mother and I routinely arrived at the airport in plenty of time to meet their flight. I'd press my face against the huge floor-to-ceiling window at the United Airlines terminal and scrutinize the activity on the tarmac until the nose of their plane crept into view. Irene and Ed would wave at me through the tiny oval windows as their aircraft taxied to the gate. When they emerged from the Jetway, I'd indulge them in a generous display of affection, for which I'd be rewarded with several complimentary in-flight tins of roasted macadamia nuts from Hawaii. Uncle Edgar was tall and lean. Aunt Irene was short and rotund. Both were always curiously perfumed with the distinctly medicinal scent of Listerine.

I helped jockey their powder blue, fiberglass Samsonite luggage from the baggage carousel into the car, and from the car into the house. As I dragged their indestructible suitcases into the spare bedroom, Irene poured two tumblers of scotch and soda over ice. Then my aunt and uncle would settle in to a competitive game of gin rummy.

Requesting the presence of my company, Uncle Edgar would hoist me onto his lap, where I would remain throughout the competition, happy but dizzy from the blended vapors of scotch and mouthwash. Usually, at the conclusion of a winning hand, after he had scratched his points onto a small pad, my uncle would say, "Want to see a crow light on a fence?" Then, without a moment's hesitation, he would squeeze my knee between his thumb and forefinger, sending a shockwave through my leg that simultaneously tickled and hurt to a degree that made me literally cry-uncle and beg him to stop. Naturally, this only incited him to further torture. He kept me in his vise lock until I laughed so hard, struggling to get away, that tears poured from my eyes. Just when I thought I couldn't bear it any longer, Uncle Ed would mercifully release his grip, allowing me just enough time to catch my breath before doing it all over again.

Several scotches and a few losing rounds later, my aunt would invariably wander into the kitchen where my mother was busy preparing dinner, often to the tune of meatloaf and mashed potatoes. I'd slide onto the empty seat across from Uncle Edgar and he'd deal me in. Despite the vast differences in our abilities, my uncle never reduced his intensity of play, and he refused to throw a hand for my benefit. Whenever I thought I had him beat, he would straighten up and say, in a friendly Midwestern verve, "I'll tell you what I'm gonna do. Tell you what I'm a-gonna do." Then he would "knock" and lay his winning hand on the table. "Looks like I got you pretty good, this time," he'd say, tallying up the points. "You can't catch me now, I'll betcha. I'll just betcha." And he was right. I'd try to conceal my disappointment, but Uncle Ed must have perceived my frustration because he'd permit me to sip on his scotch after that. I liked the way it tasted, and Uncle Edgar could be certain that the more I sipped, the more I'd linger to play his game, and lose. Overall, it was a frustrating but symbiotic arrangement. Not only did I get to hang out and imbibe with my favorite uncle, but on those rare occasions when I won a hand, the victory was particularly sweet: I knew I had beaten him fair and square.

SCRUPLES

ON MY WAY HOME from school, I stopped to remove the jacket my mother had insisted I wear that morning when the air was still cool. Third grade was almost at an end and was beginning to smell like summer. All things considered, I had a good year, both academically and socially. Boys and girls were beginning to take more than the usual passing interest in each other; discernible behavioral and physical distinctions stirred a healthy curiosity in the opposite sex, which often resulted in a conspicuous and visceral yearning in and around the vicinity of the groin. I sensed I was being noticed by girls in some unfamiliar, almost animalistic fashion, eerily reminiscent of the horrors I suffered on the playground years earlier. At first I was fearful and wanted to recoil. At the same time, I couldn't ignore my suspicion that something profound was happening, and this time I was determined (if not eager), for it to happen to me.

My neighbor Rona became very popular with the third grade female student population, which was not surprising. She was approachable and she liked to gossip. Fortunately, she lived next to me. Rona helped facilitate access to the girls whom I desired to know better, and with whom I was too shy to make a direct overture. I think she may also have facilitated access to me. It might seem like Rona was being used, but I think she enjoyed the attention and notoriety she commanded as the social middleman. I certainly appreciated what she did for me, particularly those times when she contrived to heighten my mystique by providing exclusive "inside information" to her closest friends. Although some of what she told them was true, most, I admit, was derived from her own fertile imagination. She would almost certainly have excelled as a Hollywood power broker had she chosen to go that route. Rona got invited to every party and rarely missed a single one: for her it was a necessary part of doing business. She regularly orchestrated parties at her house, and persuaded me to attend, even if I was the only boy among a dozen or more girls, which was often the case. Every afternoon I'd see her with another girlfriend, hanging out on her front lawn, presumably waiting to exchange a few pleasantries as I returned home from school.

Since my mother's concern for my catching a chill was no longer relevant in the temperate afternoon sun, I tied my jacket around my waist. The realization that warmer weather was upon us promptly lead to imaginings of summer recess, the beach, baseball, barbeques, and extended daylight hours. I inhaled deeply, accelerated the pace of my stride, and concluded that life was good.

Rona and her friend Lisa were sitting on the front lawn when I reached home. I waved, and the girls waved back.

"Whatcha doin'?" I asked.

"Oh, Brad. You don't care what we're doing. You're just asking because you're so nice." Rona was hard at work. "Wanna come inside for cold drink?"

"Sure."

Lisa batted her lashes at me, or maybe something flew into her eye, like a gnat. "Hi, Brad," she said.

I sat next to Lisa at the kitchen table. I could tell she was nervous. Rona stood at the sink pouring a packet of raspberry flavored Kool-Aid into a pitcher of iced tap water. The long metal spoon clinked inside the glass approximating the bucolic sound of a cowbell. When Rona placed the glass of Kool-Aid in front of me, I gulped the entire thing holding my breath. This was to prevent an attack of hiccups that often occurred whenever I felt trapped in a tenuous situation. Lisa stared at her drink. Rona sipped hers like a highball, talking incessantly and with great aplomb. It was clear Rona was hatching some carefully planned scheme that was only just beginning to unfold.

"I told Lisa she could kiss you," Rona bragged with a brazen sense of entitlement that surprised me.

"You did? Why?"

"She asked me if you'd mind, and I said 'no'."

"Well…" I felt an agonizing bout of hiccups coming on.

Lisa had turned a deep shade of raspberry Kool-Aid.

"You don't have to let me if you don't want to," she finally said.

"It's no big deal," Rona interrupted with passive-aggressive charm.

"It's just that… that…" I was stammering, full of mixed feelings and particularly embarrassed for Lisa. I wanted to be a loyal friend and neighbor to Rona. I didn't want Lisa to kiss me (I barely knew her), but I didn't want tomorrow's gossip to suggest I was a prude, either. That would surely constitute an unconscionable act of social suicide and tarnish my sparkling reputation. Why did Lisa want to kiss me, anyway? I thought. Rona was relentless, determined to sell me on this crazy idea. I had to think fast.

"Let's go to your room," I whispered.

Rona's eyes widened, as did Lisa's. They were smiling as we marched into Rona's bedroom.

"I'll keep the door opened just a crack, in case my mother walks by."

"Is your mother home?" I asked.

"She won't bother us. Besides it's only a few kisses."

"A *few* kisses?" I forced back a hiccup. It burned the back of my throat and tasted like a mixture of Kool-Aid and battery acid.

"I promised Lisa she could kiss you a few times."

"I'll only kiss you once, if you want," Lisa said apologetically.

"It doesn't have to be on the lips," Rona said, as if quoting some imaginary rulebook.

"Do I have any say in this?" I asked.

"Sure. It's no big deal. Just tell Lisa what to do." Rona was beginning to sound annoyed.

I requested a thirty-second time-out to consider my position. First, if I agreed to let Lisa kiss me, I had to get something in return; the kiss was no reward. Second, lips were definitely out. I intended to save my lips for my first serious girlfriend, and Lisa was not her. Lisa was not even pretty. Finally, I realized that if I could get them to do something totally outrageous in return, it might prevent any gossip from ever getting out. It would be as if the afternoon had never happened.

"Okay, here's the deal," I told them. "You can each kiss me ten times on the back of my hand, but after that you have to pull down your pants and put on a show. That's my final offer."

"I don't know…" Lisa said, wavering.

But Rona was onboard immediately. "Fifteen kisses," she demanded. Now she was selling Lisa on the idea. "Come on. It's no big deal. And he'll give us each fifteen. That's pretty good."

"I haven't agreed yet," I protested.

"Alright," Lisa said.

"Fifteen *quick* kisses," was how I qualified it, and Rona volunteered to go first. She pressed her boney lips against the back of my hand, pecked out fifteen quick kisses, and handed my hand to Lisa. Lisa's lips were soft, moist, and supple. I did not expect this, and felt the strange sensation of blood pulsating through my neck. Suddenly, this was no longer a game; it was more like a profound form of awakening. Is this what girls were about? I let myself freefall into a state of euphoria. Then Rona's mother ambled past the bedroom door. I froze.

"Relax," Rona said. "She won't bother us."

Rona was right. Her mother went straight to the kitchen to scour some dirty pots.

"What number are you up to?" I asked Lisa. I contemplated offering her some bonus kisses.

"Nine."

"Fine, hurry up," I said.

Lisa did as I asked, knocking off the remaining kisses without much pageantry. When it was over, I examined the back of my hand. It was excessively damp, but otherwise no worse for wear.

"Your turn," I reminded them.

Rona nonchalantly dropped her drawers and began parading around the room. She encouraged Lisa to do the same.

"See. It's no big deal." Rona said with a casual flip of her wrist.

Lisa was blushing as she unbuttoned her pants and let them drop to her ankles. Her underpants followed.

"It may be a little dirty," she said apologetically.

"He doesn't care," said Rona, and Lisa began her display as per our agreement.

I'm not sure what I expected, but I was won over by girls. But now they frightened me in an entirely different way.

"I've gotta go," I jumped. I hastily excused myself, jogged home, and switched on the TV.

Before long, I was engrossed in an episode of The Jetsons, entitled, "Jane's Driving Lesson." Mr. Spacely was yelling at George for something, when a test pattern unexpectedly appeared on the screen, followed by the no-nonsense voice of an announcer: *We interrupt this program for a test of the emergency broadcast system.* The TV was not broken; I had experienced this before. Each time, I was gripped by an intense, unsettling fear. Terrified of what might happen next, I listened for the drone of the air raid siren, the whoosh of military aircraft, or worse, the nauseating whistle of an incoming nuclear warhead. I imagined, with such patent clarity, the fury of the atomic blast - the violent explosion, the flash of white light, the windows blowing inward, the house collapsing in flames around me, the radioactive fallout ultimately erasing anything left standing. I thought about my mother in the refrigerated section at the A&P, my father on the phone at work, and our housekeeper ironing shirts downstairs in the den. I wanted to warn them, to beg them to save themselves. I also wanted to be near them. I wanted to experience one last contact with another human being before… but

I was paralyzed with fear, and could only do one thing. I prayed. I prayed that the air raid would not come, and girls would gloriously inhabit every available inch of the planet earth.

MY MOTHER'S HOTPOINT KITCHEN

The next morning, I awoke to the exotic aroma of kippers and onions sautéing on the stove. This was my father's favorite breakfast, and he enjoyed preparing it himself so it always came out just the way he liked it. I watched as he smiled through oily wisps of smoke, folding caramelized onions over a pair of glistening fish, their heads still intact, sizzling in the heavy iron skillet used almost exclusively for this purpose. Then my father and I would sit down to a real man's breakfast, delighting in the hearty flavor of smoked fish. The kippers were chock full of long, delicate bones which I would painstakingly remove, creating a pile at the edge of my plate. My mother would inevitably pass through the kitchen and caution me to be extra careful, and not get them caught in my throat. Eating kippers and onions with my father on Sunday mornings was one of my greatest pleasures. It was our thing, I felt close to him, and I realized I was a lot like him, too.

Our kitchen was built in 1955, the year I was born. Everything about it at the time was state of the art. All the major appliances were electric, and all were made by Hotpoint: the dishwasher, the four-burner stove, the wall oven, the exhaust fan, and the refrigerator. The refrigerator was the epitome of ingenuity, a constant source of fascination, and something which never failed to attract scrutiny and inspire pleasing conversation. What made it unique was the ambidextrous door designed to open on both sides. The refrigerator handle was a large "V" located at the center of the door. If it was rocked to the left, the door would swing open on the left. If it was rocked to the right, the door would swing open on the right.

Walking home from school one day, I was filled with optimism. It was a clear, crisp afternoon in November, and I was taking a shortcut through a neighbor's backyard; a route I had traversed many times, involving a challenging climb up a retaining wall - a series of step-like levels supported by railroad ties. Portions of the climb presented a degree of difficulty requiring the use of both hands to pull myself up; therefore, my book bag always went first. This was the most direct way home and easily shaved a full five minutes off the journey. The ground under my feet was hard and lumpy, but as I advanced up the retaining wall, each successive level presented a thicker, softer carpet of pine needles.

By the time I reached the top, the pine straw was as dense as a mattress. I rolled on my back to catch my breath and looked up at a magnificent array of conifer and birch trees on the outskirts of our property. The tall, mature evergreens provided shelter from the wind; the stillness heightened my senses, the sweet smell of pine poured over me, and the steep, angled rays of the autumn sun projected geometric shapes in the trees. A squirrel scratched at the base of a white birch. I watched him scamper up the trunk and skillfully advance to the end of a slender limb like an acrobat on a high wire. I remembered my mother once telling me that the white, peeling bark of the birch tree was used as writing paper before the invention of parchment. The squirrel blinked at me nervously, then jumped onto the limb of an adjacent tree and disappeared. I grabbed my backpack and headed for home.

Emerging from the panoply of trees, my house came into view. Like most of the houses in Saddle Rock, ours is a split-level colonial with grey cedar shingles and white trim, centered on about a third of an acre of gently rolling bluegrass. My house is the center of my Universe – a safe and indestructible fortress, the nucleus of a perfect existence. It is my beacon of light; my soul's vibration; my center of gravity. It represents eternal sustenance, shelter, warmth, and love. My house envelops me in an overwhelming sense of well being.

The day is mine! I am ebullient, joyful, and more. To my delight, my dachshund, Fritz, is tied to his tether, lying on his back, soaking up what remains of the midday sun. When he sees me approaching, his tail wags ferociously, and I hug his long, brown

body so hard, I fear I might be hurting him. All the while he is
slathering my face with warm saliva, and his breath smells like a
freshly cut lawn.

There were many occasions when I'd bring home a group
of friends after school. We'd burst into the house; enthusiastic,
loud and tempestuous. Nana never hesitated to express her staunch
disapproval of the noise. "STOP THAT RACKET!" she'd yell
from her bedroom at the top of the stairs, her voice commanding
and resolute. I was always stunned, embarrassed and terrified. My
friends were always just terrified, but we would all snicker and call
the old lady a "witch." At the age of nine, it rarely occurred to me
to consider the wishes of others. But on this afternoon I was alone,
without friends to disrupt Nana's quiet solitude.

I slipped into the house and headed for the kitchen. I had
Fluffernutter on the brain, and couldn't wait to slap one together
for myself – with extra Fluff. The next thing I know I am leaning
against the bread drawer, looking up at my mother. Her usual smile
was absent as she described how the ambulance took Nana away.
"She just stopped breathing," my mother said, "and died before we
reached the hospital."

For the first time ever, the kitchen is a somber place,
drab, without sunlight. Moments earlier, the afternoon had been
a calliope of organ music; a carousel of brightly-colored wooden
horses. It had all come to an abrupt halt. "When will she be back?"
I asked. I didn't fully comprehend death's implications, yet knew
in my heart the question was ludicrous, based on little more than
childlike wishful thinking and a desire to go back. My mother
smiled and shook her head. There was resignation in her moist,
blue eyes. And I understood, for the first time, that some things in
life are irreplaceable.

I ran upstairs to Nana's room, fearful yet curious about
what would happen next. Her bed was freshly made. The oxygen
tank lingered mute in the corner, void of the faint hissing sound
it routinely made. Everything was surprisingly neat for someone
who had recently died. Even my army men were not strewn about

the floor as usual. The double hung windows were open at the bottom, fresh air replacing the stale air of death.

Before the age of nine, I had never ridden in a limo. Yet here I was, sitting in the back of a velvety, barracuda-like vehicle that seemed impervious to the crisp November morning outside, beyond its tinted glass windows. The car is as black as night: as black as death. We drove down Bayview Avenue en route to the funeral parlor, passing under a skeletal canopy of bare oak trees. Muted daylight stippled through the limo's moon roof. The only sound was the faint rumble of tires beneath my seat, then the popping of loose gravel as we arrived at our destination and turned into the drive.

The top half of Nana's casket lay open like the upper section of a Dutch door. It was lined with ivory silk padding, and reminded me of the clouds in heaven. I asked my mother to lift me up. Nana was dressed in deep purple velvet and lace. Her hands were folded across her chest. Her slender fingers were adorned with onyx and jet stones in ornate silver settings. A thick application of rouge covered her cheekbones; the cheeks themselves appeared sunken and drawn in.

I searched intently for the slightest movement beneath her eyelids, and then felt foolish for doing so. "Can I touch her?" I asked, in a manner both tentative and eager. My mother nodded. I reached for the back of Nana's hand, but then quickly recoiled. I didn't want to know the feel of death, after all. She was my grandmother, and she was dead. That was sufficient.

Nana had reached the age of 96. After the funeral, I began to wonder where someone goes when they die. The question went unanswered. Although I didn't understand where death ended, I knew it began in the kitchen. I would learn to keep an eye on the kitchen: important things often happened there.

STRAIGHT TO THE POINT

EVERY WINTER, Ringling Brothers and Barnum Bailey Circus would come to Madison Square Garden and my mother would take me and my brother to see the show. We stuffed ourselves with hot dogs and cotton candy. We twirled flashlights attached to plastic lanyards, and flung peanuts at parading elephants. My mother made a point of arriving at least an hour before the Ringmaster announced the start of the Three-Ring-Circus; this left plenty of time to wander the Sideshow, a more intimate venue compared to the spectacle under the Big Top. At the Sideshow, everything was within reach. Elephants vacuumed peanuts off the palm of my hand. I saw a monkey scoop a handful of dung off the floor of its cage and fling it at a group of taunting kids. Men swallowed swords, ate fire, and pushed knitting needles through the folds of their skin. A woman displayed tattoos covering more than ninety percent of her body. But the act that fascinated me most was the knife thrower. He placed his beautiful assistant against a wooden board, spread her arms and legs, and from a distance of perhaps twenty feet, sent sharp steel knives tumbling in her direction. The point of each knife struck the board, embedding itself just inches from the cream-colored flesh of the beautiful assistant. Miraculously, each appendage remained whole and unscathed. I held my breath throughout. The entire demonstration was pure magic.

On the way out, we stopped at a souvenir stand and my mother bought us live chameleons. They were packed in a little box designed to look like a cage. I named mine "Blade." We glared at each other through the slats in the box and bonded immediately. (Unfortunately, Blade escaped just days after I took him home, and was discovered – looking something like a wilted string bean – in the clothes dryer at the end of the *permanent press cycle*. I was devastated.)

The Three-Ring-Circus was never disappointing. Although the clowns terrified me, I loved every minute of their act. Still, the knife throwing demonstration haunted me all the way home.

When we finally returned, I reached for the phone and called Ira.

Our basement was lined with varnished wood panels. Some of the panels were hinged and opened onto shelves where my mother stored serving trays, crock pots, vases, earthenware, spices, and a battalion of Mason jars filled with Nana's homemade watermelon pickle. Ira was not attractive like the beautiful assistant in the sideshow, but he was equally as cooperative. I positioned him against the basement paneling and instructed him to spread his arms and legs, the way I had seen it done earlier. I removed ten darts from a box and confirmed the sharpness of each tip. Then, pacing off a distance of approximately ten feet, I turned and faced Ira. Gripping a dart between my thumb and forefingers, I took aim and, squinting over the shaft of the dart, focused on a spot about an inch from Ira's throbbing neck. Nervousness seemed to briefly hijack my muscle control, but I was determined to outline Ira's body with darts. I told myself it was simply mind over matter. I would use the force of my will to send the dart to its desired destination on the wall.

I took a deep breath, cocked my arm, and let it rip. There was a strident *thud*, and the dart ricocheted off the wall, bouncing several times before landing at my feet. Amazingly, Ira didn't flinch. "Why not try a few with just the wall?" Ira said. I wisely did as he suggested, and soon I was tossing darts with the confidence of a professional. "I'm ready," I told Ira, and I began tossing darts with such precision as to outline the whole of Ira's childlike form. I threw not one errant projectile. Ira sustained not one puncture wound. I was encouraged by my proficiency, and endeavored to ramp up my act to a level of greater difficulty (for me) and greater jeopardy (for Ira). "I've got a humdinger of an idea," I told Ira, convinced he'd agree to my plan. "This time I'll try it blindfolded!"

For legal reasons, I cannot reveal what happened next.

GOT ME HYPNOTIZED

IN THE SUMMER OF '66 I was eleven, and went to sleep-away camp for the first time. It was beautiful in the Adirondacks during the months of July and August, but I found certain rigors of camp to be off-putting. Aside from riflery, which I loved, camp put me on a schedule that was, to my way of thinking, impossibly rigid. Every morning at seven, I'd be rudely awakened by the sound of Reveille blasting over the public address system. Camp was like the Army, I thought. Soothing classical music would have been infinitely better. More objectionable than the choice of music, though, was the unseemly hour at which I was forced to rise. Is it wrong, when I'm on vacation, to want to sleep until I naturally wake up (which would never be before ten, at the earliest)?

It got worse. Every waking minute of every day was stringently planned in advance: inspection, breakfast, activity, activity, snack, lunch, rest, activity, activity, free time (a whole 30 minutes in which you were expected to write home), dinner, evening activity, quiet time, sleep. As far as I was concerned, this *was* the Army. Before, when I spent summers at home, it was perfect: I slept when I was tired, and ate when I was hungry. I controlled the flow of my day – what I did, when I did it, and with whom – which was fueled by my own inventiveness and creativity. I thrived. Nevertheless, I am grateful for my only summer at camp for one simple reason: I was hypnotized. This alone made all the time I spent *not* sleeping, or shooting .22 caliber bullets at paper targets, worthwhile.

The nighttime air is unusually still and muggy as everyone piles into the Rec Hall for Evening Activity. When I get there, the place is jammed. The entire camp has come to see what had been billed as a "demonstration of mind over matter." The Rec Hall is a large, cavernous space with a stage at one end. Campers sit cross-legged, willy-nilly, on the floor. It is hot inside, and some of the counselors are using their weight to prop open side doors to let in a little breeze.

After awhile, the camp director takes the stage, and with a flourish, introduces the featured guest. The audience responds with thunderous applause. A large man, weighing perhaps three hundred pounds, appears from the wings and bows when he reaches center stage. The man asks for ten volunteers. I wave my arm in an attempt to get his attention, but he quickly points to nine other campers at the back of the room who join him on stage. Now I've got all my fingers crossed and I'm trying to psychically draw him in. It works. He points directly at me, but before I am in motion, the camper beside me leaps up and rushes onto the stage. Asshole! The hypnotist had picked me; I wasn't about to let some snot-nosed jerk rob me of this opportunity. As far as I was concerned, this was the most important event of the entire summer, if not my entire life. I didn't simply *want* to be hypnotized; I *needed* to be hypnotized, tonight.

I race onto the stage and join the other campers. Luckily, the hypnotist doesn't notice there are eleven of us when he asked for only ten. He places us in a line across the stage, facing the audience, and explains how he will test our ability to respond to "autosuggestion."

"I'm going to ask you all to relax and breathe deeply," he says. His voice is deep and soothing. "Think of some restful activity, like lying on the beach, or listening to soft music." (Definitely not Reveille, I'm thinking). The hypnotist continues methodically: "I'm going to count backwards from five, and as I do you will sink deeper and deeper into a calm, restful state. When I reach the number one, you will be in a deep trance. Ready? Five…four…"

The hypnotist's voice drifts through me like the cool mist that floats off the lake at dawn. I had already decided, positively, I was going to let this man hypnotize me. I appoint myself his partner, so to speak, in his little demonstration. I begin to focus on my breathing, dismissing all skepticism and resistance. I surrender to the power of his voice. I let go.

As the countdown continues, I am surprised to feel a physical response to the hypnotist's suggestions. My eyelids grow heavy; my breathing deeper; and the tension in my shoulders seems to disappear. I wonder if I'm not imagining it all.

"Two... One...," the hypnotist says, "Sleep." At that, my eyes close and my head drops forward. Suddenly, my body feels heavy, like I'm standing on a planet with twice the gravity of Earth.

"Good... Very good," says the hypnotist. "Now I want everyone to raise their right arm, slowly. Raise it out in front of you. Keep it straight (that's right) and parallel to the ground."

I imagine the hypnotist is speaking only to me, and do as I'm told. No problem.

He continues: "I'm going to apply pressure to your arm, but don't let me push it down. Keep your arm stiff and straight." I feel him forcing my arm, and am amazed - it doesn't budge.

Next, I hear shuffling on stage. My eyes are shut and I have no idea what is happening, but I suspect that the demonstration is over.

"Alright, you're going to wake up now. I'm going to count to five. When I snap my fingers, you'll be awake and fully refreshed. One... two... three..."

The hypnotist snaps his fingers. I open my eyes and see that I am the only camper remaining on stage. I'm also feeling remarkably alert and refreshed. There is a wave of applause. The hypnotist congratulates me, puts his meaty hand on my shoulder, and asks if I would assist him in one last demonstration – the finale. I eagerly agree.

"How do you feel?" the hypnotist asks.

"I'm fine," I admit. Actually, I am euphoric.

"If you're willing, I would like to put you in a very deep hypnotic state," he says with a wink.

"I'm ready."

"Good. This time, I want you to concentrate on my voice as I count back from ten. You will close your eyes and descend into a profound state of relaxation. Listen carefully and respond only to the sound of my voice. Ten... nine... You are feeling sleepy now."

His voice is mesmerizing. I'm not afraid. I think about nothing and surrender to his voice. As I do, I become increasingly aware of an acute connection between my body and mind.

"You are asleep," says the hypnotist. There is a short pause, and he repeats the words, "You are asleep." That he repeated himself caused me some doubt. Maybe I wasn't responding as well as I had in the previous exercise. Then I realize I'm not asleep at all, and begin to feel like an actor who has suddenly forgotten his lines. The last thing I want is to sabotage the hypnotist's demonstration and expose him as a fraud - we would both look like major fools - but it may be too late. It is too late. I realize that my only option at this point is to fake it.

"You feel your body getting stiffer," the hypnotist says.

My eyes are closed. I'm standing with my feet together and my arms at my side.

"You are stiff as a board," he continues, "as straight and strong as an iron pipe." I do my best to appear stiff and straight and strong to the audience.

I feel a gentle shove and I'm tipping backwards. Someone has caught my head and someone else is lifting me by the ankles. My body is now horizontal, and, although my eyes are still closed, I can tell I'm being carried across the stage, as two carpenters might carry a large wooden plank to their workbench. I'm astonished I'm not collapsing in the middle. I sense I've been placed across two chairs; my head on one, my ankles on the other. I am spanning the chairs with no means of support. This is, to say the least, unsettling. In my mind I am scrambling to focus on the iron pipe suggestion. I concentrate on the words (stiff, straight, strong), when a subtle force begins to bear down on my stomach. I feel an acute awareness of everything around me. I imagine that the hypnotist is bearing down on my stomach with his palms. A series of "ooh!s" and "aah!s" rise from the audience: but why? This goes on for about thirty seconds. Sometimes the pressure on my stomach increases, but I'm able to resist. Finally, I hear a booming round of applause as I'm lifted from the chairs and returned to an upright position.

"I am going to count to ten, and you will begin to awake. When I reach ten, you will be fully awake and refreshed. One...

two… three…," the hypnotist begins.

The pressure to perform is off. I'm relieved, and allow myself to awake at my own pace. I open my eyes before the hypnotist has finished counting to ten, but he counts to ten anyway and says, "Now you're awake and fully refreshed. How do you feel?" I say, "Great."

The applause turns explosive, and the entire auditorium is on its feet. It is my first (and only) standing ovation, and it's hard to believe I am the center of all this attention. I take a bow, and the frenzy grows in multiples. I can't help thinking: What's everyone so excited about?

The three hundred pound hypnotist rests his arm on my shoulder. Heat is radiating off his substantial, three-hundred pound frame. His cheeks are lined with trails of perspiration. He seems shorter to me, and I notice he isn't wearing any shoes.

"Do you know what happened?" he asks.

I look at the two folding chairs at the center of the stage. On the floor between them is an inverted milk carton.

"You were placed between those chairs," he says. "I removed my shoes and I stood on your stomach."

I'm confused. How could I have possibly supported a three hundred pound man while suspended between two metal folding chairs?

"The milk crate was under you, just in case," he adds.

It really happened. What I thought were his palms pressing on my stomach, were actually the hypnotist's stocking feet. I really was hypnotized. As the campers filed out of the Rec Hall, several of them approach me and ask how I did it. They all thought it was some sort of trick. I assure them it was not a trick, but no one believes me.

That night, I lay in bed satisfied I had advanced one more step along the path to enlightenment. I placed my transistor radio under my pillow and drifted off to the music I would forever associate with the summer of '66.

Gimme a ticket for an aeroplane; ain't got time to take a fast train; lonely days are gone, I'm a going home; my baby just wrote me a letter... Camp was coming to an end and I couldn't wait to be home again. I told myself to hang on; it won't be long.

You ask me if there'll come a time when I grow tired of you: Never my love; never my love... I thought about the one and only thing I truly loved - my dog Fritz.

Cherish is the word I use to describe, all the feeling that I have hiding here for you inside... How I missed Fritz! I needed to be with him, and hug him, and watch his hindquarters wiggle with excitement at the sight of me. I ached for him.

During the five-hour drive home from camp, my mother broke the news that Fritz had died. She explained that the veterinarian was forced to put Fritz to sleep; he had developed a problem with his back which left him paralyzed in his hind legs. The condition was irreversible and could not be corrected, either by medication or surgery. I was devastated, particularly when my mother revealed that the euthanasia had occurred more than a month earlier. (She didn't want to tell me while I was at camp and risk spoiling my summer.)

Though I knew no one (except perhaps God) was responsible for this tragic turn of events, it was more than an eleven year old with a deep love for his dog could handle. After that, I regretted having gone to camp for the summer. *Don't go away! Don't go away! Don't ever leave the house!* Maybe I was responsible, I thought, as my heart was breaking.

TURBEYVILLE

BY THE TIME I had entered the fifth grade, it was clear who my best friends were. Everyone had a nickname that stuck like flies to a glue strip: Cohen, Bozzie, Sylvan, Ash, Moose, Mattesau, and Lebo. Everyone had their own walk. Cohen was handsome, outgoing, and athletic. He was also shaving by the time he was eleven, which made him eligible to date older girls. Bozzie was into martial arts before Bruce Lee was into diapers. His intense dedication quickly earned him a black belt in Karate. Sylvan had a reputation of always packing the greatest lunches: meatball heroes, Italian combos, chicken cutlet with bacon and barbeque sauce, corned beef on rye with spicy mustard. Ash wanted to be everybody's friend, and for the most part he succeeded. He was kind, easygoing, and remarkably accepting of other people. And Moose, well, he was just Moose. He was big, and he was strong, but he still took his Louisville Slugger to bed every night to guard against intruders. Mattesau's father owned a bowling alley, which made him popular on weekends when everyone got to play for free. He had this involuntary movement disorder, and was perpetually rocking back and forth, back and forth. This hurt his popularity at school, but mysteriously made him a better bowler. Mattesau was simply unbeatable at the game of tenpin. Lebo was the novelty kid. His father owned a business that licensed everything from Beatle wigs to Soupy Sales ties. He also imported novelties like itching powder, sneezing powder, stink bombs, and even authentic-looking rubber dog poop – the kind of stuff you'd see ads for in the back of comic books. Lebo was somewhat of an entrepreneur himself, and occasionally offered the latest of his father's wares for sale during lunch.

This was the gang. We had spent our entire elementary careers at Saddle Rock School together, gained notoriety among students and faculty, and by the time we reached fifth grade we felt like we owned the place. Every day at lunch, we claimed the same big round table at the far corner of the cafeteria. Each table was identified by a number. Ours had the number "8" scrawled across the top in wide permanent marker. Table eight might just as well have had the word "reserved" written on it. No one outside of our group dared sit there unless invited. If we were all absent from school, the table would remain empty. We were never challenged by any of the kids during lunch, and it was cool, but there was a price to pay. As a result, we remained under the close scrutiny of Old Miss Turbeyville, the all-time Grand Pooh-bah of cafeteria disciplinarians. Old Miss T. was a force to be reckoned with. The cafeteria was her domain; anyone within its confines was subject to her rules and, if those rules were violated, her form of retribution.

When Saddle Rock Elementary School broke for lunch, it was mayhem in the cafeteria. School administrators realized that Miss Turbeyville's presence was an absolute necessity if any semblance of order was to be maintained. The decibel level in the room would inevitably swell to earsplitting proportions; only Turbeyville had the divisiveness to choke the shrillness, and the authority to do it whenever and however she pleased.

Her weapon of choice was a large, brass bell with a black, tooled lacquer handle. It was her battleaxe, her bowie knife, her claymore, her cutlass, her dagger, her tomahawk missile. Turbeyville could swing that bell with the force of Zeus raising thunder for the heavens. The effect was awe inspiring. Everyone in the cafeteria, including the elderly hairnet ladies who quietly spooned globs of whatever to hordes of ravenous kids, went instantly mute. Turbeyville ruled by intimidation, and instilled the fear of God in everyone; everyone, that is, except the gang at table eight.

* * *

KIDS FILL THE LUNCHROOM to capacity as colorful lunchboxes are unsnapped and little hands reach for edible treats in brown paper bags. One of the kids yells "Custodian!" and a hush falls over the room. Lebo, looking pale and infirm, is wiping his mouth and staring at the floor; a fresh puddle of chunky pink vomit is staring back. The custodian (Mingo was his name-o), arrives with bucket and mop in hand. Turbeyville orders the cleanup while doing her best to comfort poor, sick Lebo. But when the mop strikes the ghoulish puke, it merely rolls end over end like a rubber pancake. Lebo had just cleverly orchestrated a brilliant marketing ploy for his father's latest novelty, fake vomit. It fools everyone, and we all howl, except for the custodian who is taking slightly longer to register the ingenious illusion. I am already feeling inside my pockets for cash - this was something I knew I must have, today. Surely Lebo had others to sell. Old Miss Turbeyville snickers but is not amused. She rings for SILENCE, restoring the lunchroom to a modicum of noise and confusion. Stragglers carry the last vestiges of cafeteria food to their tables, hovering over plates that smell to me like canned asparagus (i.e., dirty socks) - a sad tribute to government-approved nourishment.

Back at table 8, Sylvan senses something is wrong. His mother had promised him a fresh roast beef hero with Russian dressing and a piece of her famous chocolate cake. Earlier in the day, he had told me how much he was anticipating lunch, so much so that he was finding it hard to concentrate in class, on top of Mattesau's incessant rocking. Now, sitting beside him at lunch, I watch as Sylvan's face twists with a look of disgust as he dumps the contents of his brown paper bag onto the table. There lay a flattened sandwich of Swiss cheese (between two haggard slices of Wonder Bread), and a Hostess blueberry pie. It is not at all the lunch he expected. Sylvan is confused, but hungry, and forces down a few bites. "This sucks," he says, dejectedly returning his sandwich to its crumpled square of wax paper. He next removes the wrapping from the blueberry-filled Hostess pie and nibbles sadly on the sugar coated edge.

"I don't know what happened," Sylvan tells me. "This was supposed to be the greatest lunch of the century. And my mother knows I hate Swiss cheese."

"Maybe there was some kind of mix up," I offer. "Whose name's on the bag?"

Sylvan smoothes the brown paper bag on the table, but sees no name. "My mom always writes my name on my lunch!"

I smile. "Then that is not your lunch."

Sylvan looks up, as if suddenly shocked by my harsh, yet astute, deduction. There, sitting directly across the table, is Moose, smiling broadly between huge mouthfuls of roast beef on a hero, and slurping gobs of bright pink Russian dressing off his quivering chin. Old Turbeyville had managed to silence the house to a blissful whisper, but Sylvan is oblivious. He jumps up, points an accusatory finger at Moose and shrieks, "You stole my fucking lunch, you asshole!"

Dead silence. Turbeyville's ears stand up. She sneers, squinting as she scans the room, slowly and deliberately, for the source of the expletive, but it's obvious. Peter is standing alone, his face as purple as the filling in his Hostess blueberry pie. Like a wave, the awkward silence swells into laughter, erupting from every corner of the room, at which point Turbeyville's colossal bell clangs into action. But the din of the crowd is overwhelming, reducing the characteristic punch of her bell to a murmur. It is ineffective at roping in the calamity. Frustrated by her inability to stem the tide, Turbeyville rings harder, slamming the open end of the bell on a nearby table with astonishing force. It quells the noise, but only temporarily.

"Hand over my lunch, you little shit!" Sylvan's fury is monolithic. Apparently, he is not intimidated by Moose's imposing figure.

Moose begins to laugh, further aggravating the situation. He licks his fingers from the last of Sylvan's succulent roast beef hero. Turbeyville strides toward our table, her long skirt billowing above her waist revealing a pair of old-fashioned, lace knickers. As the scene unfolds, I pray for a harmonious outcome though it seems unlikely. Sylvan's arm is cocked and ready. In his hand is the Hostess Blueberry Pie. Moose can see it coming. He pushes back from the table and stands as Sylvan lets it rip. Surprisingly, the blueberry bullet stays whole as it speeds across the table, but then grazes Moose's ear before splitting in two. One half catches the back of Laurie Praver's golden hair. The other lands with a splat, blueberry filling and all, on the fancy laced boots of Old Miss Turbeyville.

Turbeyville is suddenly looming over us, ready to pounce. She raises her bell high in the air, pauses briefly, and then brings it down hard on the surface of table 8. She proceeds to bang the open end of the bell until it seems she will knock a cookie cutter hole straight through the wood. Instead, Turbeyville's Bell, in all its fury, strikes a thundering blow to Mattesau's right index finger;

a direct hit. The resulting sound which emerged from Mattesau is neither human nor animal, but so startling that it immediately silences every person in the room. The cafeteria gets so quiet that you can hear the faucet dripping from the janitor's closet down the hall.

Incredibly, a livid, purple nodule begins to rise on Mattesau's knuckle; first the size of a pea, then promptly swelling to resemble a colossal blood turnip. Everyone watches, marvelling at the miracle of the human body. And everyone concludes that Mattesau will no longer be unbeatable at the game of bowling.

The automatic bell signals the end of lunch, and Mattesau is carried out strapped to a chair. I notice that his mouth is open, but he isn't making a sound. I also notice something else: Mattesau had stopped rocking.

Moose offered to make peace with Sylvan by returning, untouched, the large piece of his mother's famous chocolate cake. Sylvan accepted. They shook hands at the bell, and to everyone's surprise, Moose took the full hunk of chocolate cake straight to the face. Sylvan made sure he smeared it on every inch above Moose's neck. His hair was matted; his eyes and ears were frosted shut. Even his nose was plugged with devils food. But Moose was Moose. He delighted in it all; because, in the end, he ate the cake.

TWO IN THE BUSH

THE SIGNS OF SPRING are everywhere: verdant trees thick with leaves, green grass and the whir of gasoline-powered lawn motors, vivid colors and perfumes bursting from every flower bed, and the territorial birdsongs that sweeten the morning air. Fifth grade is almost over, and there is a feeling of excitement and anticipation among me and my friends. Soon we will be upperclassmen entering sixth grade. We've finally grown up.

It's a warm Friday afternoon when the last bell rings and everyone spills onto the school grounds. I'm standing in the commons, searching out my friends, when I receive word that a sixth-grader is organizing a party at his parent's house that evening. It's a make-out party. I'm invited, and I'm told I can bring a guest. Immediately, visions of Maddy Ackerman drift through my mind. Lately, I was beginning to think I was in love with Maddy, and had even considered asking her to go steady. I can feel my I.D. bracelet weighing heavily on my wrist now.

Maddy was adorable, and I desperately wanted to adore her close up. I had never attended a real make-out party, but since I was soon to become a sixth grader, I felt ready. Until now, it had been nothing but endless rounds of Spin-the-Bottle. I had spun that Coke bottle so many times my arm ached; the game seemed like kids stuff to me now. At this stage my sex life was clearly inadequate, and I needed something more. This party offered me a chance at greater intimacy. Honestly though, I was nervous. I didn't know what to expect.

Maddy accepted my invitation and agreed to meet me at the affair. When I arrive, a bunch of kids are milling around an aluminum folding table, filling their cups with soda and ice. Maddy is standing alone, sipping something through a bright red straw. I watch her briefly from a distance, studying her pursed lips and the upturned corners of her mouth. She looks beautiful - light and buoyant in her summery dress. I can't believe she agreed to be my date at a make-out party (although I'm not sure she knew it was a make-out party). She smiles as I approach her, and I'm suddenly nervous. I jam both hands in my pockets.

"What are you drinking?" I ask, fearful that I had just asked Maddy the dumbest question in the world.

"Seven-Up. Want some?" she replies.

"I think I'll grab a Coke," I say, though I really want a sip of hers.

"I'll be right back," I add, and head for the refreshment table.

I'm hoping I'll run into Cohen, certain he could tell me exactly what to do. But Cohen is nowhere to be found. I recognize almost no one, which is unsettling. But when I look back at Maddy my worries disappear. I pour myself a glass of Coke and return to my lovely date. Maddy is easy to talk to, and good looking. She is also generous, feminine, and deferential. She makes me feel in control, affording me a satisfying taste of manhood.

At last, I see Cohen in the distance, holding hands with a sixth grade girl who I don't recognize. I ask Maddy if she knows her, but she just shrugs.

"Do you want to go over and say, *Hello*?" I ask. Maddy shrugs again. I interpret this to mean "no," which is fine with me. I didn't mind having Maddy all to myself.

About fifteen minutes pass when I realize Maddy and I are alone in the yard. Where had everyone gone? I hear Cohen's voice next; not his real voice, but a voice in my head, paraphrasing something he had told me a year earlier, after he had attended his first make-out party: "Couples disappear behind the bushes and kiss... or whatever else they want to do." Cohen had told me the bushes act as camouflage, providing a temporary haven for young lovers. Now I understand what he meant, and subtly proffer Maddy an invitation to accompany me in the bush. Amazingly, she accepts.

I take her hand and lead her into a row of pink azaleas along the side of the house. Beneath a cloak of flowers and leaves, we find a cement step below an inactive door. Maddy sits and I sit beside her. I hear a ringing in my ears, which means I'm nervous - very nervous.

"What do you want to do?" I ask, swallowing hard and almost choking on my words. My face feels hot and flush.

"I don't know. What do you want to do?" Maddy asks. She speaks softly, but in a straightforward manner. She is either way more courageous than me, or concealing her fear more effectively.

I pick at a branch. I am too nervous to say anything. My words refuse to surface. With each passing moment of inaction I grow more self-conscious. I rub sweat from the palm of my hands. I know there will never be a better opportunity to make out with Maddy Ackerman. It's now or never. I take a breath, as if preparing to swim underwater, and say, finally, "How about a kiss?"

Maddy smiles, ever so sweetly. "Okay," she whispers. I feel

as if a jumbo marble has become lodged in my gullet. I do not want to give Maddy any indication that I'm nervous, and resist the urge to swallow. Instead, I clear my throat and take her hands in mine. Her fingertips are electric. When I draw her near, our mouths come together like opposite poles of a magnet. I feel the rush of her breath; it smells like strawberry gum. Her skin is soft, like my lucky rabbit's foot, and I detect the subtle perfume of lotion on her cheek. It's frighteningly wonderful.

Then it's over.

"What do you want to do now?" I ask. Maddy smiles and shrugs her shoulders. There's a long silence as Maddy waits for my suggestion. She clearly wants to follow my lead, but I'm not sure what my next move should be. The kiss has left me totally flustered, and as the silence mounts, I can't help wondering: *What would Cohen do now?*

"Let's get out of here," I finally say, and I duck out of the bushes without looking back.

I'm a cauldron of mixed emotions: a glutinous stew of pride, humiliation, desire, fear, accomplishment and defeat. I compare the experience to taking my first injection at the doctor's office: Not knowing what to expect, the fear of pain is usually much greater than the pain itself; still you come out shaken. Such was the case of my interlude in the bushes with Maddy Ackerman. Maybe it was a necessary step along the road to becoming a man. Fortunately, I could take solace in the fact I had graduated from the juvenile pastime of Spin-the-Bottle. This, at least, was a step in the right direction.

LUCKY FELLOWS

THE FOLLOWING WEEK at school, I go to great lengths to avoid Maddy. I walk in the other direction when I see her coming toward me. I sit with my back to her during lunch. When she tries to make eye contact, I look away. I do this because I like her.

One afternoon at lunch, I see Bozzie eyeing Turbeyville like a tiger stalking prey. Today, she was on *his* radar. Bozzie catches me looking, and I make a face, as much to say, "What's up?" He points to a table of girls, where Maddy is sitting, at the far corner of the room. Seconds later, someone at that table lets out a loud scream. Turbeyville abandons her bell on our table and goes to investigate. Then, Bozzie springs into action. Turbeyville's bell briefly disappears. Seconds later it's back where she had left it, and Bozzie is sporting a wicked smile.

The commotion at the girls' table was all Lebo's doing; he had planted the fake vomit at Maddy's feet. Lebo's fake vomit never failed. The cafeteria erupts with laughter. Some kids start throwing raisins. "You?" I say to Bozzie over the din. He snickers. "Wait," he says.

Turbeyville is enraged; the veins on her neck are protruding like giant slugs. Her face is fire-engine red. She reaches for her bell. (My head already hurt from the impending, relentless noise from that bell). I'm pissed at Bozzie for instigating her torturous wrath. Turbeyville grabs her bell and shakes it with wild abandon, and... nothing. Not so much as a tinkle comes out of that bell. Turbeyville is astonished. She shakes the bell again, but the result is the same - utter silence. Then I realize the cafeteria is silent, too; as silent as if the room were completely empty in the dead of night, after the janitors had all gone home. Bozzie jabs me in the ribs and directs my attention under the table to his clenched fist. He slowly opens his hand, and there, in his palm, is Turbeyville's brass clapper.

I look up to see Miss Turbeyville, arms akimbo, towering over table 8. "You will either tell me who did this, or you'll all suffer the consequences," she says. Moose raises his hand and says, "I don't know anything, I swear." Moose is telling the truth, even though he looks like he's lying through his eyeteeth. Cohen, Ash, and Sylvan all look guilty – they had known about the scheme, even before me. Ironically, Bozzie, the guilty one, is the only one at our table who looks like the perfect angel.

"Stand up," Turbeyville orders, and we all stand. "Not you," she says, to no one in particular. "You…" She grabs Bozzie's sleeve and drags him out of the room. The rest of us sit down and wait in silence for her return.

"Where do you think she's taking him?" I finally whisper.

"Probably the Principal's office," someone says.

"Do you think he'll tell?"

"*He* stole it."

"Stole what?"

"Turbeyville's clapper," I say, and I slide it across the table to Moose.

"Hey, get out of here. I don't want it," Moose complains.

Ten minutes later, Bozzie returns to the cafeteria followed by Miss Turbeyville. As she escorts him to the table, Bozzie subtly purses his lips and shakes his head. I interpret this to mean he didn't talk, and I expected nothing less. Bozzie was tough. He was unlikely to crack under any kind of pressure or duress, even if it came from the Principal himself.

"You're lucky fellows," Turbeyville says. She dismisses Bozzie, who strolls out of the cafeteria looking once over his shoulder before he turns a corner and disappears.

"Your friend has refused to implicate any of you," Turbeyville says, smiling. "Therefore, you will *all* be required to serve detention for at least two hours after school; longer, if I catch anyone talking."

Everyone, except Bozzie, suffered for his transgression that day. Bozzie was lucky to have friends like us.

We continued to stick together, even after we graduated from the confines of elementary school and escaped the menacing wrath of Old Miss Turbeyville. But Junior High would present a whole new set of challenges: there was the future to consider, friendships would be tested, and girls would play an increasingly bigger role in my life.

MELTING POT

Saddle Rock was just one of many villages that comprised the town of Great Neck. Most, if not all, had enough young baby boomers to support their own elementary schools. Undoubtedly, the most affluent part of town was Kings Point. The famous comedian Alan King lived there, and for a long time, many of us kids believed the area derived its name from him. (This, of course, was not true.)

Seventh grade was when all the elementary schools in town were combined into one. My world, which previously existed exclusively within the confines of the tiny village of Saddle Rock, now included all of Great Neck. My peer group grew enormously, and Great Neck North Junior High was like one giant melting pot.

Though I was maturing in many ways, I still suffered daily anxiety attacks at the stroke of noon, and the paralyzing drone of the air raid siren. TV was no fun either; the Emergency Broadcast System announcements were always looming, ready to signal the prospect of a devastating nuclear attack. Though I had grown expert at concealing my fear, I was privately embarrassed by what I knew was an irrational fear - something I felt powerless to control. On the first day of seventh grade – a milestone, because I was starting Junior High, in a whole new school, with a whole new group of "Neckers" – I again disappointed myself (deeply) when the noon siren wailed. I was the only kid in the cafeteria who stopped chewing his sandwich, and reflexively peered out the window looking for a flash of white light. *What is wrong with me?* I thought. Thank God I didn't "duck and cover" under the lunch table and embarrass myself, although the impulse was undeniably there.

As I began developing friendships with kids from all over town, I was exposed to lifestyles which were vastly different from what I had previously known. At first it was like culture shock. The kids from Kings Point were notably different because they often came to school with newly-minted quarters in their penny loafers. For the first twelve years of my life, I believed I had grown up with the best life had to offer. I yearned for nothing. My life was as close as one could get to heaven on earth. I lived in a three thousand square foot split-level house on a third of an acre. My parents drove a '57 Oldsmobile before trading it in for a used Cadillac convertible. We had a housekeeper who cleaned and ironed twice a week. We rarely dined at fancy restaurants because it was never as good, or as comfortable, as our own home. We didn't require extravagant vacations. We didn't require vacations at all, but when we took them we traveled by car and slept at roadside motels. Nothing could have been more fun.

My friends from Kings Point didn't live in houses – they didn't need houses - they lived in mansions; with elevators, bowling alleys, billiard rooms, tennis courts, squash courts, indoor swimming pools, horse stables, projection rooms (which doubled as fallout shelters), and Italian fountains spread across several acres of beachfront property - all with private boat docks. These homes were so big it was easy to get lost inside.

It was fun visiting the homes of my wealthy Kings Point friends, but I never felt envious or jealous. At the end of the day, I was always relieved to return home. Lots of my friends had more than me. But were they happier? I don't believe so. The truth is; you don't need a lot to be happy.

THE ULTIMATE FAMILY VACATION

SUDDENLY, it was the middle of August, 1969. In September I would be entering the ninth grade. My family and I sat at the kitchen table having dinner. I was talking about the classes I'd be taking, school supplies, my friends, and the like. "I can't believe you'll be fifteen in February," my mother said. "Where does the time go?" my father said. "I don't want the summer to end," my brother complained, at which point my father reached inside his suit jacket and pulled out a colorful folder, slightly larger than a #10 envelope. On the front was the picture of a ship. He handed the folder to my mother, and when she opened it, a huge smile appeared on her face. He had just presented her with four first-class passages on a cruise to the Caribbean. The ship was sailing from New York Harbor the very next afternoon. Tomorrow! I could barely sleep that night. I had never been on a cruise before, but knew that my parents had taken many cruises together, before my brother and I were born. They always said it was their favorite type of vacation.

When I awoke the next morning, a white stretch limo was in our driveway waiting to take us into New York. It was only the second time I had ridden in a limousine - the first was at my Nana's funeral, five years earlier – and thought it curious that limos seemed to be employed only on extreme occasions, both happy and sad. Whatever the reason, it was a fun way to ride.

Soon we were approaching the passenger ship terminal on Manhattan's West Side. The limo pulled up to the berth at Pier 90. Hundreds of passengers scurried about, porters pushed dollies stacked high with steamer trunks, pallets of cargo and supplies swung from cables guided by massive cranes, and yellow cabs converged from every direction. I was overwhelmed by the display of activity.

I gazed up at the ship's imposing bow. Painted in big letters were the words, "S.S. Santa Maria." My mother had told me that the ship was owned by Grace Lines, the preeminent luxury cruise ship operator of the time. It was awesome.

Aboard the ship, my father hosted a "bon voyage" party in our stateroom. Many of my parent's closest friends were there, including Ethel and Gus Gabriel from the penthouse in New York City. A waiter balanced hi-balls on silver trays. I was served a "Shirley Temple;" rosy and sparkling, with a shimmering maraschino cherry perched on top. My father wore a festive, silk Hawaiian shirt in red and black. I wore a blue Nehru jacket which had a bit of sheen to it. Rex had on a navy, double-breasted sport-jacket with gold buttons. Each button was embossed with the image of a ship's anchor.

As we approached our scheduled departure time, a porter began walking up and down the corridors striking three distinct tones on a handheld chime while bellowing, "All ashore that's going ashore!" over and over. It was time for all visitors to leave the ship. We were handed rolls of colored paper streamers. When the gangplank was lifted we pressed ourselves against the rail of the ship, towering above a crowd of people on the dock. They waved at us and we tossed our streamers. Suddenly a flood of multicolored curlicues spilled down the side of the ship.

The ship's horn sounded: a violent and sustained column of air blasting through two enormous black smokestacks towering above the mid-ship decks. The walls shook and the floors rumbled. Then we were underway. Amazingly, the minute our ship pulled away from the dock, she became so steady it seemed the island of Manhattan was moving away from *us*, instead of the other way around. Soon we were steaming past the Statue of Liberty. Grasping the cool metal rail on deck, I peered at the horizon until the last sliver of land dipped below the surface of the water and disappeared.

We spent the next several days cruising on the high seas, cutting a smooth course through the dark choppy waters of the Atlantic, and then the bluer, friendlier seas of the Caribbean. The Santa Maria was a wonder to behold, and, it seemed, nothing was unattainable aboard this floating, bustling metropolis.

On our first night aboard ship, a porter delivered an invitation to our stateroom requesting the honor of my parent's company at the Captain's table for dinner. Naturally, they accepted. My mother wore a black, beaded gown with the Nathanson Dress Company label. My father wore a formal white dinner jacket and black baggy slacks. Together they made a stunning couple. As they bid me and Rex a good night and headed out the door, I couldn't help feeling proud that these were my parents. Left to our own devices, Rex and I wandered freely about the ship, and soon bumped into two cute girls from Darien, Connecticut who happened to be doing the same thing as us. They were friendly enough, so we decided to join forces and wander the ship together. As it happened, the girls were twins, and looked identical except that one had a tiny beauty mark on her left cheek. It just so happened I liked her best. The girls were fifteen, a year older than me and a year younger than my brother, which suited us fine. After exploring the ship for about an hour, we ducked into a dark, unoccupied room. It had a parquet floor and a bar, and was obviously a dance club which probably didn't open until much later. Behind the bar was a refrigerator, and in the refrigerator were several bottles of champagne. Rex and I took this as a sign from God.

I quietly peeled the heavy foil off the cork. Underneath was a twisted wire cage. "Does anyone know how to do this?" I asked. The girls shook their heads. Rex said: "I do." So I handed him the bottle. He proceeded to extricate the cork in expert fashion, and the four of us passed the open bottle around. My first champagne! It tasted vaguely like ginger ale. The bubbles sprang up through our noses. Soon we were all giggling. The champagne had me under its spell, and the effect was delightful. It ignited something charming in my personality. I felt clever. I acted silly and made everyone laugh. We played "spin-the-bottle" with the empty bottle, and I got to kiss my favorite twin on the cheek (just below her beauty mark), several times. After a few hours, Rex and I decided to return to our room, but vowed to meet up with the girls again. I was very much in love with life aboard the S.S. Santa Maria.

Everyone but my father slept late the following morning. When I woke up he was not in the room, my mother was suffering from sea sickness, and my brother seemed to be reeling with similar symptoms, induced by either an excess of sympathy for my mother, or an excess of champagne from the night before. I brushed my teeth, excused myself, and ventured outside in the hopes of finding my father.

The morning breeze was cool, and I considered turning around to get a sweatshirt, but the sun felt warm. The sky was perfectly clear and bluer than any blue I had ever before seen. It was going to be a hot one. I heard someone say, "Excuse me." I turned around. A porter was balancing an excessive amount of fine china precariously on a large silver tray: someone's room service, no doubt. I stepped aside, giving him plenty of space. I didn't want to contribute to what appeared to be a disaster waiting to happen. But it never did. "Good morning," he said, as he slipped past. Not a single teacup as much as rattled. Amazing, I thought. We're floating on the ocean, and it feels like we're standing still.

When I spotted my father he was shooting clay pigeons off the rear of the ship. The pigeons were launched from a spring loaded device. Whenever my father would yell, "Pull!" a terracotta disk the size of a salad plate would catapult into the air. A fraction of a second later, my father took aim and pulled the trigger on his shotgun. I stood back and watched for awhile, mesmerized. I hadn't been aware that my father was such a good marksman, but this was not his first cruise, nor his first time shooting clay pigeons. He hit them all dead center, blew them to smithereens, and the pieces dropped like stones into the ocean. I felt small next to him, and when he took a break to light a cigarette, I tugged on his jacket. He seemed pleased to see me.

"Wanna try?" he asked.

"Can I?" I asked.

The man in charge handed me a loaded rifle and winked at my father. "It's got some kick," my father told me. "You've got to watch out for that."

He instructed me to squint down the barrel of the gun with my right eye. "Shut your left eye. Follow the clay pigeon out of the gate, and lead it just a little with the gunsight. Stay relaxed and balanced," my father advised. "And keep the gunstock snug between your cheek and shoulder. Yell 'Pull!' when you feel ready."

I took a deep breath, readied myself, and yelled, "Pull!" The clay disk spun out over the water. I followed it with the rifle. A split second later I squeezed the trigger. There was a deafening blast and I almost fell over backward. The clay pigeon splashed into the ocean in one piece. "That's alright. Try again," my father urged. I thought to myself: I can do this. "Pull!" I yelled again. The clay disk whirred past and I fired. This time the clay pigeon shattered into a million pieces, and then disappeared with hardly a trace. "Great shot, son!" My father put his arm around me and squeezed, just a little. Then it was his turn to shoot. He raised the rifle and steadied it against his cheek, squinting through the smoke of the Pall Mall pressed between his lips. "Pull!" he yelled through the other side of his mouth. The target whizzed over the ocean. My father spun and fired, missing the clay pigeon entirely. Looking somewhat perplexed, he slowly lowered the gun, removed the stub of his cigarette, and flicked it downwind. "That usually means it's time to stop," he said. He offered me the rifle. "No thanks," I said. My shoulder ached from the recoil, but still I wanted to stay there forever, to freeze the moment in time. It was perfect.

Onboard ship that evening, there was a cocktail/costume party in the main lounge. Kids were not invited, but my parents assured me and Rex we could attend if we promised to keep a low profile. Thus, we sat quietly well-behaved at a small booth sipping Ginger Ale through narrow red straws. A live band played music from the forties while a mirrored ball rotated on the ceiling, etching fiery drops of blue light around the room. Rex and I watched with interest as a conga line of costumed adults paraded past us. They wore lavish costumes. Some had feather boas, elaborate hats, sequined garments, and theatrical makeup. I didn't see my parents, and wondered what they had planned. I knew they hadn't left our stateroom wearing costumes. "Where are Mom and Dad?" I asked Rex. And at that moment I caught a glimpse of them at the rear of the line. When they strolled past, I could see my mother was wearing a muumuu with a pillow stuffed in front. It made her look nine months pregnant. My father wore another one of his loose, colorful Hawaiian shirts. Each of them was holding a sign; my father's said "CAUSE," my mother's said, "EFFECT." It turned out, my parents won first prize for "Most Original Costume."

We weren't aboard ship more than two or three days, but by this time it seemed almost everyone knew about my mother's career as a vaudeville singer (probably because my father liked to brag about it), and eventually someone asked my mother if she would sing something. "I don't sing anymore," my mother said modestly. My father egged her on, as did everyone else in the lounge. But it wasn't until the bandleader himself beseeched her that she finally acquiesced.

Someone handed my mother a microphone. She smiled graciously at the roomful of people and cleared her throat. I felt nervous for her, but she didn't look nervous at all. My mother was in her element. I saw her look at my father with loving eyes, and he winked back. She turned to the bandleader and nodded, and as the music began to swell, she lifted the mike and, like a bird taking flight, she began to sing:

Bésame, bésame mucho,
Como si fuera esta noche la última vez.
Bésame, bésame mucho,
Que tengo miedo perderte,
Perderte otra vez.

Quiero tenerte muy
Cerca, mirarme en tus
Ojos, verte junto a mí,
Piensa que tal vez
Mañana yo ya estaré
Lejos, muy lejos de ti.

Bésame, bésame mucho,
Como si fuera esta noche la última vez.
Bésame mucho,
Que tengo miedo perderte,
Perderte después.

Kiss me, Kiss me a lot,
As if tonight was the last time.
Kiss me, kiss me a lot,
Because I fear to lose you,
To lose you again.

I want to have you very close
To see myself in your eyes,
To see you next to me,
Think that perhaps tomorrow
I already will be far,
Very far from you.

Kiss me, Kiss me a lot,
As if tonight was the last time.
Kiss me, a lot,
Because I fear to lose you,
To lose you later.

Naturally, I had heard my mother sing before, on more than one occasion. However, something about tonight was different. Her voice was warm, soothing and mellow as always, but as she sang, her gaze held my father's as though they were the only two people in the crowded room. My mother's eyes were moist, and as blue as the surrounding waters of the Caribbean. My father's eyes seemed to twinkle like a clear night sky in the middle of the ocean. Only then did I fully comprehend the depth of my parents love; this was the look in their eyes the night they met, as my mother performed on stage at the Copacabana, more than twenty-five years earlier.

The next morning, Rex and I met the twins at the pool. I had stuffed an athletic sock in my Speedo to appear more mature, but it slipped out during a dive and wound up in the middle of the deep end. Rex disappeared with his twin for an entire night, never to reveal what had transpired between the two of them.

The cruise seemed to go on forever, and it was pure bliss. Rex and I continued to explore the ship on a daily basis. We'd investigate every corridor, so that by the end of our vacation we could probably have drawn a detailed map of the vessel. We also continued to double date with the twins on a nightly basis. Rex continued to disappear with his twin halfway through the evening, leaving me alone with the other, who never seemed receptive to my romantic advances. Alas, the girl from Darien was the only wish I had aboard the Santa Maria that went unfulfilled. But it didn't matter much, because something else wonderful happened on that cruise, something I didn't expect: I began to see my father in a new light. He was more than simply someone for me to admire. He was a real person, and I was growing up. I considered the possibility that we might become friends, and that appealed to me. That's how I remember the Grace Line cruise in the summer of '69. It was a wonderful thing for me and my family to experience together… truly, the best that could happen.

TRACY

NOT COUNTING my short lived relationship with Maddy Ackerman, punctuated by the awkward kiss on the cement steps behind the azaleas at my first make out party, Tracy Lieberman was my first real girlfriend. She wore my ID bracelet for almost two years; a relatively long stretch when you're just fourteen. In that time we played countless rounds of "seven minutes in heaven." I practiced unhooking her bra with one hand until my hand was mangled with muscle cramps, and stole second base (under her shirt) on several glorious occasions. We listened to the Beatles "White Album" until the grooves wore out.

It was New Years Eve, our second auld lang syne as a couple, and Tracy's parents were out of town for the long weekend. We had made plans to celebrate at her place, and I was stoked. Already

I had begun the countdown that would rocket me into 1970 and leave my virginity behind.

In preparation for the evening, I rode my bike to Leeds Drugstore and locked it to a sign displaying the hours for the parking meters. Next to me, a cop was eyeing a car with an expired meter. He was also eyeing me, strangely, like I was some kind of juvenile delinquent or something; which I wasn't. I reached into my pocket for a nickel, fed the meter he was about to ticket, and walked away, feeling as though I had just, simultaneously, committed disparate acts of both defiance and charity.

Inside Leeds, I browsed the aisles, waiting for the store to empty, and backed into an employee stocking a shelf with toothpaste.

"Sorry," he says.

"Sorry," I say, then notice the nameplate pinned to his chest. "Sorry, Jimmy," I correct myself.

I had sex on the brain, and the only thing standing between me and Tracy was the three-pack of Trojans on the shelf in front of me. I had never bought condoms before, and I was nervous. With any luck, the store would remain empty and my transaction would unfold quickly and without incident. The cashier would be the only eyewitness to my purchase.

I carry the little box to the register, feeling like a hardened criminal. Why is this so difficult? I tell myself to relax; there's a first time for everything.

The minute I hand the Trojans to the cashier, everything turns to molasses. She slowly, (ever so painfully slowly), inspects all six sides of the box for a price. While I wait, a studious-looking woman enters the pharmacy asking for a package of Juicyfruit gum. She proceeds to dig vigorously in the bottom of her oversized bag for change. I recognize the woman as Miss Collins, my fifth-grade teacher. She looks curiously in my direction, but before I can say "hello," she looks away. Fortunately, she seems to have forgotten who I am. But then I wonder: Was I that unremarkable in fifth grade?

"Just a minute," says the cashier. "I have to check the..." I cut her off. "That won't be necessary." The cashier stares at me.

I stare back. At first I consider making a run for it, but quickly change my mind. I wasn't doing anything illegal. On the contrary, it was rather gallant of me to take responsibility for birth control. As strong as my urge was to have sex, I would not risk getting Tracy pregnant. No way. I was doing the right thing - the only thing - and decided to step up and be a man.

"Jimmy, can you get us a price on this box of *lubricated* Trojans, please?" I yell to the back of the store.

"Three pack or twelve?" Jimmy yells back.

* * *

AT SEVEN O'CLOCK that evening, I step out of a hot shower, wrap one towel around my waist, and use another to wipe steam off the mirror above my sink. I studied my reflection in the mirror. It was important I look my best this evening. I lean close to the mirror to see if a shave is necessary. It's not, and I blow-dry my hair instead. Finally, I reach in the medicine cabinet for my secret weapon: English Leather. I dab some behind my ears, replace the substantial wooden screw-top, and give myself one final look. I was ready.

An hour later, I'm standing across the street from Tracy's red brick apartment building. As usual, her doorman is outside, wearing his long grey coat and cap. His hands are clasped behind his back, and his nose is pointed skyward. He appears to be sniffing the air, as if trying to identify something that might soon arrive; the way a dog sniffs a headwind to locate food or another animal. Doormen, by their very nature, are a suspicious lot. They look for intrigue behind every door they hold ajar. They make deductions based on random clues: the comings and goings of residents, the sex and appearance of visitors, packages left in their provisional custody. They are watchful observers of the hoi polloi, adept at recognizing hidden motivation in subtle behaviors, and sometimes transmitting that information to others, especially if it seems likely to sweeten their end-of-year Christmas bonus. As I approach

Tracy's building, I decide I do not want to be part of that equation. It would be disastrous if Tracy's parents learned I had entered Wednesday night and departed Thursday morning.

I pause to look at the fire escape; it clings like a vine to the side of the red brick building. The rust-pocked iron had been slathered numerous times with black enamel paint. Some of the bolts bored into the brick were partially unthreaded or absent altogether. Still, it looked secure enough, and offered direct access to Tracy's fifth-floor bedroom window. She had agreed to leave her window unlocked. Hopefully, she remembered. I had only grasp onto the bottom rung of the ladder and pull myself up. Suddenly, I was Prince Charming, climbing Rapunzel's tower. No doubt about it: this would truly be a night to remember.

We dined on cold pizza and diet soda. I would have preferred Champagne, having developed a serious taste for this scintillating libation just four months earlier on our Caribbean cruise. Unfortunately there was none to be found, so Tracy and I settled on Tab. We passed the first part of the evening in front of the TV, wrapped blissfully in each other's arms. She let me kiss her whenever I pleased, which was often. Her smell was intoxicating, fresh.

The hands on the clock seemed to leap ahead in huge blocks of time, but this was often the case when my principal activity was making out with Tracy. We were no doubt ready to take our relationship to the next level. A quick check of the clock indicated that midnight, and the New Year, was less than an hour away.

"I think I'll take my last shower of the year," Tracy says.

"Want me to join you?" I chide, aware that showering together was far too fast for a couple of kids in the eighth grade.

"Yeah... right." One of the things I loved about Tracy is the way she evoked perspective by mingling propriety with sarcasm. I poke my tongue out playfully, then, when her back is turned, flip her "the bird," thus expressing my true feelings.

I sink into the sofa and check my back pocket. The rubbers are still there. Had I mentioned them to Tracy? I couldn't remember.

I can hear the shower roaring in the next room and imagine

the water touching Tracy's body. I am jealous of the water. I want to be the water. After the flow stops, I hear the drone of her hairdryer.

"The excitement is building here in Times Square," say the perpetually youthful announcer from the crossroads of the world. "The ball will begin its descent in less than twenty minutes."

Tracy returns wearing a pink chenille bathrobe. Her hair is still damp, and she looks very sexy. I pat the sofa cushion next to me, proffering an invitation to cuddle.

"You smell good," I say, and I give her a hug. I can feel the rush of excitement building in my loins as Tracy melts in my arms. She closes her eyes, her lips part, and I kiss her softly on the mouth. It feels incredibly natural. Soon our breathing assumes a profound synchronicity; our chests seem to heave as one.

The television cameras continue to beam live images from Times Square. A sea of drunken revelers are staring skyward at the Allied Chemical building as the traditional glass ball begins its sixty-second descent to signal the start of 1970.

"Fifty-seven, fifty-six, fifty-five…"

I reach beneath Tracy's robe, exhilarated by both the contour of her breast and the start of new decade.

"Thirty-three, thirty-two, thirty-one…"

Slowly, I peel her robe off her shoulder, the blue TV light exaggerating the forbidden nature of the act.

"Fourteen, thirteen…"

One of Tracy's breasts is now fully exposed, and my mouth wanders there.

Tracy's reaction is involuntary and immediate. Her thumb catches the inside of my mouth, forcing it back and momentarily choking me. Her fingernail slices through my palette, and my tongue is suddenly infused with the salty taste of blood. She's got quick reflexes, I thought to myself. But I am very disappointed. The evening had taken a turn for the worse.

"Happy new year," I whisper, not knowing what to say next, and somewhat taken aback by the violent nature of Tracy's action.

"Happy new year, lover," she replies, before kissing me on the lips.

Little was said after that. Tracy fell asleep on my arm, and I was unable to wake her. I couldn't sleep, except for the arm Tracy was lying on; it was the worst case of "pins and needles" I had ever felt. In the morning, Tracy offered to make eggs and bacon, but I left immediately after downing a glass of orange juice.

As I walked home, my mind was racing. Several kids at school had been bragging about going all the way for more than a year. The thought of being left behind with some prude who wouldn't even let me see her naked was unbearable. It was hard enough lagging behind in height and facial hair, unlike the most popular boys, some of whom were already capable of growing full beards. But sex was something I could control, or so I thought. Several times throughout the night I attempted to loosen Tracy's robe (while pressing my lips tightly shut). I desperately wanted to explore what lay beneath, but she was like a guard dog that slept with one eye open, foiling my every attempt with a determined wave of her arm; even her belt had been double knotted.

I broke up with Tracy two weeks later. I didn't want to break up with her, but I had to defend my honor; protect my reputation. The day we returned to school, all the girls rushed to comfort Tracy. All the guys rushed to pat me on the back. Despite the gender-specific support from my friends, I remained unresolved about the evening. I was upset that it did not go according to plan, and this was not the way I wanted the New Year to begin.

It took several weeks, but I finally grew up. I realized my failure to have my way with Tracy didn't mean that I had failed. We had fun that night. It was a memorable New Years Eve. My relationship with Tracy may have changed, but we could still be friends. It was not the worst that could happen.

THE WORST THAT COULD HAPPEN

THE NATHANSON DRESS COMPANY flourished for more than thirty years. But by the mid-sixties, the labor unions began demanding too much for their members, and, along with dozens of garment makers at that time, my father was forced to close his doors. It was a difficult period for my father, but once he accepted the inevitable, he seemed to step a little lighter, having also left behind the stress that comes with owning his own business. But with two sons still to raise, my father needed an income. He turned eagerly toward the excitement of Wall Street where he decided to reinvent himself as a stockbroker. As before, he took the train into the city every morning, but now he'd return home with books and study guides. For months, he worked late into the night preparing for his broker's license, and when the time came he aced the exam. Within months, my father rose to become Vice President at a firm on Wall Street. He seemed content with this new line of work - conversing with clients on the telephone, engaging in high-level meetings. There was a social aspect to the job, providing another outlet for my father's gregarious personality.

On a clear morning in February, 1970, I lay in bed enjoying that peaceful, semi-conscious state, neither fully asleep nor fully awake, when I hear my mother's mellifluous voice creep into a dream.

"You hoo," she intones sweetly. "Come on, Snooky; time to get up."

I kick the covers, (an acknowledgment to my mother that she has been heard), but keep my eyes closed and follow the sound of my mother's footsteps as she heads down the hall and into the kitchen. Soon, coffee beans are churning in the Hotpoint grinder.

My window is opened a crack, allowing unseasonably mild air to spill past the chiffon drapes in my bedroom. The fresh air lifts my spirits, and mixes with the song of a robin protecting its nest. Could springtime be just around the corner, I wonder? Next I hear the familiar sound of my father's knuckles rapping against my doorframe.

"Seven o'clock," he announces in a deep, commanding voice. "Get up."

I take no liberties with my father's demands. I force my eyes open, and there is my father's towering figure, smiling down at me - my daily dose of reassurance. Seeing him is all it takes to convince me that all is right with the world. His smile tells me not to worry, to embrace the miracle of another glorious day. His eyes tell me he will always be there, no matter what. I don't question his unspoken promise. As his son, I know it is my birthright - something to which I am permanently entitled.

I fling the covers aside. "I won't be home for dinner," I explain. "There's a basketball game after school. Everyone's going."

"Well, then I'll see you tonight when you get home. Have a good time."

"I will, Dad." I wasn't accustomed to telling him I loved him. I assumed it would embarrass him because it wasn't the manly thing to do. Instead, I simply add, "Goodbye."

The basketball game was a runaway victory for Great Neck North. They beat Plandome, 72 to 55. When it was over, several of us wandered into town and ordered burgers at Kreigers, the local soda fountain. I got home at nine.

The house is dark. I follow a light into the kitchen where my mother and brother are leaning silently against the cabinets. Their faces are grim, and I'm suddenly confused. I imagine my father already upstairs in bed - he sometimes turned in early when his ulcer was bothering him – but my mother informed me otherwise. "Your father is in the intensive care unit at North Shore Hospital."

"What happened? Is he alright?" I ask, biting my lip. My mother was not an alarmist. She calmly explains that he'd had a heart attack, was being monitored, and that he'd be fine. I believe her. I want to believe her. I need to.

My father had suffered a massive heart attack while returning home on the four-twenty-two from Penn Station. He collapsed at the Great Neck Station climbing the steps from the platform. My brother was there to meet the train. Someone had called an ambulance, but my father regained consciousness before it arrived and insisted my brother drive him home.

My mother helped my father into bed. Although he assured her he was fine, his color soon turned ashen, he went into shock, and lost control of his bodily functions. At that point my mother didn't wait for an ambulance. She rushed him to North Shore Hospital in the back seat of her car.

As I stood in the kitchen listening to the story, I wasn't panicked, and I didn't feel like crying. Somehow I knew my father would be fine. He was still young (only 68), strong, and had recently been given a clean bill of health by his doctor.

"He's hooked up to a lot of equipment," my mother tells me. "But he squeezed my hand, and his grip was powerful."

"When is he coming home?" I ask.

"The doctors want to monitor him overnight. I'm sure he'll be home in the morning." My mother's voice is full of conviction. She tells me and Rex not to worry. She tells us to get a good night's sleep.

"The doctors will call if there's a problem," my mother concludes. After that, we got ready for bed.

I awake to the muffled sound of my mother's voice. She's back in the kitchen, talking on the telephone. Although I can't make out what she was saying, the message is unmistakably clear: my father would not be coming home. I would soon discover that his condition had worsened in the middle of the night. He slipped into unconsciousness, and his heart stopped. Doctors were unable to revive him.

I don't attempt to get out of bed, but roll onto my stomach and bury my head in my soft feather pillow. It is a moment that would define me: first there is hope, and a world full of possibilities; then, suddenly, I'm standing alone in the dark, with barely enough clothing to keep me warm. The soft, plush rug my father had lovingly placed beneath my feet at birth had been yanked from under me. Just days before my fifteenth birthday, without warning, my father and I ran out of time.

Mom quietly enters my room, not appearing as though she'd been crying. I know she had composed herself for my benefit. "He didn't make it," was all she said. But her words were unnecessary, and I could tell from her sullen expression, she knew it, too. "Where's Rex?" I ask. She tells me he's in his room. I should give him some space. Then she says she has to make some calls and returns to the kitchen. I bury my head in my pillow and cry.

In an instant, the carefree feeling that had always guided my spirit was replaced by something less friendly: a voice, a constant reminder of the randomness and fragility of life. And it was impossible not to become a more cautious person, always trying to anticipate whatever tragedy was lurking just out of sight, in the darkness.

I didn't expect to see so many friends at the funeral. I remember my reaction upon seeing Tracy, who had thoughtfully come to pay her respects. I asked, "What are *you* doing here?" The moment the words floated out of me (I was in shock, after all) I realized how dumb I must have sounded. But that's when I knew I had broken up with someone who had far more to give than her virginity. Tracy was a friend, and friends are forever.

"What are *you* doing here?" I kept hearing myself say. But so many unexpected faces somehow helped relieve the ache in my fractured soul.

Following the burial, the ordeal continued at our house. There was food everywhere. My neighbor Harold came by with his younger brother Marshall. He handed me a tape for the portable eight-track player my parents had given me for Christmas. It was the new Jefferson Airplane album, "Volunteers of America." The song, "Good Shepherd," took me deep inside myself to a place of curious contradiction, where equal parts of serenity and hysteria occupied one space at the same time. Yesterday I held the world in the palm of my hand. Today it was rapidly slipping away.

Several years passed before my mother allowed herself to disturb the garments in my father's closet. His suits still hung neatly, facing in one direction, just as they had when my father was alive. Several of them, worn once or twice before going to the dry cleaners, still retained the faintly fruity smell of tobacco and Old Spice. Oftentimes I would enter my father's closet, bury my head in an armful of his suits, and he would miraculously return, almost as vividly as in real life.

I watched the red Salvation Army truck back out of our driveway. As it disappeared down the street, I knew I would have to find some other way to restore the memory of my father. Then the tears came again - apparently, I had not finished grieving.

I realized I had lost something which could never be replaced, not ever, and there was nothing I could do to change that. It was out of my hands. It was out of my hands as it had always been, except now there were no illusions. From this point forward, and for the remainder of my life, I could only experience my father as a continuous Technicolor loop in my mind. Sometimes he would surprise me, showing up in an occasional dream. Ironically, that's when it felt most real: when it was only a dream.

My mother did not skip a beat. Like the realist she was, she continually asserted that life would go on. "Try this, darling," she said, reassuringly. Then she put my hand on my chest and said, "You can feel him with every beat of your heart."

I took my cue from her. I trusted her. But despite my early attempts to elevate this tragedy into something positive, sadness enveloped me like a heavy shroud. No one seemed to fully understand. If I could have fun every so often and laugh, I was not doing too badly; would it not, to embrace more than a brief moment of happiness from time to time, constitute a gross betrayal of a son's love?

After my father died, I was no longer startled by the piercing blast of the air raid siren or alarmed when my favorite TV show was interrupted by a test of the emergency broadcast system. As far as I was concerned, the bomb had already dropped.

BOOK THREE

UNCERTAINTY

SMOKING POT

THERE IS ONE great disadvantage to growing up in an affluent community: kids and cops have it too easy. Both groups have too much time on their hands. It creates a stressful dynamic, because we are always rivals in an ever-changing game. It can be calculating like chess, or deceptive like poker. Sometimes it's a fast round of checkers. Whatever the game, there is always a winner and a loser. And there is always a price to pay.

It was the winter of 1971. One night, Cohen, Moose, Ash, and I were walking from my house to Pete's, when a Great Neck cop pulled up beside us in the familiar blue and orange squad car. It was past eleven on a frigid, snowy evening in the middle of January; cold enough to produce frostbite to any exposed part of the body. We were all wearing winter coats, but since Pete's house was only a few blocks away, none of us were sufficiently bundled against cold weather like this. At best, we were good for ten minutes, tops. Now, some old geezer of a cop was stopping us in the most ceremonious fashion; lights flashing and siren blaring, as though he were apprehending four dangerous criminals. One would think our pictures were hanging prominently in the main vestibule of the Great Neck post office.

We were shaken - scared shitless, in fact – as any 15-year-old would be who was concealing a large bag of marijuana in his coat pocket. The situation amounted to nothing less than a bad hand in a game of poker. We had no ace in the hole. Only our best poker faces stood between us and a night in the local jail. It was time to bluff.

The cop lowers his window, and we're struck with a blast of heat, and the smell of gin. He removes his hat and tosses it on the dash, revealing a head of thinning, matted gray hair. "You know, when I was your age, my buddies and I would hang out past midnight, sometimes drinking. You boys aren't drinking, are you?"

"No sir," we echo in unison. We look at each other in the cold. From the tone of the officer's voice, it's apparent this is something other than official business. On this quiet, frigid night in the dead of winter, it seemed the officer was desperate for companionship - more than the alcohol had to offer.

Moose tries charming the officer. "We were just at his house watching some television and decided to go visit our friend, Pete."

"Whose house were you at, son? His?" The cop points to Ash.

"It was my house, sir," I admit. My hand is in my pocket clutching a baggy filled with a substantial quantity of marijuana. Despite the cold, my palm feels hot and clammy.

"What's your name?" asks the cop.

"Nathanson."

"Nathanson? You have a first name?"

"It's Brad."

"Nathanson..." The cop rubs the white stubble on his chin. "Oh yeah, I know your family. Over on Grist Mill Lane."

"Right," I admit.

For some reason I had lied. I actually lived down the block on Cooper Drive. I immediately begin to regret my hasty and dishonest response. What if he's testing me? Fear chokes me and sends blood rushing to my head. Keep cool, I'm thinking. The last thing I want is to get busted and blow it for everyone else. I look at my friends and feel the pressure of everyone's eyes upon me.

The cop flattens his tongue, licks the meaty part of his hand, and smoothes his chaotic hairdo. "Parents are home, right?" He was testing me again, looking for a hole in my story, no doubt.

"Yes. They are. We just left them. But I think they're sleeping by now," I say, pleased with the candor of my reply. The cop looks at Cohen who is vigorously patting himself, trying to keep warm.

"What's your name?"

"The name's Cohen, sir. Brad Cohen."

"Oh, I see, another Brad. Your parents are Norman and Millie. Is that right?"

"That's right. And I was just headed home, you know, 'cause it was getting late, so I was gonna walk a few blocks with these guys and go home 'cause it's sort of on the way, if you know what I mean."

Cohen tends to talk incessantly whenever he's terribly nervous. And it was obvious, very obvious, he was terribly nervous now. He had every reason to be. Cohen's happy-go-lucky nature usually worked to his advantage, (he had an uncanny ability to smooth-talk girls and get anything he wanted), but sometimes it got him in trouble. He tended to leave incriminating evidence in plain sight, particularly around his room, and his parents were naturally always finding it. I hoped now that he hadn't forgotten the bulging pocket of his winter coat filled with a baggie containing several ounces of pot. Of course, if the cop were to bust any of us that night, Cohen would likely do his best to convince him that we were holding it for a friend who he would refuse to name.

An hour later, we were still standing outside the squad car, frozen from head to toe. Heat continued to radiate from inside the squad car. Although we were pleased the officer was toasty and warm, we were not doing so well. Ash was shivering. Moose could not stand still. Cohen was blowing into his bare hands in a futile attempt to stay warm. My cheeks were on fire and my feet were numb. I began to wonder if the cop knew we were carrying contraband. Perhaps he was keeping us in the cold to teach us a lesson. Nevertheless, by now I was angry and had lost patience with the game. I looked at my wrist, pretending to check the time, though I was not wearing a watch.

"I really need to get home," I say. "My mother expected me thirty minutes ago."

"Yeah, me too," Moose chimes in. He and I were the recalcitrant ones, which would explain why, at school, we were no strangers to the office of the Principal. We also had a decent sense of injustice and despised the misuse of authority. Just because someone is an adult, or a cop, or wears a uniform, or has a title, doesn't necessarily make them right.

After Moose speaks, there's a long pause. We stood there, frozen, altogether forgetting we could be busted at any moment, perhaps thinking a warm jail cell might be preferable to our present situation.

The cop yawns and returns his hat to his head. "Go home, boys. What I need now is a cup of coffee and a donut. Get home safe." At this point, the cop closes his window and speeds off in a white cloud of exhaust.

We look at each other, incredulous. The cold air is all that's left of the night. We part without words, cutting through yards, scaling fences, each of us taking the shortest possible route to the warmth and safety of our respective homes. No jail tonight.

SITTING DUCK BLIND

MY MOTHER'S HOT CHOCOLATE is better than any powdered mix from the store; she always uses real ingredients, shaving bits of cocoa into simmering milk, then adding heaping spoonfuls of sugar, and topping it off with a dollop of fresh whipped cream she prepares in advance. I lick the syrupy remnants from the rim of my mug, thank mom, and head out to the garage. "Zip up. It's cold," I hear her say as I pedal my ten-speed Tour de France down the driveway. Cohen, Ash, and I had made plans to meet at the Saddle Rock dock after lunch, and I was late.

The sun shone brightly, but I can't appreciate its warmth. Gliding swiftly on my bike, the frosty air is stinging my cheeks. My eyes water profusely. But I don't slow down. Cohen and Ash are waiting. When I arrive at the dock, I lay my bike on top of theirs and scale the locked fence, indifferent to an official-looking sign warning trespassers to "Keep Out" or risk criminal prosecution.

We had experienced a number of exceptionally cold winters in recent years, but the Long Island Sound never looked like it did now. The water was completely frozen, all the way from the beach to a fringe area, perhaps two hundred yards out, where the ice broke into large chunks and bobbed in the choppy waters beyond. Cohen, Ash, and I needed only to traverse half that distance to reach the duck blind.

The duck blind (a small wooden shed built atop a floating platform), materialized for the first time in early autumn. It had been purchased by a local group of hunters who had anchored it roughly a hundred yards offshore; this, after all the sailboats, catamarans, and motor craft (the adult toys in which our neighbors cheerfully frolicked throughout summer) were removed from their moorings and placed in storage for the winter.

A communal four-man dinghy (now padlocked and overturned on the small, grey dock where Cohen, Ash, and I stood), would ferry the band of hunters to the platform on weekends before dawn. They would row out wearing floppy camouflage hats and insulated coveralls, hide inside the duck blind until a southbound flock came within range, and, sportingly (of course) ply our unwitting feathered friends full of buckshot, all for the thrill of watching the wounded, incapacitated birds drop awkwardly out of the sky to no uncertain death. On some mornings, as I lay in bed, I could hear the reverberation of the hunter's double-barreled shotguns exploding raucously over the proximate banks of the Long Island Sound.

Now, the duck blind sits quietly abandoned, frozen in a thick layer of ice and snow, empty like a spent shell casing, painted white with the collected spatter of seagull droppings. Cohen, Ash and I gaze at it from our position on the dock. We'd been harboring a perverse interest about the duck blind for months, probably because it was on our turf. This was our beach; we grew up here; we were intimately familiar with every inch of shoreline. The duck blind seemed not only an abhorrence of purpose, but a territorial breach which, we felt, entitled us access. It was time to confront our prickling curiosity. It was time to scratch the itch. Although we had considered exploring the platform sooner, we were deterred for several reasons. For one, we had no way to get there (none of us held a key to the dinghy). Secondly, we weren't anxious to get our heads blown off. Our characteristic "balls of steel" notwithstanding, we thought it prudent to exercise caution where firearms were concerned, particularly when those firearms were in the hands of grownups that "got off" on killing for sport. At the moment, however, it seemed unlikely that the hunters would arrive unannounced. We also recognized we could access the duck blind by simply walking across the ice. It certainly looked solid enough to support our weight, which made this a ripe opportunity to finally proceed with our long-standing investigation. We were aware that entering the duck blind would, technically, constitute an act of trespassing, but considered this a trivial misdemeanor compared with others we had perpetrated in the past.

I offer to lead, and clutch a turnbuckle fastened to the dock as I lower myself gingerly onto the ice. I'm greatly relieved when I let go and stand up; the ice doesn't yield, even after repeated stomping, and I'm confident it's as robust as it appears. "Let's go boys," I say, and just like that the three of us are walking on top of the Long Island Sound!

The trouble begins as we're about fifty feet from the dock. Cohen had enthusiastically slid past us and is in the lead. I'm in the middle, and Ash is close behind, when I hear the sound of sloshing water, followed by crackling, and more sloshing. When I look up, Cohen is on a frozen teeter-totter, hopping frantically from one slippery slab of ice to the next, just an instant before it fractures under his weight, exposing a rabid chop of unmercifully frigid water.

I raise my arm, signaling Ash to freeze (no pun intended), and when he does, the ice cracks beneath us. Suddenly we're wobbling like two men on a child's surfboard, riding the wave of a Tsunami. Our survival instinct kicks in, and we double our efforts (as Cohen is attempting to do), clumsily hopping across jagged shapes of ice, as the heaving waters snap at our feet. Although a slip and plunge could only result in an untimely hypothermic death for both of us, at no point do we consider turning back; we were already halfway there. However, we are in no way lacking a sense of urgency about our predicament.

Miraculously, as if some higher power had intervened, the three of us reach the duck blind, which is now bobbing freely in the water, surrounded by wet slabs of ice. We grab the float and climb inside, aware that we might be fated to remain for some indeterminable length of time, which is unsettling. Even more unsettling is the fact that the duck blind is less interesting than we had expected. It smells sour like (what else?) fish and seagull droppings. There were no cool artifacts left behind by the hunters: no shell casings, nothing carved onto the walls. And the proportions of the float itself are unimpressive: it feels like a baseball dugout designed for a paltry team of four midgets.

"Not much happening here but the view," Ash says. He lights a Newport cigarette and offers me a drag, but I'm in no mood to smoke - menthol, in particular.

"How we gonna get back?" I say. "My feet are friggin' freezing." One thing was certain; we could no longer go back the way we came. The frosty waters of the Long Island Sound were blasting through the cracks we'd precipitated when crossing the ice.

Cohen proposes a solution: "Look," he says, pointing toward the beach. "The ice there is solid, all the way in."

Cohen was right. "Let's blow," I suggest, but Ash wants to finish his cigarette. "Chill out. We just got here," he says, screwing up his face at his poor choice of words.

Cohen reminds us that it will soon be dark. He has a point. It got dark fast and early this time of year. The sun has already dropped below the span of the Throgs Neck Bridge, and it's only four o'clock. By the time Ash flicks the butt of his Newport onto the ice, the shoreline is enveloped in a pinkish-blue haze.

One by one, we step off the duck blind, focusing on the precarious platform of ice under foot, and advance toward the beach. The ice does not acquiesce as before, but our wet sneakers rob us of much needed traction. We slide quickly, but carefully. With approximately thirty yards to go, Ash's feet slip out from under him and he lands violently on his back. The fall seems to unfold in slow motion. Cohen and I hold our breaths, and pray that the ice does not succumb to the impact of Ash's body. Fortunately, our prayers are answered. The ice holds. We shuffle over and help

Ash to his feet. As we brush the slush off his back, now soaking wet, we hear several blasts of a siren followed by the muffled shrill of a man's voice.

The shore road runs parallel to the beach atop a ninety foot embankment (the result of many years of erosion). Parked on the road, and clearly the source of the commotion, is a shiny red hook and ladder, its lights flashing. The Fire Chief is standing at the rear of the truck, flailing his arms and shouting something which, by the time it reaches us, is unintelligible. Cohen, Ash and I look at each other, dumbfounded. It would have been nice to be rescued at this point, but none of us can imagine how a hook and ladder was going to reach, especially since it looked so tiny on top of that high ridge. We laugh at the absurdity of the situation, but continue toward the shore. Then, we hear the whirring of another siren; this one louder and more persistent than the first. A familiar blue and orange Nassau County police cruiser has pulled alongside the fire truck, and two uniformed cops are getting out.

I hear one of them yell: "You _ids. Get the _ell _ver here, _ow!"

"Guys," I say, feeling deflated, "who thinks they can fill in the blanks?"

We hasten toward the shore, and a second cruiser appears – siren wailing, lights flashing – then a third.

"Are we in trouble, yet?" Ash says, as a hoard of police officers scurry down the embankment. It's clear we are being targeted for imminent apprehension, and we knew we were on thin ice. Luckily, we reach solid ground before the cops reach us. Then, we do what any reasonable teenaged kid would in the face of public humiliation and jail time: we run. We double back to my house, cutting through a network of backyards. We're certain of only one thing: this was our turf. We knew every shortcut, every hiding place, and every nook and cranny in the neighborhood. The cops didn't have a chance in hell of catching us.

We arrive at my house, somewhat out of breath, to find my mother unloading groceries from the trunk of her Caddy. "Hi kids.

Where are your bikes?" she asks. I tell her the roads were slippery, so we left them at Cohen's. "Hmmm," she murmurs. Usually I can tell, but (was it something in her voice?) I'm not sure if she's buying my story.

     We didn't go near the dock for several days after that. We had seen enough episodes of "Dragnet" on TV to know that criminals always return to the scene of the crime - where they are often apprehended. But when we finally did return, our bikes were gone.

     "Where is your bike?" my mother would ask whenever I needed a ride somewhere, and I would concoct some elaborate story regarding its mysterious whereabouts. Each story was as contradictory as it was implausible. My mother didn't believe a word, of course, but always accepted my explanations in good faith. I believe she had a motive. She cared little about what happened to my bike; it was just a bike. More likely, this was an opportunity for her to cultivate a trusting relationship, and encourage me to share, honestly, the experiences of my youth.

     Finally, I spun a prodigious tale so convincing, my mother saw fit to call police headquarters and report my bike stolen. The story was supposed to have a happy ending: the police would believe my bicycle had been stolen from our garage by a band of marauding juvenile delinquents, taken for a joyride and abandoned at the dock. My impounded bicycle would be returned henceforth in perfect working condition. But like most fairy tales, this one didn't come true. I never saw my bike again; it vanished, along with the bikes of Cohen and Ash. But it wasn't all bad. Fortunately, the duck blind also vanished, and this was an ending we could all live with.

CENTER OF GRAVITY

AFTER MY FATHER DIED, I couldn't stop feeling I was alone in a dinghy, hopelessly adrift in the middle of the ocean, without oar, anchor, or compass. At once, all control, direction, and security seemed to vanish. I had lost my way. I was in search of something;

not a replacement for my father, which I knew was impossible, but rather, what he represented. I needed something to ground me; something good to guide me. I tried TM, but that didn't cut it anymore; I had long ago put my mantra on a shelf, where it continued to collect copious amounts of dust. Cohen and Ash were feeling a need for something, too. We were increasingly on the edge of serious trouble, it seemed, too close for comfort in most cases. We all needed grounding before we did something we would someday regret. So it is not surprising that when someone told us about the Meher Baba spiritual center in New York City, we rushed to see what it was all about.

It was Cohen's older brother, Robert, who suggested it. Robert was not into it for himself, but his girlfriend at the time, Eva, had been planning to check it out. Although we were only fifteen, Eva was seventeen and had recently procured her driver's license. She agreed to drive us to and from the Meher Baba center, located on Barrow Street in Greenwich Village. It may seem insane that a couple of 15-year-olds would be permitted to go unescorted into the city to attend what, on the surface, appeared to be some kind of cult. My mother seemed unconcerned. But Cohen's parents made their own pilgrimage in advance to assess the situation. Though they were perplexed by the whole idea (the Cohens were Jewish), they couldn't find anything overtly objectionable to prevent their son from going.

It was a stormy night in March when we set off for New York to attend our first meeting. Eva found a parking spot on the street, about a block away, and we raced to get out of the rain, finally ducking into the three-story walk-up. We shook water from our clothes and hair in an effort to look halfway presentable to the group of people we were about to join. We were all aware of the importance of first impressions.

We climbed the narrow stairway to the third floor. When we saw several dozen pair of shoes piled outside one particular door, we knew we had found the right apartment. Affixed to the door was a poster; a large, sepia-colored photograph of Meher

Baba. He wore a friendly smile. Below his likeness were the words, "Don't worry; be happy."

We looked at each other. "Are we sure we want to do this?" I asked the group. They nodded, smiled, and we all kicked off our shoes, adding them to the top of the pile.

An older man with a heavy white beard responded to our decisive knock. "Jai Baba," he said in a resonant voice as he greeted us. We introduced ourselves. He introduced himself as Paul, and invited us inside.

People were milling about the room, talking softly and hugging each other. They looked like recovering alcoholics and drug addicts, but I felt safe enough. Presumably they were here to help themselves, same as me. If they were recovering alcoholics and drug addicts, far be it from me to judge them. After all, I was recovering from something too: the loss of my father.

Paul walked us across the room, and introduced us to a woman named Linda Beighle. She looked about twenty-six, and had strawberry blond hair cut in a shag style. She had blue, wide-set, almond-shaped eyes, and a welcoming smile. She seemed to possess that nurturing gene. I was immediately drawn to her.

Linda explained the customary protocol of the weekly meetings. There would be readings, silent meditation, and the evening would conclude with a song. Soon, people began sitting cross legged on area rugs, and faced the front of the room. We found a patch of carpet and followed suit. Paul stood before us and began reading from a paperback book. The book had a blue cover, the color of a robin's egg, and contained the teachings of Meher Baba.

For more than an hour, Paul read about love, and truth, and freedom - freedom from things like greed, aggression, fear, worry, drugs and alcohol. He read about life's illusions, and man's struggle to know God and understand himself. Everything he said resonated with me; it seemed to make sense. I looked around the room, and everyone was smiling. The answer seemed simple; be tolerant of others, respect yourself, practice moderation, engage in meditation, express gratitude, love God.

When the meeting ended, there was a table set up with pamphlets, books and other items for purchase. I left with some pamphlets which explained Baba's philosophy. Those were free. I purchased a small photo of Baba; black and white, encased in a Plexiglas disk, and attached to a leather cord so it could be worn around the neck.

The four of us were naturally high as we drove back to Great Neck that night - so much so, in fact, no one noticed we had been driving without our headlights on – that is, until we were pulled over by a cop. Luckily, Eva is very charming, and was easily able to sweet-talk her way out of a ticket.

The weekly meetings became a regular occurrence, and I was delighted to discover the positive effects of our new found spiritualism on my damaged psyche. My favorite album became George Harrison's, "All Things Must Pass." I listened to it incessantly. It was unendingly beautiful - and meaningful. Meanwhile, Linda and I grew to know each other better. Something happened to me whenever I was in her presence: my heart would race a little, and I felt happy. Linda was a free spirit, and had the power to carry me along. Her love was complete and unconditional, but never exclusive. She could not be confined to a single relationship, but it was clear she had reserved a special part of herself for Meher Baba, and for that reason she remained celibate. There was a price to pay for loving Linda, but as far as I was concerned it was worth it.

As spring approached, and the days grew longer and warmer, we noticed that Linda had been absent from the meetings for several weeks in a row. When we questioned Paul, he informed us that she had embarked on her yearly pilgrimage to the Meher Baba Spiritual Center, located in Myrtle Beach, South Carolina. She would probably be gone for at least a couple of months. The news was disconcerting to me. I was missing her already. I also felt slighted that she hadn't thought to tell me she was leaving – but it was part of the price. A few days later, my phone rang. It was Linda, calling to invite us to join her at the retreat for a week - a week which happened to coincide with spring recess.

3 A.M.: Cohen, Ash, Eva and I are on a Greyhound bus bound for Myrtle Beach. It's a grueling, non-stop, eighteen hour trip. Eva is sleeping next to me, with her head on my shoulder. The pale moonlight strikes her face, enhancing her high cheekbones. She looks beautiful to me. I'm wishing she were mine, but know it's impossible, so I try to absorb this closeness: the smell of her hair; the weight of her head of my shoulder. Unfortunately, the intimacy is not shared. It is mine alone. I finish the jug of cheap wine I'd been drinking since noon. It's too much, and I begin to feel sick. The queasiness grows. I try to fight it, and finally burp - a long, vile eructation, rising out of my depths like a fiery serpent. I feel enormously relieved, and fall asleep within minutes.

Early the next morning we arrive at the Greyhound Bus terminal in downtown Myrtle Beach. When I step off the bus, I immediately notice restrained tension between blacks and whites. The blacks yield, but hesitatingly so, as if coyly grasping for entitlement. There is an unworldly ambiguity on the street; remnants, perhaps, from the Civil Rights Movement of the '60's, or the whisper of further change in the wind.

The Meher Baba Center is a camp for searching one's soul. This place is quiet. We sleep in tiny log cabins, take cold showers outdoors, eat brown rice with wooden sticks, take long walks, and meditate on hallowed ground.

We find our sleeping quarters, and hike to the dining room. Linda Beighle is there, looking radiant, and steaming vegetables in a large pot. Her sweet Irish face seems to glow. With her strawberry blond hair, and shag cut, she looks a lot like Jane Fonda in the movie, "Klute." But most striking is her inimitable spirit. I am in its grip once again. And it catches me, like it had already caught, I could plainly see, so many of the guests already in the room. I needed to be close to her, again. I approach her, and my heart begins to race. The essence of musk mingles with her personal scent, producing an infusion more beautiful and enchanting than anything in nature. The attraction is irresistible. All I want is to stand next to her and breathe.

Linda and I quickly get reacquainted, and before the night is over we make a date to watch the sun rise. I rise at 4am and take an iced cold shower. Moonlight guides us along a narrow wooded path to the beach. We romp along the trail, often skipping, like two free spirits. Linda tells me about her auntie, pronouncing it, "Onti," for which I make fun of her. We are out of breath when we reach the shore, and the sun has yet to rise.

Great plumes of sea foam blow in from the breakers, and roll onto the huge, expansive beach. We run, skirting the edge of the water, holding hands, and kicking at the knee-deep foam. At first the sun is a sliver on the horizon, then an enormous ball, the color of a cut blood orange.

After seven days, our time at Myrtle Beach had come to an end. Linda drives us to the bus terminal in her tan VW minivan - the original hippie mobile, with faded brown drapes on the windows. I don't want to leave. Mostly, I don't want to leave Linda. I needed her in my life. She is like a breath of fresh air, happiness, lightness of being, freedom. I bum a Camel cigarette off of her, non-filter. She lights it for me and says, "Smoking too much will kill you."

"Sometimes I want to hurt myself," I say.

"Yeah...," Linda says. "I know." And I can tell she knows exactly what I mean.

I watch Linda return to her van and drive away.

For the next 18 hours we rumble north on highway 95. There is sunshine and rain, light and darkness. I look out my window, and take it all in. I don't drink wine, or make idle conversation, or pine for Eva. I don't wax romantic. I don't dream.

Though I would continue to cling to the teachings of Meher Baba and all the goodness he represented, I knew I was done with the meetings, and the posters, and the books, and the songs. I would take his lessons with me, but I was ready to move on.

ALL I WANT

I'D NEVER SEEN her before because our town had two high schools, Great Neck North and Great Neck South, and she was from South. Because of the geography, kids from the two schools normally didn't mingle, but that changed as soon as we got our driver's licenses. Sylvan, the oldest, and first in our group to receive full driving privileges, was expanding his circle of friends to include some of the kids from South. He was the one responsible for bringing us together.

It was a balmy spring night. The school year was almost over, and about a dozen kids from North and South had gathered at Cutter Mill Park. Sylvan was organizing an activity called "falling" - born from the practice of "sensitivity training," at the height of popularity in the early '70's - which purported to strengthen the bond of trust between people.

Harmony stood atop a large boulder, preparing to fall, spread-eagle, into our outstretched arms. I am gazing up at her, her dirty blond hair framing the soft contours of her face. There is a glow to her expression, to which I am instantly attracted. From where I stand, I can smell her lilac perfume. I want to taste her lips. This girl is casting a spell over me.

Harmony suddenly goes limp. Her body falls forward. And, were it not for the bond of trust between us, Harmony might have struck the ground with such force as to disfigure her adorable face. Fortunately, we, her trustworthy group of new friends, are prepared. She touches down safely into our outstretched arms. To my added surprise and delight, Harmony's well-formed, pert breast settles gently into the palm of my outstretched hand. Then it's my turn. I, too, fall bravely and with total abandon. Twelve pairs of outstretched arms catch me, and when I look up, there is Harmony, smiling, just inches from my face. Thus began a deep mutual trust between us. We had fallen for each other.

* * *

A FEW WEEKS LATER, we are preparing to make love in her parent's king sized bed. A cool summer breeze filters through the laced bedroom curtains, turning everything white and lovely. I can tell she's nervous; to be honest, so am I. But my main concern is for Harmony to have the best possible first experience. To be sure, I lie and tell her I am not a virgin. Though I feel badly about lying, I am sure it will put Harmony at ease. I want to convey an air of confidence, so everything will be just right.

I am sitting on the edge of the bed, with my back to Harmony. Despite my nerves I manage to achieve sufficient readiness below the waist, but I'm still trembling as I rip the condom from its hermetically-sealed package and roll it into position. It's an awkward moment, but I don't think Harmony is aware of my fumbling.

I feel like a toddler taking my first baby steps, unsure whether to hold on or simply let go. I decide to let go, moving steadily but gently. I look into Harmony's eyes: they are moist and beautiful. When she winces, I remain still until her face relaxes again. I feel myself getting close, and reach down to make sure the condom is securely attached. A short while later I climax. Harmony bleeds a little, then cries a little, and finally turns away. I try to console her. "Why are you crying?" I ask. But she offers no reply. So I hold her in my arms until calm returns and she is ready to put on some clothes.

The radiant character of the day slowly fades; replaced by a glow in my heart, one which seems to grow every moment we're together. It's unlike any feeling I've ever known.

We made love repeatedly after that, sometimes less than ten minutes separating each act. This is one of the miracles of youth, when biology is on your side. It is a blessing - unless, of course, you're the girl's parents.

Harmony's parents had always treated me like family. They took me to restaurants, loaned me their car, took me backpacking, and invited me to long weekends at the beach. With respect to my relationship with my girlfriend's family, things couldn't have been better. One weekend in October, when the foliage was screaming at its peak of Autumn hues, Harmony's father purchased expensive backpacks – the type with aluminum frames – and other camping gear, and the three of us spent a weekend hiking along the Appalachian Trail. We pitched our tent in a secluded area of the woods; at the site of a real Civil War battle. We found remnants of cannons and cannonballs, dark and pitted from the ravages of time. An old wheel with wooden spokes was leaning against an ancient stone wall nearby. I ran my fingers along the rust-stained band of metal still clinging to the rim after all these years. The place was hauntingly beautiful. I swear I could hear the echo of battle cries, and smell the gun powder which seemed to fill the air around me. It was experiences such as these that distinguished Harmony's family from my own. My parents were a generation older than hers; I never did things like this with my family, even when my father was alive.

The bottom line was this: I loved Harmony, and I believed she loved me. All I wanted was for our love to bring out the best in each other. And I believed it was possible.

Then, one day, Harmony's mother discovers her diary in a drawer and reads every word of it. I don't know what it said (I wasn't even aware Harmony kept a diary), but I am certain it contained some specific reference to our intemperate sexual activities.

After that, Harmony's life became a living hell. Her parents excommunicate and force shame upon her. She is summarily alienated, put under house arrest, and forbidden ever to see me again. Occasionally, Harmony would escape to find refuge at a friend's house. There she would phone me, always distraught and choking back tears. I beg her to meet me back at Cutter Mill Park. We steal about forty minutes by the rock where we first met. She tearfully describes how her parents had turned their backs on her, refusing even to acknowledge her presence in the house. I can't comprehend their cruel form of punishment, but it is terribly clear how thoroughly Harmony is tortured by it.

What high crime had we perpetrated? I did not know. I knew only this: I loved Harmony with all my heart. I was careful with her, always. Her parents were wrong to treat her this way. She didn't deserve it. I was determined to act in her defense and, if possible, make things right.

"You're crazy," Ash says, when I tell him my plan. "Her father will kill you. I've heard he keeps a gun."

"Only the good die young," I reply bravely. "Fuck 'em. I'm doing this."

The next day, Saturday, I wait until afternoon and follow the stone path to Harmony's house. The Tudor style home, once inviting, now appears dark and ominous. Still, I try to focus on my objective, and hold my head high as I ring the doorbell. Her mother greets me with a smile, but it isn't a warm smile, it is forced and condescending. I wonder if she's surprised by my unannounced visit, but I'm not overly concerned. What matters is what I've come to say.

"We need to talk." I begin, in a manner that is sincere and businesslike.

"Come in." Her voice is flat and cold; her face expressionless. I didn't care. I was in the door.

I follow her into the living room. As we cross the area rug in the foyer, I hear the thump of footsteps overhead and imagine Harmony's father pacing the floor above, wrestling with his temper, (possibly fingering the trigger of a loaded gun). I'm sure he wants to kill me, and the only way to contain his rage is by physically separating himself from me. I'm not insensitive to his feelings. In fact, I can't help considering whether I had, indeed, perpetrated some heinous act against his daughter. Did I coerce Harmony into having sex? Did I debauch her? Did I misrepresent myself or my intentions? I didn't think I had - not intentionally, anyway – except for that one small, white lie about my being a virgin. If that was my only crime, I thought, maybe this whole mess was nothing more than a simple misunderstanding.

Harmony's mother offers me a seat on the sofa, and sits opposite me in an armchair. The drapes (a heavy paisley material in earthy shades of plumb, moss and burnt umber) are drawn;

they hang like armor down to the sable floorboards, obscuring all evidence of the sunny day outside. The coffered ceilings add to the dingy ambience of the room, imbuing it with a melancholy which seems unnatural and oppressive. I want to leave, but knew I would not, could not, until I'd said everything I'd intended to say. There was no plan "B."

"You're making a terrible mistake," I begin. "You're daughter is miserable." Harmony's mother looks at me as though I had just said something so obvious as to be absurd.

"She deserves it," her mother spits back. "She was sneaky, and she lied."

Her remark seems no less absurd than mine, and I find myself fighting off a sudden wave of indignation. How dare you, I'm thinking, as a one-sided conversation begins to plow through my brain like a runaway freight train: You're the sneaky one! You invaded her privacy! You sleaze bag! You bitch!

I want to scream these words out loud; tell this woman off, but for Harmony's sake I decide to eat humble pie.

"It's my fault," I say, "and I'm sorry to have caused all this pain to you and your family."

"So kind of you to say so," she replies, each word infused with hatred.

"I'll do anything to make things right. Please stop condemning you daughter."

"Why should I?" she asks, with an almost perverse sense of cruelty. I had never seen this side of Harmony's mother, and it frightens me.

"She doesn't deserve to be treated this way," I say. "Tell me what I can do."

"Haven't you done enough, already?"

"I love your daughter, and I hate to see her suffer."

She laughs out loud, mockingly. "You don't know anything about love."

But she was wrong. I did know something about love, though it seemed unlikely she would ever believe it. I change the subject. "Is your husband home?" I didn't intend to be bold, rude, or presumptuous, but she ascribes all three to my question.

"He doesn't want to talk to you," she snaps. When she sees I am not intimidated, it infuriates her.

The conversation continues, albeit one-sided, until it is clear all good nature had left the room and my visit was over.

"Please don't treat your daughter this way. She doesn't deserve it." I implore Harmony's mother in a most highly impassioned demeanor, knowing this is my last opportunity to say anything further on the subject.

"We'll see," she simply says, as she hurries me toward the front door.

I thank her and depart, unable to tell if my visit would have any effect, positive or negative, on Harmony's situation at home.

Ultimately, I knew there was only one antidote powerful enough to counteract the poison our love had introduced into that family: time. I felt good about confronting Harmony's mother. It was something I needed to do. Harmony was my first love, it's true. Maybe I was too young. Maybe I was still too inexperienced to know much about love. But I did know this – and the pride I felt having confronted Harmony's mother confirmed it: that love means standing by the one you love.

I was unprepared for the detour our relationship would take when we parted to attend separate colleges. Harmony and I had never seriously discussed what would happen after we graduated from high school. Our tastes in colleges were varied enough. I registered as a freshman at Boston University, a huge institution with a sprawling campus in the heart of a big city. She entered a small, artsy college in rural New York. Love is blind, and so was I - blind to the possibility of change, and temptation, and pain. Throughout my freshman year at college, I watched something once beautiful wilt and die. There was little I could do to save it, and by the middle of my sophomore year at B.U., my feelings for Harmony had deteriorated from love and wonderment to bitterness and disdain. The distance wasn't insurmountable

- only two hundred miles separated us - but where our love was concerned, we were light years apart.

I realized I was not good with loss. With Harmony out of my life, I was left with a fierce pain in my heart. It lingered for several years while I lived and attended classes in Boston. Oftentimes it paralyzed me, and I thought the pain would never end. But it did, eventually dissolving into a harmless whisper; quiet enough to allow me the freedom to roam, yet sufficiently apparent to reminisce on that smell of innocence, when sweet love percolates within you for the very first time.

DIVINE INTERVENTION

I AM AWAKE to witness the light of dawn brushing back the evergreens. The song of a robin has lulled the crickets to sleep. Leafy silhouettes appear on the canvas roof of the tent; dappled projections of the early morning sun. The smell of mountain dew is intoxicating. I am wearing a light t-shirt and boxers as I crawl from my tent onto the soft, damp earth. The air is motionless and mild. Our campsite is pristine and undisturbed. A ghostly veil of white mist levitates over Berry Pond, its mirrored surface reflecting puffs of fair-weather clouds. I am reluctant to disrupt this tranquil balance by imposing myself on the scene, but having spent the long night cocooned inside of my sleeping bag, nature calls.

Ash is sleeping off the Southern Comfort from the night before. I creep outside our tent without disturbing him, zip him inside, (sealing him off from potential, hairy four-legged intruders), and follow a narrow path leading into a vast acreage of state-sanctioned woodlands. After ten minutes, I spot a young couple headed in my direction.

"Morning," I say cheerfully.

"Morning," the couple says in hushed unison. They seem nonplussed by this friendly happenstance and do not stop to chat, but pass along the narrow trail without further word or pleasantry.

I'm taken aback, momentarily dejected by the couple's lack of affability toward a fellow nature lover, but dismiss it, convinced it best that our encounter resulted in nothing more than a transient disruption of my impending morning constitutional.

"Have a magical day," I offer, feeling at once superior and embarrassed by my allusion to Disneyland. But the couple is oblivious. Like me, they evidently had an urgent need to be alone.

I hang a left off the beaten path and jog toward a flat marshy area where several young birch trees had taken root. Soon I am far from the path, sufficiently hidden to indulge myself in the privacy of the forest. I designate the most comfortable, convenient, and environmentally sound site for toxic waste disposal, and get into position; dropping my smiley-face boxers to the ankle, knees flexed, hands grasping at the trunk of a young birch tree. Suddenly something appears that makes me freeze. Less than ten feet away and looking me square in the eye is the prodigious form of a North American black bear. It rises on its haunches and flares its nostrils. Judging by its size, I estimate the bear weighs over five hundred pounds. The animal growls and then yawns. Slowly, I reach for the elastic waist band on my shorts and pull them up, careful to avoid any sudden movement which the animal might mistake for an act of aggression. Then, in a brief moment of clarity, I realize that the bear is probably as terrified of me as I am of him. I decide to remain calm and do what any experienced outdoorsman would do. I run.

I bolt like a mad wildebeest in heat, and don't look back; thrashing my way through thorny thickets, hurtling fallen logs, skirting jagged rock formations, vaulting babbling brooks. I run harder and faster than I have ever run before. I run for my life.

When I'm relatively certain I've ditched the carnivorous beast, I pause to look over my shoulder. The bear had stopped chasing me. I watch it do an about-face and lumber deep into the woods, out of sight, and out of my life. This is not my day to die, I muse.

Back at camp, Ash is heating a pot of coffee over a small fire.

I rest on a log and proceed to describe my harrowing encounter with the bear.

"Far out," Ash exclaims, not fully cognizant of the danger I'd escaped. "Good thing you're a runner," he adds.

Good thing. We eat a breakfast of scrambled eggs and cheese, and we're ready for a peaceful day in the great outdoors. Despite my precarious encounter with the Black Bear, I'm still anxious to explore the wooded trails. I unfold the map the park ranger had given us when we arrived.

"We'll begin here." I point to a bold, jagged line representing several miles of cleared woods. This is where the Appalachian Trail and the Long Trail converge. The map detailed other minor paths branching off randomly like the varicose veins of an octogenarian. We decide on a circuitous route requiring only a modicum of exertion, then gather our daily essentials and stride blissfully into the woods.

The map indicates we're traveling in a northeast direction. A succession of white "blazes" painted on the side of the trees indicates we're following the Appalachian Trail. We're headed for Balance Rock - a 165-ton limestone boulder balanced on bedrock. "Maybe we can take some pictures," I suggest.

We walk for miles in silence, the stillness of the wilderness broken only by our labored breathing and the steady plodding of boots against the rocky trail. I'm awed by the wonder of nature and the miracle of creation.

Hours pass and we come upon an active stream jutting through a picturesque section of the woods. After consuming a hearty meal of Slim Jims and Mountain Dew (the soda), we settle in for a well-deserved nap, and are lulled swiftly into slumber by the sound of rushing water.

* * *

I'M SITTING IN A POOL OF BLOOD, which I knew was my own. It could have been in the middle of a highway. My legs are paralyzed so I could not move. I do not scream because I feel no pain. I am more confused than anything else. I remember being struck from behind, as though by a car or truck. There was a loud thud. Then I felt like I was dissolving into another dimension. I was without form or substance. I simply was. It was as if my entire being were spread over an entire universe. I was nowhere and everywhere. I could see everything, but saw nothing. All around, I could see nothing but silvery blackness.

Then I begin to panic. What does one do here to occupy the time? I didn't want to spend the rest of my life in this state of nothingness.

Soon I calm down, realizing how safe I am. Nothing could harm me because I was everything. Only I could harm myself. I realize I needn't worry about time because time does not exist here. There are no days, months, or years. Everything is infinitely equal. Time and space are one.

I begin to feel comfortable. In a strange way, it is like lying on the beach in a warm sun.

* * *

WHEN I AWAKE, a family of deer is drinking from a stream, not ten feet from where we lay. The shadows from the trees have grown longer. "We should head back. The trail can disappear easily at dusk," I say wearily.

We gather our trash, carefully reassemble our backpacks, and rejoin the trail. To the west is a striking panorama; a fiery sun slices the mountain ridge, imbuing the horizon with an oily opalescence before dissolving seamlessly into the chrome blue sky. Beyond that, a star-spangled twilight threatens to consume another day with the tarry blackness of night.

Ash leads us back to camp. I feel euphoric, grateful for the gift of life, and promise myself I will try to appreciate every day, taking nothing for granted. Then it occurs to me we have completely forgotten about Balance Rock, our designated goal, and conclude that our reward hinged not on the final destination, but on the journey itself. I am so thoroughly intrigued by this epiphany I don't notice that the trail has turned uncharacteristically narrow and ragged. Ash must have inadvertently strayed off course.

"This is not the Appalachian Trail," I utter, in a loud but conciliatory voice.

Ash stops, mid-stride, and takes inventory of our surroundings. He looks confused. "Sure it is," he says, but he is unable to back up his conviction. There is not a blaze in sight; nothing. Straining against the darkness, I peer into the distance. Ahead, I see a double blaze, one above the other, typically used to designate where two trails converge. I run toward it. Ash is not far behind. Do I really see something, or is the light playing tricks on me?

"Stop!" I yell, as the mirage disappears. Then I realize that the two of us have abandoned the last place in the woods where we were *not* lost. I do a slow three-sixty, carefully studying the landscape in all directions. Nothing looks familiar. I feel like I am going to be sick.

"What?" Ash pleads.

"We're lost." My acute sense of direction which has served me with uncanny precision my entire life, was crumbling like a mud hut in an earthquake. Suddenly I'm weak in the knees and disoriented.

The forest floor appears to melt into a solitary tangle of roots and vines. I am unable to distinguish the outline of a path or trail anywhere, despite the fact I had been standing on one, moments ago.

It is neither safe nor fun to be lost in the woods at night. There are too many variables; too many things to go wrong: dehydration, hypothermia, animal attacks, snake and insect bites, starvation, injury from falling (sprains, fractures, concussions, internal bleeding), disorientation, panic, seizure, heart attack, stroke, parasites, intestinal viruses, and shock. Anything can happen (quicksand?), which, without medical attention can easily result in serious complications, and even death. Ash and I were strong, healthy twenty-year-old men, but this was no guarantee of immunity.

The light of dusk is slipping away, and I am having serious doubts about our chances of extricating ourselves from the woods before total darkness sets in. Fortunately, we had the foresight to bring along flashlights, and the batteries were new.

The veil of a slow moving cloud eclipses the moon, pilfering the already scant light it provided. Ash and I are tired and thirsty but we don't panic, and keep our hopes alive. We knew, at least, if we could hold on until morning, the odds of our returning to civilization would be greatly improved. But, as the minutes turned into hours, our flashlights and our spirits dimmed. Then my flashlight dies.

"Shit!" I scream, hoping my cry will carry to the nearest Ranger station. Ash is about thirty yards away, poking around the pitch-black forest as the anemic beam of his flashlight slowly fails. "This sucks," he utters, with mournful resignation and a mouthful of cotton. We needed a plan.

I suggest we regroup and take inventory our belongings. Perhaps we'd find a whistle, or a compass, or some extra batteries. Or maybe Tinkerbell will magically appear and illuminate our way back to camp where two Norwegian sex kittens are waiting to pleasure us until dawn. Wishful thinking, it seemed, grew on trees, especially those obscured by darkness.

"Did you hear something?" Ash whispers. "Don't move."

"I'm not moving, though you'll have to take my word for it since you can't see me," I say jokingly.

"Don't breathe."

"Now you're going too far. Next you'll insist I stop eating and drinking beer." Ash shoves me. "Alright," I say. "You don't have to push." I hold my breath as long as I can (about seventy-two seconds; a respectable time, even for a wishful thinker) before I have to gasp for air.

"Shhh…," Ash admonishes.

"Hey listen. If I stop breathing altogether, I'll die," I remind him. "I'll probably die here anyway." Ash's face seems to morph into a kaleidoscope of caricatures, none of them pretty. I keep quiet, even though my patience is wearing thin. "I don't hear anything. I don't see anything. And I'm hungry," I finally say, and then I take a seat on the stump of a tree. Silence comes at last. Ash and I linger motionless and mute, like trees in a petrified forest; lost in thought, lost in nature, just lost.

"Ash?"

"Yeah?"

"Do you think this is how horses feel when they sleep?"

"Shut up."

"I'm serious."

Ash refuses to indulge me. He is obviously in a bad mood, and it was going to be a long night; I had no intention of sleeping next to him in the same stable.

"Listen, we're getting out of here, now," I announce, as definitively as springtime follows winter. I am surprised and encouraged by the level of my conviction, which seems to emerge from the deepest recesses of my mind as a flash of indelible white light. Whatever the source of this insight, I am ready to act. I don my backpack and start walking. I am not on a trail: there are no trails, only the uneven, tangled web of an overgrown forest. There is only one way to go, one direction to travel. I follow my heart.

Ash is not sharing my passion; he saunters lethargically in my direction, but when I look back, his entire form has been swallowed by the night. I keep an ear on him and, despite my fatigue, lacerations and thirst, trudge ahead with single-minded determination. It is impossible to see where I am going. Even my hands, bloody from scratches and covered in mud, are barely visible to me. But I know I am making headway; I can feel it.

The faint gurgle of water, possibly a nearby brook, energizes me. I hasten my pace, colliding with a branch which nearly skewers my eye, but grazes my cheekbone instead. Still advancing, I wipe away blood with the back of my hand. I step into a void and suddenly begin a headlong tumble down a steep embankment. There is nothing to grasp. I feel my body accelerating down the hill. But before I can think about contusions, broken bones, internal hemorrhages, or a fractured skull, I land on a level surface as clear and wide as…

The opalescent blaze sparkles like a splendorous "Welcome Home" sign. I had inadvertently, literally, stumbled upon the Appalachian Trail. I scream and hoot and holler. And before I am anywhere close to regaining my composure, Ash spills onto the trail beside me, covered in mud and leaves.

It wasn't long before we were back at camp kissing the mossy earth. We were dirty, wet, hungry, and dehydrated, but alive. Somehow providence had smiled upon us and guided us back to camp. We had been lost for almost six hours. Ash made a small fire while I hung our wet clothes on a nearby line. Then we crawled inside the tent for the night. My body ached all over.

"I didn't think we were going to make it," I say, rolling onto my sleeping bag.

"I almost shit in my pants, man," Ash admits.

We both fall silent, listening to the sound of the night forest mingling with the soft crackle of burning wood. I think about the meaning of true friendship as something that never dies, even when separated by time or distance. True friends keep you from getting lost in the world. So, maybe we were never really lost tonight. "You know something, Ash?" I whisper. "I would have lost it if you weren't there." I feel a strong surge of emotion, but push it away. Then I say the thing I really meant to say: "I'd be lost without you, my friend." But Ash doesn't hear me. He is fast asleep and snoring. I shrug, and zip together the flaps of our tent. My slumber would come later. Lying on top of my sleeping bag I thought about my dream of dying… then, finally, drifted off to sleep, as leafy silhouettes appeared on the canvas roof; dappled projections of the early morning sun.

BOOK FOUR

DISCOVERY

COLLEGE BUDDY

I HAD ALWAYS BEEN told you meet some of your best friends in college. While still in high school, I found this notion difficult to accept. I asked myself: Is it possible (or even desirable) to make new friends, when the ones you've already made, dating as far back as nursery school, are perfect? I was skeptical, but eventually discovered it *was* possible. I met some of my best friends in college.

It is the beginning of my junior year at Boston University, and the first day of class is greeted by an unseasonably warm September day; the kind of day which provokes notions of Indian summer, or tempts you to skip school altogether and go to the beach. But I'm eager for school to start. All summer long, I had been looking forward to my first filmmaking course, and the day had finally arrived.

I enter the small screening room, which doubled as our classroom, with my eyes wide open. The walls are covered in acoustic drapery, and the room is filled with rows of theater-like seating screwed to the floor. There is a large projection screen on the front wall, and in front of that, a teacher's lectern. I take a seat in the back row and observe as a wave of animated students fill the room. They are slow to take their seats, and chat nervously with each other. Meanwhile, I am growing increasingly impatient. I just want everyone to shut up so the class can begin. Eventually the professor asks for quiet, and when the students settle down, he proceeds to outline the course curriculum. For our first assignment, he wants us to work in teams of two or three. Each team will collaborate to make a short film, the subject or theme to be of our own choosing. "You may take a few moments to break into teams," he says suddenly. I'm wondering: Now? Immediately, the classroom erupts. Like a swarm of ravenous ants on a mound of fresh breadcrumbs, everyone clamors to find a partner. It is pure pandemonium.

I remain seated in the back row - alone, shocked, and alienated. I am certain that when the smoke clears I will be the odd man out; the only student without a partner. I feel flushed and embarrassed. I'm beginning to perspire. I do not belong here, I'm thinking. Maybe my personality isn't suited to a career in show business, after all. As I'm wiping my brow, I look to my right and see, a few seats away in the back row, the pallid countenance of someone as dejected looking as I, and, as it turns out, the other half of my filmmaking team – by default. He looks at me, and I know exactly what he's thinking. And I know he knows I know what he's thinking. And he knows what I'm thinking. And I know he knows what I'm thinking. And he knows I know he knows what I'm thinking. It is uncanny. And when we finally reach the end of this logic, I speak.

"I guess this means we're partners," I say, reluctantly.

"I guess so," he reluctantly agrees.

He tells me his name is Rick. Rick and I made two short films that semester, both critically acclaimed. Our final film is entitled, "Loneliness a Leaf Falls," based on a poem by e.e. cummings. It's about a desperate loner who can't find a job. We worked tirelessly to produce the film. We were innovative. We even created a soundtrack which we mixed on whatever crude equipment was available – a first, at the time, with student filmmakers. Our hard work seemed to pay off. The film was hailed as the best student film of the year, and became the featured presentation at the Boston University film festival.

Rick and I believed our futures in filmmaking were secure. But on the night of the public screening, everything changed. The projectionist failed to load the film correctly. At first, it's disastrously out of sync. Then the film became entangled in the projector's sprockets, and is finally melted by the intense heat of the projector's lamp. At the end of the evening, our film was returned to us in a brown paper bag; useless, molten celluloid, inextricably twisted inside a bent, metal take-up reel. It was pathetic. No one ever got to see our movie. It was a sad, unfortunate outcome, but Rick and I were determined to maintain a positive attitude. Though it was over for our film, our careers in filmmaking (and our friendship) were just beginning.

Rick and I agree to register for the television production course being offered second semester. We meet Don when teams of three were required, as part of a class assignment, to orchestrate a multi-camera studio production - one we would produce, write and direct. How we ended up with Don eludes me, but his palpable enthusiasm seemed to complement our low-key approach to show business, and could conceivably give us an edge.

After weeks of preproduction the day of our taping had arrived, but our principal actor, a friend of Don's, had not. Rick and I are infuriated, but Don, insisting "the show must go on," hastily assumes the role himself. While his performance was admirable, Don seemed to have all the fun while Rick and I scrambled behind the scenes to coordinate the technical aspects of the production. It wouldn't have surprised me if Don had planned this outcome from the start. He always impressed me as a natural performer with a great sense of humor.

We were nearing the end of the final semester of our senior year. Spring was only a month away, but Boston was getting hammered by a heavy snow storm. I'm sitting alone in my apartment contemplating my impending future, when I'm suddenly struck with what seems like a brilliant idea. I pick up the phone and call Don.

"You home?" I ask.

"Of course I'm home, dumb ass. I picked up the phone, didn't I?"

"Stay there," I say. "I'm coming over." I grab several relevant items, slip into my Timberland boots, and trudge out into the blizzard. When Don opens the door, I plow past him, dragging snow and mud into the living room. I don't bother with formalities. With Don it was never required, and I liked that.

"What's up, Dude?" Don asks. I open a map of the United States and smooth it out on his wobbly coffee table.

"See this?" I say.

"It's a lousy map of the country," Don says.

"That's not all," I retort. I take a Sharpie, circle Boston on the map, and draw a straight line to Los Angeles. "That's where we're going when we graduate," I announce. Don and I shake on it, sealing our agreement to relocate to Hollywood, become roommates, and find our fortunes together – as soon as our college diplomas are in hand.

I coast through the remainder of the semester and final exams; all the while I'm imagining my life on the west coast; sunny days, palm trees, expensive cars, platinum blondes, and a glamorous career in movies. My fantasy grows increasingly detailed after several weeks, and when I describe our imminent lifestyle to Rick, I paint such a rosy picture that he proposes joining us. I think it's a great idea, Don has no objection, and a departure date is set.

MANIFEST DESTINY

RICK, DON, AND I decide to caravan across the country in three cars on June 13th, 1977. Unfortunately, as the day draws near, Rick injures himself at a friend's graduation pool party; he had hurdled over a diving board and landed on top of a tall cocktail glass. The glass shattered, impaling his foot and severing several nerves and tendons. He was treated at the local hospital and sent home on crutches. Rick was in no condition to travel, but Don and I decide to leave as originally scheduled. Rick would join us in California as soon as he was well enough to make the trip.

Meanwhile, my Uncle Edgar had called my mother a few weeks earlier to say he needed help. Aunt Irene had slipped on ice the previous winter and hit her head on the frozen ground. It was a serious fall, and it left her in a coma. Given her age at the time, 77, the doctors didn't expect her to live, but they were wrong, sort of. She regained consciousness, but required intensive rehabilitation. My uncle transferred her to the best facility in Omaha, where full-time help was available. There she seemed to improve, but lately encountered some setbacks. Uncle Edgar thought my mother's presence would renew my aunt's will to live. "Why not drive out west with me?" I suggested to my mother. "We'll pass through

Omaha, and we can both visit Aunt Irene. I'll stay overnight. You can fly back to New York whenever you're ready." My mother loved the idea. I only had to convince Don to agree to a small alteration in our plans.

Don had met my mother on several occasions when she had come to visit me at college. He was always asking her about her days in vaudeville. She'd tell him stories, and the two of them would laugh until tears rolled down their cheeks. I think Don saw something of himself in her. Anyway, I noticed a bond from the moment they first met. So, Don had no problem with the last minute change. In fact, he told me he loved the idea, and was thrilled that my mother, who was sixty-five at the time, had the "gumption" (as he put it) to drive half-way across the country crammed into the passenger side of a Toyota Corona. He admired her spirit.

Both of our vehicles were suspect with regard to their ability to sustain a 3500 mile journey from the Atlantic Seaboard to the Gold Coast. Don had a '68 Volkswagen Beetle. My car was a 1970 Toyota Corona. Each automobile had already logged more miles than was generally expected of them. Both cars were running on borrowed time. Still, we believed in our machines. We believed in their ability to facilitate our impending encounter with destiny. We were young and optimistic. We were also inexperienced and naive.

In preparation for the trip, Don and I install CB radios in our respective cars. This would enable us to communicate with each other while driving, without having to stop. The signal strength was rated at fifteen miles in any direction, but we never expected to be separated by more than one or two, and for the most part we agreed to maintain visual contact whenever possible.

On a cloudless morning in June, I back my white, five-speed, four-door Toyota with a powder blue vinyl interior out of the driveway. It's packed to the hilt with all my stuff. I reserved only the passenger seat for my mother and enough vertical clearance for an unobstructed view out my rearview mirror. The glove compartment was stocked with roadmaps. Our first stop: Sandusky, Ohio.

The ball of the stick shift feels good in the palm of my hand. I feel hopeful and eager – the optimal state of mind for anyone beginning a long journey. Don had left from his home town in Connecticut a few days earlier to visit relatives in Sandusky. We had planned to rendezvous with him there on Tuesday. Then we'd caravan the remaining 800 miles to Omaha. We didn't care if it took two days or ten. We all agreed there was no reason to push it. We would take our time and enjoy the ride. It was impossible to predict what we would encounter along the way, but as I shift into drive, I can feel a smile widening on my face. My mother, I notice, is smiling, too.

I drove nearly 575 miles that first day, the most I'd ever driven in one stretch, and we ended up in a sleazy motel outside of Cleveland. For twenty-two dollars plus tax, Mom and I were permitted to share one double bed in a room which had two. To make sure we didn't cheat, we were handed a single blanket - after we had paid in advance.

Dinner consists of Big Macs and coffee. I am extremely tired and can't wait to finish eating so I can finally get some sleep. When the time comes, my mother and I push the double beds into the middle of the room, and share the blanket, (which turns out to be plenty big for the two of us).

As I drift off to sleep, I think about how my Toyota had performed that day. For the most part it had run smoothly, cruising like a Cadillac on the highway, but it stalled at every tollbooth. There is probably no need to worry. I resolve to relax and enjoy the scenery, as I did today, and I replay the landscape of today's movie. The Buckeye State is flat; rich in farmland, sprouting acres and acres of corn, alfalfa, and wheat. It is very beautiful; very, very beautiful.

My mother and I are awake by sunrise. By six-thirty we're sitting in a downtown Sandusky diner having breakfast with Don. We pore over roadmaps while the waitress pours us coffee. I'm glad the three of us are finally together. It made it seem like our journey had "officially" begun. "We're really doing this, aren't we?" I say to Don. "I guess so, pal," he replies. While my mother paid the check, Don and I check our cars. His Beetle is so crammed with stuff it seems to sag in the middle. "It's definitely heavy," he admits. "My mechanic warned me not to go faster than sixty, or I might melt a valve." This does not sound good, but it doesn't dampen my enthusiasm for the trip. Both our cars were subject to some type of mechanical breakdown. Something bad could happen at any moment, but we could cross that bridge when we came to it. For now, we were anxious to hit the road.

I take the lead. My mother navigates. Don follows close behind. We're on the road for about a minute when Don's voice crackles over the CB radio. "Breaker one-nine," he says. "How long before we reach Nebraska?"

Normally it would have taken 12 hours to drive to Omaha, but out of deference to Don's auto mechanic, I keep well below the recommended sixty miles per hour, even though the speed limit is sixty-five. I don't want Don to feel any pressure to drive fast, and then have his engine explode on us.

Driving slowly may have put less of a strain on Don's car, but it had the opposite effect on me. By the time we reach Des Moines, I am exhausted. I pull into a gas station to fill up and inquire about a decent place to stay overnight. The attendant points to a shadowy hotel across the street, then to a murky spot beneath my Toyota. "You've got a nasty oil leak," he says. "But I can fix it." I hand him my car keys and we check in across the street.

When we start out the next morning, my mother offers to drive. Watching her behind the wheel reminds me when, as a young preschooler, I'd accompany her on her daily rounds to the bank, the cleaners, the post office and the supermarket. Not since then had I spent so much quality time alone with my mother, particularly within the small confines of an automobile. Let me tell you: it was fun. We listened to rock and roll music on the radio, and my mother admitted to getting "quite a musical education." She told me about the time she took her father's car out for a joyride before she had her license, and I, in turn, confessed to smoking pot "once or twice." Sometimes we'd just stare in silence at the endless road; an elusive mirage shimmering in the distance like the placid surface of a lake. "It's a big country," my mother finally says. "Isn't it beautiful?"

"Yes it is, mom. Beautiful."

* * *

WE ARE INSIDE Omaha's city limits. My mother quickly locates her sister's house from memory. When we arrive, the front door is open but no one is home. Then we discover a note Uncle Edgar had left on the kitchen table apologizing for not being there to greet us: He is at the hospital, and will be returning soon. I wander from room to room. This is the house my Uncle Edgar and Aunt Irene had lived in all their married life. The house has two bedrooms separated by a single bath, a large open living room, and a tiny but workable kitchen. Everything is on one level except for a huge unfinished basement attached to a two-car garage.

I can remember being here only one other time; in 1965, when I was ten, and our family flew out to spend Christmas. Rex and I were relegated to the basement during our stay. Tucked in an alcove behind the stairway was a queen sized bed and a tall dresser for us to use. At best, the basement provided bleak accommodation. Worst of all, the basement was not heated and became unbearably cold at night. Even with the extra blankets we discovered in an old trunk, it was almost impossible to sleep, but because we had our own space away from the adults upstairs, we were basically pleased with the arrangement.

My parents are conspicuously absent from this recollection - maybe it was their time to be free and leave the kids to the supervision of the aunt and uncle (who never had any children of their own) – but, nevertheless, my memories of the visit are happy ones. Snow was plentiful, making it a gloriously white Christmas, and wherever music could be heard, mixed in among the holiday classics, was the just-released single, "Turn, Turn, Turn," by the

Byrds. In 1965, slot car racing was sweeping every city in the country, and Omaha was no exception. Uncle Edgar devoted many an afternoon driving me and Rex to the monster tracks around town. In the evenings, my brother and I put on jackets and ties and dined at the Happy Hollow Country Club, where my aunt and uncle were longtime members. A magnificent Christmas tree with gold garland, colorful ornaments, and hundreds of bright lights greeted guests as they entered the lobby. A huge frozen pond behind the main building was illuminated for night skating. Just before bedtime, Aunt Irene would bake fresh cookies and sprinkle them with red and green sugar crystals.

Suddenly it is twelve years later.

* * *

UNCLE EDGAR RETURNS about an hour after we arrived. I'm surprised to see him looking so thin and pale. He has a two-day growth of white stubble on his face. His shoulders are slumped, and he seems tired. He looks like he is about to melt a valve. My mother prepares a pitcher of Lipton iced tea and pours four tall glasses. This rejuvenates us all, including my uncle, who seems anxious to return to the hospital. My mother and I accompany him. Don comes along to lend his support, but remained in the waiting room while the three of us visited my aunt.

Irene was one of my favorite aunts, and it was a treat whenever she came to visit us in New York. I think she was fun because she was slightly eccentric. While my uncle Edgar taught me to play Gin Rummy and Cribbage, she was full of other quirky ideas. One summer they drove to New York and we caravanned to Cape Cod, staying several nights at a motel called the "Now Voyager." We'd go digging for clams on the beach, and eat hardboiled eggs sprinkled with a mixture of salt and pepper in a plastic bag. One morning, Aunt Irene had the iron out and was waiting for it to heat up. She cautioned me about hot irons, and then showed me how to tell when the iron was ready. "Put some saliva on your index finger," she said. "Then lightly touch the bottom of the iron, like this." When her finger touched the iron it made a loud sizzling sound.

"It's ready," she smiled.

I asked, "Can I try?"

"Okay, but don't hold it there too long or you're liable to get a nasty burn."

With a mix of excitement, fear and trepidation, I wet the tip of my index finger and touched the scorching hot iron. I felt a warm rumbling as my saliva boiled under my fingertip before evaporating almost immediately. It made that loud sizzling sound. "Cool."

Aunt Irene spoke with a subtle Midwestern drawl which became increasingly pronounced on afternoons when the scotch began to flow. But I loved the drawn out pace of her vernacular, and always felt a deep affection for my mother's older sister.

Nothing could have prepared me for what I saw upon entering my aunt's room at the hospital. Five beds are pushed against the walls. There are also several wheelchairs, and miscellaneous lifesaving equipment. The room smells strongly of urine and sour milk. A few of the beds are occupied by elderly women lying on their sides, barely moving. One woman is naked from the waist down. They look emaciated; pallid skin stretched over skeletons, eyes too deep in their sockets to be clearly visible. One woman is moaning. Another is meowing like a cat. The windows have bars. (Is this a hospital or an insane asylum?) Banks of fluorescent fixtures hum on the ceiling, and everything has a sickly greenish cast. Thank God my aunt is not here, I'm thinking. But I am wrong. At first she is just a silhouette, parked in a wheelchair before an open window, where sunlight pours into the room. I would never have suspected it was her, but Uncle Edgar confirms it. He swings her wheelchair out of the blinding light and pushes her toward us. I notice Irene is strapped in. Food stains cover the front of her robe. She is wearing only one shoe; the other had apparently fallen off and was placed, perhaps by an attendant, on her lap. A nurse in a white uniform kneels beside my aunt. "Hello, Irene. Is this your family?" she says in an unnecessarily loud voice. My aunt gives no response. Then the nurse turns to my mother and says, "She did her hair for the occasion. We just came upstairs from the beauty parlor." Turning again to my aunt, the nurse says, "Didn't we Irene?" My aunt struggles to speak, but can only produce an unintelligible groan.

Aunt Irene looks only vaguely familiar to me. There is nothing behind her eyes. At one point she seems to grow panicky. Finally she manages a few words. It sounds like she says, "I'm too high."

It's impossible to say if Irene recognizes us, or is even aware we are there. I want to believe she knows, but my heart tells me otherwise. When we leave the room I feel sad and scared. Then my mother begins to shake all over and collapses into Edgar's open arms. She begins sobbing violently, and it is so foreign to me to see my mother in this condition.

We stood in the hallway for a long time, until my mother had no more tears to cry. I notice Don in the waiting room watching a TV bracketed to the wall. Occasionally, he'd glance in our direction. Later he told me he had been watching an episode of the Muppet Show. The guest host was the famous model, Twiggy. As we entered the hallway, Twiggy was singing, "In My Life." Unbeknownst to me at the time, Don was somehow sharing this poignant moment in my life, experiencing some deep, unforgettable emotions of his own.

As we walked away from the hospital, I realized I would probably never see my aunt Irene again. I hadn't seen her today, really. It was not my aunt in that room, I thought.

I'm glad to wake up the following morning, knowing Don and I will break fresh ground on our journey to California. I'm also relieved to have a valid excuse to get away from the painful reality of Omaha. We spend the morning preparing our vehicles. We scrape bugs off our windshields. Mom and Edgar come out to say goodbye. I hug and kiss them both, lingering for awhile, while Don waits patiently idling in his VW with his elbow hanging out of the window. Soon his patience runs out and he taps his horn. "Come on man, let's roll before they close the border," Don yells. California is beckoning.

I hold my mother's image in the rearview mirror as I drive away. There is love in her eyes, a broad smile on her face, and she never stops waving. When she's out of sight, I am unexpectedly ambushed by an intense feeling of dread. It catches me by surprise, and I am suddenly filled with apprehension. The road ahead seems full of uncertainty. Can I handle it? This is not as simple as my four year stint at Boston University. I am *relocating* to Los Angeles; a move which is, potentially, permanent. This time I am truly severing the ties - to home, and to my mother. I feel nauseous. What was I thinking? I begin to panic. I want to call the whole thing off, even if it means abandoning Don. (At least I won't be abandoning my own mother.) But, somehow, my foot stays firmly on the accelerator; really, it's too late to turn back.

The vile feeling in my gut remained sharp for many miles, but the highway begged my attention, relentlessly, offering assurances I was not ready to concede.

THE GREAT DIVIDE

NEBRASKA IS LONG and flat. We have to stop often for coffee to break up the monotony. At about 2pm we stop in the town of Cozad. It smells of manure. "Let's make it quick," I say, as we fill our tanks. "We'll get coffee next time," Don agrees. The odor is powerful and inescapable. Coffee can wait. We jump back in our cars, eager for a breath of fresh air.

Entering the on-ramp to Interstate 80, thick black smoke begins to pour from my dashboard, then fire. I pull over, whip off my shirt and use it to beat at the flames. The entire incident takes less than a minute. I inspect under the dash and am soon able to determine the source of the fire.

"It looks like a short in the fuse box." I relay this to Don as I lay on my back, head against the brake pedal, looking up. Two of the fuse receptacles are melted, charred, and hot to the touch. I wonder what those two fuses are for. "Only the brake lights," Don says, studying the legend on the fuse box cover. This will not do. Driving without brake lights is not only dangerous, it's illegal. "I have an idea," I say, always the resourceful one. I remove the silver wrapper from a stick of Juicy fruit gum and wedge it between the prongs which previously held the now burnt fuses. I depress the brake pedal. "It works," Don yells from the rear of the car. We high-five it and return to our respective vehicles. Then I notice something amiss on Don's car. "You turkey," I say. "You left your gas cap back at the filling station." But Don doesn't bother returning for it. He simply stuffs a rag in the opening and we begin the next leg of our journey.

"Wasted Away in Margaritaville" is on the top 40 list that summer. Wherever we are, if our cars are in range of a radio station, we know we'll hear that song. The tune gets my blood pumping, raises my speed at least another ten miles per hour, and I never tire of it. It's on the radio now. I crank up the volume, open all the windows, and pop a stick of gum in my mouth. I marvel at the feat of engineering that somehow enables the road to appear perfectly straight, and continue for as far as the eye can see.

There are two lanes going in either direction, separated by a wide strip of dry grass. All around, the landscape is unimaginably flat. For some reason, there are very few vehicles headed west, so Don and I feel like we own the road. "Breaker one-nine." Don's voice echoes over the CB radio. "Go, breaker," I say, careful to obey FCC regulations regarding proper CB protocol.

"Got any more gum?" Don asks.

"Sure," I reply. "Pull up alongside me and I'll pass you a stick." Never mind that we are barreling down the road at 65 miles an hour (with Don's car ready to blow). With all the driving I'd recently done, I'm feeling "at one" with my machine, as though it were an extension of my body. I'm certain Don feels the same, and am confident of our abilities to accomplish even the most subtle maneuvers. Without stopping or slowing down, I'm intending to pass a stick of gum through my passenger side window to Don. "You jackass," Don screams through his laughter. "If the cars touch, they'll bounce apart like two pucks on a shuffleboard court." Yet despite the inherent danger (or perhaps because of it), Don is eager to try. We take our time, carefully synchronizing the speed of our machines as we move into position. The hardest part, for me, is holding the wheel steady while stretching across the passenger seat and far enough out the window so that Don can grab the stick of gum.

We are forced to abort the first few attempts because our cars keep drifting apart. But with each successive try we get closer and closer until Don finally grabs the prized stick of Juicy fruit by the tips of his fingers and holds on. Amazingly, at the precise moment of engagement, the split second in which the transfer is made, it seems as if our two cars are standing perfectly still. Don says it is the juiciest piece of Juicy fruit he has ever tasted, I say it is the boldest motorized stunt I have ever attempted, and we are both energized as a result of our accomplishment.

We cross the Colorado border. We had been driving into the sun all day, and now it's beginning to drop like a shiny coin in the slot of a one armed bandit. What I see both shocks and surprises me. I rub my eyes. It's still there. Was I seeing a mirage? Don is a good distance back, perhaps a quarter-mile, and I decide to pull off the road. I leave the car idling and get out, not believing the vision before me, even as it begins to reveal itself with increasing clarity. I hear Don's voice on the CB. "What's the matter, man? You got a problem?" But I'm too enthralled to respond. I wait until he pulls up behind me.

"Look," I scream, pointing straight ahead.

"Yeah, so, big deal… The sun is setting behind some clouds," Don says.

"Look again," I admonish. "Those aren't clouds, they're mountains!" Sure enough, the snowcapped Rockies loomed ahead in all their majesty, seemingly close enough to touch. We are both dumbstruck, and stare in awe, not speaking. At that moment, I thought I could sense the presence of God.

This feeling of the divine began to dissipate shortly after we crossed the Rockies, and had diminished almost entirely, two weeks later, upon our arrival in L.A.

HOLLYWOOD KNIGHTS

RICK, DON, AND I entered Tinseltown intent on a conquest of mythical proportions. We had each thrown down our personal gauntlets, and were committed to enduring all hardships, physical or psychological, until we had successfully secured our place in the annals and lore of Hollywood. We decided we would not quit or lower our guards until that victory was ours. We were smart and motivated. We had time on our side. It was our destiny. At the very least, we were certain that, in time, we would be discovered – either for our good looks, our amazing talent, or both.

Rick arrives with a paperback tucked under his arm. It's called, "Notes of a dirty old man," by Charles Bukowski. Rick is so enthusiastic about the book's contents that I ask if I can read it when he's finished. It turns out to be one of the most brilliant works I have ever read. Bukowski wrote about life. In many ways, he seemed to be writing about *my* life. He is like a religion to me, and his stories make me feel like I am not alone in the world; someone else actually understood.

We move into a decaying, three-bedroom stucco house in a tumbleweed section of North Hollywood. The house has a terra-cotta roof and a detached, two-car garage which is entered through a back alley that doubles as a channel for flood water. Inside the garage, we discover a well stocked toolbox. On the wall, balanced across two hooks, is a well-preserved fireman's hatchet.

The house is ours for three hundred a month, plus utilities. We split the cost equally, except for food. Each of us has our own shelf in the pint-sized refrigerator. We claim whatever space we can of the freezer - which has little room for anything, due to years of neglect and caked-on frost. There's a working fireplace and a bar in the living room. The backyard has a fruit-bearing orange tree. Another tree produces real pomegranates. The house itself is a dump, but we take pride in the place, and we're determined to make it work. We clean, paint, make repairs, and mow a few patches of crabgrass which have managed to break the surface of our sandy yard. We spend a day buying cheap furniture: box springs, mattresses, dressers and a sofa. A kitchen set is on display outside a discount store on La Cienega Boulevard, and we buy it for a song. With a few left over dollars we purchase an assortment of plastic flowers and a glass vase. Our dump of a house begins to feel like a home.

At first there was something romantic about our new lifestyle: school (and homework) was finally a thing of the past, the sun was always shining in L.A., and we felt a daily rush of independence. But our bliss didn't last long. Change had not come as expected; it was not inevitable. Hollywood didn't know we existed. The days seemed to drag. While we did not regret our admittedly impulsive move to L.A., things are not as warm and fuzzy as they had been when we were in college. The stress we endured during final exams was nothing compared to what we were experiencing after several months of unemployment and uncertainty in Hollywood. We were running out of money, and bad things kept happening.

Although it rarely rained in Southern California, the first night in my new bed I could hear the faint pitter-patter of precipitation hitting the rooftop. The sweet smell of honeysuckle floated through my bedroom window. As I drifted off to sleep, I thought about how smooth and effortless our relocation had been: it should bode well for things to come. It was still dark when I felt the faint pitter-patter of precipitation on my face. The lullaby of rain on the roof still echoed from above, but the honeysuckle perfume had been displaced by the acrid smell of wet sheetrock and lumber.

As I'm slowly returning from the unconsciousness of sleep,

I notice that my head is cradled in a soggy pillow. My sheets and blanket are wet. I open my eyes, and see splotches of water soaking the walls and ceiling. Huge drops of rain are dripping onto my bed, my dresser, and me. My first impulse is to go back to sleep and deal with the problem in the morning. I try, but to no avail. Blocking all awareness would have required a focus and inner-strength beyond my present mental capacity. I am drenched and cold. The steady drip from the ceiling worsens into a steady stream. I can only imagine what fountainhead lurked in the attic, but I'm not anxious to find out. I mash my palm into the soggy mattress. It feels like a supersaturated sponge. Yellow water seeps through my fingers. Alright, enough is enough, I thought. It's time to get up. I slosh out of bed and look outside. The rain is coming down hard. My room appears to have sprung several fresh leaks. Despite the early hour, I rationalize that it is imperative to rouse my roommates, alert them of the disastrous rise in humidity, and enlist their help to reverse the condition (if possible).

Don wearily hoists me through a trap door into the attic, and the weather inside goes from bad to worse. Water is streaming in from several large gaps in the roof, gathering in pools on the sheetrock over my bedroom. Straddling the ceiling joists, I describe the situation to my roommates below. Soon I'm at the end of a water brigade, placing pasta pots, sauté pans, and the like beneath the most extensive breeches in the in the roof, until our limited supply of cookware had been exhausted. The soft pitter-patter of rain turned into a sharp tang-tang and, thankfully, daybreak gave way to a placid blue sky. Don made a fresh vase of coffee (our pot was in the attic), while I tried to pull together something for us to eat.

"Sue the bastard," Don says, referring to our landlord.

"I'd like to," I say. "But I don't want to do anything that could get us evicted. We're lucky to have a roof over our heads, even if it is sieve-like." We had been in L.A. for three weeks and hadn't seen a drop of rain. Nevertheless, when I called the landlord in the morning to complain, he refused to mend the roof, saying, "It never rains in Southern California. You won't have that problem again." I gave him the benefit of the doubt and didn't make an issue of it.

"Holy shit!" Rick was yelling in the front yard. Don and I thought a portion of the roof had collapsed, and race outside.

"There's mountains out there!" screams Rick. Sure enough, the rain had washed away the smog, and the majestic San Gabriel mountain range appeared, like a mirage, at our doorstep. It's a magical sight, and quickly restores the romance of living in Los Angeles, and the dream we so desperately yearned to embrace.

Within a few days, our house had returned to a damp but livable condition (save for the sour stench of mildew blooming on my bedroom walls), and the forecast looked bright. Don began working days hawking appliances at a department store in the Valley. I was working the late shift at a roast beef sandwich franchise on Hollywood Boulevard. Rick was earning an hourly wage from a major record label, driving a forklift in their main warehouse.

Rick is not sleeping at all. It seems he has become an insomniac. For me this is good because it gives me someone to talk to in the wee hours of the morning when I return from work. For Rick, however, it is not so good: operating heavy machinery in a somnambulistic state is dangerous and not recommended, but he did it anyway.

I clean the fryers before punching out for the night. There is so much caked-on grease at the end of the day, cleaning requires a harsh chemical solvent. Even with rubber gloves, my hands burn like they've been dipped in military-grade napalm. (It takes five minutes under cold running water to alleviate most of the sting.) When I finish, I call Rick, certain he'll still be awake.

"Hello?" he whispers suspiciously into the phone.

"You up?" I ask.

"Watching, 'Invasion of the Body Snatchers'."

I make a mental picture of him kicked-back in his green patent-leather recliner in the living room, gazing into our 23-inch black and white television, the antenna wrapped in aluminum foil (which somehow dramatically improved reception).

"How's the reception?" I ask.

"Not bad. I get a little ghosting, sometimes."

"Want some roast beef?"

"Sure! I'm four cans into a six-pack of Molson. I should probably eat something."

"See you soon."

I hang up, stuff several handfuls of sliced roast beef into a paper bag, and clock out. The meat feels wet and heavy, but the bag is still intact when I toss it into my car and head for home.

The short trip is usually uneventful. There is little traffic at three in the morning, even in L.A., but this night it's different. As I'm driving through Laurel Canyon, (a narrow road, with only one lane in each direction and no shoulder), I'm suddenly blinded by a pair of headlights. It's disorienting and unnerving to see, especially at three in the morning. I check to be sure that I'm in the proper lane, and that I'm not seeing things. (I am, and I'm not.) There's a car in my lane and it's headed directly toward me! I'm petrified. I imagine the other driver is some coked-up California junkie trying to impress his girlfriend, challenging me to a game of *chicken*. But it's three in the morning, I'm tired, and my roommate expects roast beef. I'm in no mood to play games.

The car is speeding up and getting closer. I can see from the style of headlights that it's a small sports car, and I realize I have a problem (which the driver coming toward me at sixty miles an hour obviously hasn't thought of yet): If I swerve left, then neither of us will be certain what course the other will take after that. On the other hand, if I stand my ground, and the other driver doesn't flinch, we will both die. I judge we are about ten seconds to impact, and jerk my wheel to the left. The other car swerves left, then right, then left again. It now seems like anybody's guess where either car will end up. I hold steady, but so does the sick, brain dead shithead coming at me like a bullet. We are right back where we started from, only now he is in the correct lane, and I am in the wrong lane headed toward him. Six seconds remain before there is roast beef splattered all over my windshield, when I flash on an insight: I am behind the wheel of a ten year old, beat up Toyota with over one hundred thousand miles, and badly in need of a new engine; it's a piece of junk. The asshole in front of me is sporting a much more expensive vehicle. It's obvious who values their car more. But the real question, I suppose, is "who values their life more?"

I lock my hands on the wheel and slowly but firmly press on the accelerator. I am going to give this little California prick a run for his money. I am going to call his bluff. Soon I'm doing sixty on a windy section of road. I remain calm, focused, and decide I am not going to surrender my lane, period.

Our cars are about three seconds from impact. I yell, "Goodbye sucker!" to no one in particular. With one hand on the wheel, and the other on Rick's soggy roast beef, I pray it will live long enough to be enjoyed by him. And then, the little hot sports car with the little-prick driver and his little whore of a girlfriend swerves to the right. "Chicken shit," I yell as I blow past him. In my rear view mirror, the sports car is fishtailing, trying to recover after careening off the road in a hail of dirt and rocks. Victorious, I ease back into my lane - with my life and Rick's late-night snack fully intact.

Turning into the alley behind our house, I feel a strong desire for levity and friends, and I know I am just minutes away from both. On my approach to the garage, I kill the ignition and headlights and roll stealthily inside. The light from the TV flickers in the windows like cannon fire. The screen door into the kitchen opens silently and with ease. A colander with dried spaghetti mortared to the sides, sits on the cracked tile counter near the sink. Beside it is the petrified rind from a hunk of stale parmesan cheese, an empty can of Molson (still tethered to its plastic six-pack carrier), and the crumbled remnants of frosted, devils-food cake.

I inch down the dark carpeted hallway, stopping at the doorframe directly behind the leatherette recliner holding the shape of my friend Rick. I'm looking over his shoulder, and from where I stand we have identical views of the television. Rick is utterly absorbed by the images on the screen; the original and haunting, black and white version of, "Invasion of the Body Snatchers." The sound is barely audible, but I know Rick has adapted to the quiet of the house and can hear the audio very well. Rick is holding a beer in one hand. There is a ceramic bowl filled with popcorn on his lap. I am relishing the moment; waiting for the precise moment on film when the terrified man realizes the "pods" have invaded everyone in town except for him. I take a deep breath, hold it, slither within a whisper of Rick's ear, and, and...

"Wahhhhhhhhhhh!!" I scream - intent on waking the dead.

Amazingly, Rick levitates several feet above the recliner. The bowl of popcorn slams against the ceiling and shatters. Beer sprays everywhere. Rick looks down at me from the ceiling, certain it is someone or something else he is seeing. His face is stark white. His bloodshot eyes bulge from their sockets like an animated cartoon. His mouth is wide and gurgling; frozen in a silent scream. By all accounts, it looks like I have instigated my friend's untimely death by incidence of a massive myocardial infarction. He will be dead, and either myself, or (if I am clever in my account to the police) the producers of the "Invasion of the Body Snatchers" movie will be held accountable and get the death sentence.

"How'd you like a nice roast beef sandwich?" I ask. But Rick is too busy catching his breath to respond. I place the food on the arm of the recliner and sit down, continually evaluating Rick's condition in the event a call to 911 becomes necessary. Fortunately, Rick recovers shortly after he gets a whiff of the warm roast beef. While he enjoys his snack, I relate my encounter with the asshole in the sports car, and we commiserate over the realization that Hollywood is a more terrifying place than we had ever imagined. Little did we know that this was just the beginning; before the night was over, it would rain once more.

It rained for four weeks straight.

A FOOT IN THE DOOR

FOR A FEW deserving smart guys with freshly minted diplomas from a prestigious university, we were hopelessly lost and desperate. I don't know what the three of us were thinking when we decided to abandon our roots in the Northeast and move to Hollywood. None of us had any friends, relatives, or even acquaintances that could help us get jobs in the motion picture industry. It would require luck (and lots of it), even to break into an entry level position. At the moment, no one knew we existed.

One afternoon, as we strolled down Hollywood Boulevard flirting with the imaginings of fame and stardom, I am filled with a masochistic pleasure; the painful yearning that arises when intimately confronted with something both intensely desirable and virtually unattainable.

"One hundred bucks says my star will be on the Hollywood Walk of Fame in two years; in front of the Chinese Theater," Don predicts.

"Yeah, right," says Rick.

"Those spots have all been taken," I laugh, "by dead people."

"When this town recognizes my legendary potential they'll bump some old corpse," brags Don. "Who wants to bet? One hundred clams."

"That's a full month's rent," I say.

"We don't want to take your money," says Rick. But Don is insistent. "Guys, this is Hollywood, the city of dreams. Anything can happen here - amazing, wondrous things. You never know. Talent doesn't even have to factor into it."

"Which in your case it does not," Rick says under his breath.

"Shaddup. Come on, guys."

At first I'm feeling sorry for Don, thinking he had deluded himself into believing he'd succeed despite the millions of others who come to Hollywood for the same reason. Then I realize it's me I'm feeling sorry for. "Maybe he's right," I say, with a sudden change of heart. "Why go around with a negative attitude? Good things happen to positive thinkers."

It wasn't always easy, but I became a positive thinker. As an exercise in revisionism, I made a point of habitually changing bad thoughts into good ones. Day after day, I stuck with the plan. If I was on a diet, I would have lost weight - I was that committed. And it paid off. I began to notice my past feelings of desperation and despair were turning into hope and optimism, and I owe it all to Don.

Two weeks later, I call my mother with some news. "I got my first job in show business, Mom, with a major motion picture studio: United Artists!" My mother is beside herself with pride, and we agree that my four years at Boston University was finally paying off.

"I gotta go to work," I say. "Don't want to be late the first day. I love you."

"Love you too, darling. And I'm so happy for you."

My mother's long-distance praise lingers as I shower and get dressed. United Artists had furnished me with a new, standard issue uniform; a bright red sport jacket and black slacks. Both are made of a highly durable, virtually indestructible and impervious synthetic polymer. The uniform both commanded authority and protected me from the elements. As I admire myself in the mirror, I feel like a five-star general encased in Kevlar, ready for action. I hop into my car and drive south to Westwood; widely known as home to the main campus of UCLA, and for its abundance of first-run movie houses.

The marquee at the UA Westwood sparkles like a jeweled fortress. Inside, I will spend the next eight hours sweeping popcorn spills and attempting to correct the behavior of discourteous moviegoers. It's a thankless, low paying job, but I resolve to maintain a positive attitude. I had heard numerous stories of famous people starting out as network pages, or tour guides at Universal Studios, and believed my situation was similar by comparison. Why not an usher turned movie star or director? The idea suggested an odyssey of mythical proportion and grandiosity - something to justify a coveted star on Hollywood Boulevard, maybe, someday.

LET THEM EAT CAKE

A GOOD AND PLENTIFUL meal was a rarity at our house. Aside from the care packages sent to us by Rick's mother (that included sticks of pepperoni, Vermont cheddar, and Labatt's beer in cans), we mostly consumed spaghetti with salt and butter. One night, a large colander of steaming ziti I had just made tipped over in the sink and disappeared into the infinite, mildewed bowels of our burned-out garbage disposal. I watched in horror as Rick reached in, retrieved a handful of spoiled ziti, and shoved it into his mouth. He caught me looking and glared back, unselfconsciously, stridently proclaiming, "I don't care where it's been, I'm hungry!" This left me thinking: Something has got to change.

On a lazy afternoon in August, I discover an interesting ad in the classified section of Daily Variety. The Preview House on Sunset Boulevard is looking for volunteers to test market television commercials, offering the opportunity to win free prizes. The ad says participants will be asked to respond to advertisements and give their opinions in the atmosphere of "a comfortably appointed, air-conditioned theater." None of us were working that day. Instead, we had been lazing around on our uncomfortable furniture in our stiflingly hot living room, essentially broke, with nothing to do but commiserate. We had a free day. What we didn't have were comfortable appointments and air-conditioning.

When we arrive at the Preview House, we join the end of the line (which is already winding around the block), and wait for the doors to open. We pass the time reviewing how each of us had progressed since arriving in Hollywood. This is a short discussion, so we switch to the topic of where our next meal might come from.

"Once, when I was a freshman at college, I got so sick of cafeteria food I lived an entire week on Beef Jerky and Mountain Dew," I tell my friends. "It wasn't bad, really, very economical, and I could do all my grocery shopping at almost any gas station." But it's now four years later and we all agree our tastes have grown considerably more sophisticated. The thought of going a week on a similar diet was ludicrous, and my suggestion to engage in this inferior level of sustenance, at least for the moment, is immediately dismissed.

The line starts to move. As we shuffle through the main entrance, we're assaulted by a blast of frigid air. We're each handed a pink ticket, like those sold at stationery stores in large rolls with the word "Ticket" printed in the center. At either end of each ticket is a matching serial number.

The lobby has all the amenities of a regular movie theater, including a concession stand selling popcorn, soda, and candy. While the prices are reasonable, we have no money, so we forget the snacks and find our seats in the theater. We surrender our tickets to a poised young man with a distinctive all-American appearance (an aspiring actor/model, no doubt). He rips each ticket in the middle, drops half into a slotted metal box and returns the remaining halves to us. "Hang on to your stubs," he advises. "You'll need it to claim a prize if your number is drawn." We thank him and find our seats. The place soon fills to capacity.

The theater looks like a typical movie house with one exception: in front of each seat is a hand-held dial used to gauge the individual reactions of each audience member. We are instructed by a moderator to turn our dials in direct response to what we see on the screen at any given time: clockwise to indicate positive, and counterclockwise to indicate negative. The degree to which we turned the dial (either positive or negative) indicates the intensity of our response. The activity is recorded, and the results are computed in real time.

A series of thirty-second commercials are projected for our consideration. Images dance across the screen, literally. There are dancing fruit, dancing elves, dancing cereal boxes, and dancing toothpaste. I rotate my dial with rapt intensity, responding to the stimulus of light and sound like a baby in an air conditioned Skinner box. The dial is an extension of my brain. The system seems to work brilliantly, and it is satisfying to be part of some higher, communal intelligence, directing the course of consumer affairs. Judging from their smiling faces, I presume the audience feels the same. Rick, however, looks preoccupied. While Don watches the screen and reacts, I watch Rick carefully yank the plug from Don's controller, terminating his connection. The cord sags to the floor. Unbeknownst to Don, he is no longer wired to the communal mind; his input will not be factored; he is irrelevant.

In the space of three hours we watched roughly fifty commercials for a variety of products: hamburgers, soft drinks, make-up, dog food, popcorn, paper towels, underwear, mouthwash, automobiles, and sanitary napkins (to name a few). The complexity and style of each production ranged from elaborate live-action spectacles with hundreds of extras, to simple animated clay figures gesticulating atop kitchen tables. Some employed humor, while others were more avant-garde. In one commercial it was actually unclear what product they were trying to sell.

When the screening was finally over and the data had been collected (minus input from Don), the MC saunters onto the stage accompanied by an attractive young woman with an all-American smile, (an aspiring actress/model, no doubt), carrying a large Tupperware container. Inside are everyone's pink ticket halves. The MC thrusts his hand into the bucket, mixes, and randomly removes a single ticket stub. He squints as he holds the stub at arm's-length and reads the serial number aloud. There is a brief, suspenseful moment of silence in the room. The next thing I know, Rick is on his feet and shouting, "Bingo, Bingo, Bingo!" while brandishing his pink ticket with the ferocity of someone lost at sea signaling a distant passing ship. His number had been called, and the prize is a certificate redeemable for one hundred dollars worth of groceries at any Ralph's supermarket. In that brief winning moment, we couldn't have been more excited if we had won a trip around the world. (I say "we" because it was understood that any individual's good fortune would be shared three-ways.) We had hit pay dirt. With coupon in hand, we were soon perusing the well-stocked isles at Ralph's.

Our cart almost wheels itself to the refrigerated section

where every conceivable cut of beef is mooing for our attention. Don, a self-proclaimed meat and potato man, immediately begins rummaging inside the case, indiscriminately tossing package after package of meat into the cart until it's brimming. He is breathing heavily, sweating, and has a wild look in his eyes. We wait for him to finish, then Rick and I explain that a hundred bucks won't cover even a fraction of the cost of all that beef: we would have to tame our carnivorous impulses and approach our purchasing strategy with rational thought and practicality. Don knows we're right, but food had become paramount to our existence. Food-seeking behavior occupied many a waking hour, and diluted our self-control. With one hundred dollars of free food in our grasp, it was especially difficult to wander through a supermarket with a clear head. We realized we could either blow it all on one spectacular meal, or purchase items to consume slowly, over time. (I pictured my mother adding breadcrumbs to her meatloaf recipe as an "extender" – by doing so she'd maybe eke out one additional slice - and I finally understood her logic.) Rick does some quick calculations and identifies, conclusively, the one food item which will yield the biggest bang for our hundred bucks. Our final purchase would fill three shopping carts, provide ample sustenance for at least two months, and came from just one reliable source; Betty Crocker.

We became deeply ensconced in the culinary art of baking. We baked white cakes, chocolate cakes, coffee cakes, shortcakes, Bundt cakes, angel food cakes, devils food cakes, pound cakes, sponge cakes, spice cakes, lemon cakes, jelly roll cakes, cupcakes, gingerbread, sticky buns, brownies and muffins. We even baked bake-less cakes. For several months, dinner was never so sweet - nor breakfast or lunch. When the oven was engaged the house radiated like a French bakery, and I could swear there were times when the aroma slowed traffic out front, on Laurel Canyon Boulevard. This experience was so rewarding, I resolved to name my first born, "Betty." (Ultimately, this would not come to pass, as my first born was a boy.)

Had we been really smart, we would have taken pause to

look no further than our front door and open shop. The result may have given rise to a new variety of baked goods rivaling brands like Drake's, Hostess, Tasty Cake, and Little Debbie. Unfortunately we were too busy baking to see the dough for the batter, failed to recognize the entrepreneurial possibilities at hand, and the enterprise never materialized. We remained commonplace consumers and, like most, consumed until the last box of Betty Crocker cake mix was gone. Once again, we were forced to rely on our meager wages to survive.

Meanwhile, I learned from Cohen - back home - that Linda Beighle had left the east coast and moved to Redondo Beach where she had opened a macrobiotic diner. I grew very excited at the news, and made up my mind to contact her, soon. I was lonely, and Linda was one of the bright stars in my life. Although it had been more than five years since our time together in Myrtle Beach, I was certain she'd remember me.

It was easy to get her phone number from information, and when I called...

"Of course I remember you, Brad!" I heard Linda say. Her voice was the same. Her spirit sizzled through the phone line, striking me like a bolt of lightning. I couldn't wait to see her again.

We made plans to get together on a Friday. I would drive down to her house, about an hour south of North Hollywood, and she would prepare dinner for me. I offered to bring a bottle of Chardonnay.

I arrived early, pulling up to a modest house on a small plot of dusty grass not far from the beach. I climbed a few stairs leading to a wooden porch, and knocked on the frame of her screen door. As I waited, I cautioned myself not to expect too much. What we had in Myrtle Beach was in the past. Things would be different now. But when she came to the door, Linda's glowing smile, her welcoming embrace, and her smell – that fresh smell – brought me right back. My heart was beating for her again.

We had a wonderful time at dinner. Linda made steamed

vegetables and brown rice. We sat cross-legged on the floor and ate with beautiful ivory chopsticks. We lit candles and drank wine. She told me about her restaurant. I told her about my adventures in Hollywood. When dinner was over and the wine had all been consumed, we fell back onto big pillows and kissed. When things began to get heated, I followed her into the bedroom. She pulled me onto her mattress (that, too, was on the floor), and we began making out. I got the sense she wanted to take our previously abstinent relationship to another level, and I put my hand under her peasant dress, but something stopped me. I don't know if she stopped me, or I stopped myself, or what it was, but I couldn't have sex with Linda. Whatever happened, I was freaked-out, and the date ended shortly thereafter.

The next morning I woke up in my bed with a temperature of hundred and five, aching all over my body, and the worst sore throat I have ever had. I was so sick, I had Don take me to the hospital where I was given large doses of antibiotics for the flu – and it wasn't even flu season.

I never saw Linda again after that. I assumed that Meher Baba wanted me to leave her alone.

THE VIEW FROM HERE

THE COGNAC is perfect: Remy Martin, Louis XIII. I swirl my oversized snifter, hold it to the light, and study the molten amber liquid as it slinks down the sides like a delicate coating of molasses. I inhale the vapors. The aroma is a moist stone cellar with oak supports, berries, pine, and uncut diamonds. One glass cost more than a full day's pay. So what? I'm enjoying it. Isn't that what life is all about?

I had met some friends at the new hot spot in Westwood, just several blocks from the United Artists Theater where I worked. It's one of the few after-hours establishments in town, and when I get off work at one in the morning, the place is still jumping.

Normally, I would have gone straight home. I'm tired, because in addition to my regular job as an usher, I recently began working as a cameraman at Channel Z, the first and only cable outlet serving Los Angeles in 1977, providing a variety of movies and locally originated programming. But it's Saturday night, and I feel like indulging.

Ten of us are seated at a round table on a balcony which offers a bird's-eye view of the bar and main dining area. I'm quick to catch a second wind: the energy in the room is high, and the night seems full of possibilities. Roger sits to my left. He is the staff director at Channel Z, and my boss. He's the one who calls the shots from the control room, barking instructions through a headset to the camera operators in the studio. He tells us when to zoom in, zoom out, pan, tilt and focus. Of all the camera operators who work there, I am the only unpaid volunteer. Despite this, my camerawork receives the greatest amount of praise from Roger. He says I have a "good eye"; meaning, I possess a natural ability to compose a shot. Because I agreed with him, I considered becoming a professional cameraman, but quickly dismissed the idea because it would have required me to stand on my feet all day. So, rather than subject myself to a life riddled with varicose veins and sciatica, I set my sights on becoming a director, like Roger. I believed that Roger was a "real" director from whom I could learn how things were really done, in the real world, outside the college classroom. This is the reason I agreed to work for free: to learn, and gain valuable experience.

Even when I wasn't called in to operate a camera at the studio, I'd show up anyway and shadow Roger throughout his workday. I'd attend pre-production meetings, look over his shoulder in the control room, and sit in on edit sessions. He seemed to welcome my presence and delight in my curiosity, pausing to answer questions or explain things. Sometimes he was unable to explain what he was doing. "All artists work differently," he'd say. "Directors have individual sensibilities; it's their job to express their unique vision."

It wasn't long before the director in me began to emerge, and I realized I had a unique vision, too. In meetings, I would sometimes challenge Roger's creative decisions and propose alternatives. Roger was always dismissive, even when everyone else in the room responded enthusiastically to my ideas. Several weeks later, Roger called to inform me that my services at Channel Z were no longer needed.

It was hard not to take this rejection personally, especially after all the time and hard work I had donated. I wondered if there was something wrong with me. Maybe I just didn't get it. Maybe my ideas sucked. Maybe I had nothing to offer, after all. Maybe I should find something else to do with my life. But the more I thought about it, the more I was convinced it was not *me* who had the problem. I began to accept the notion that perhaps Roger was a pompous fraud, and given the opportunity I could do a better job than he. I once read somewhere that 87 percent of all people in all professions are incompetent – a disheartening thought. Well, maybe I *was* a better director. Unfortunately, Roger was the one with the job; he had the leverage and held all the power. Talented or not, Roger was in the driver's seat: that's the bottom line.

But I've gotten ahead of myself: It's Saturday night, we're having drinks at this hot spot in Westwood, and Roger is rambling on about the screenplay he's writing...

"It's very similar to Chinatown, so I'm trying to get it to Jack," Roger says of his screenplay. When I hear this I almost laugh; but, as ridiculous as it sounds, he's serious. He actually believes he's writing the next *Chinatown*, and expects Jack Nicholson to agree to play the starring role. Yeah, right. Roger, it seems, has managed to elevate self-delusion to an art form.

Below us, the main floor is swarming with beautiful blondes buzzing the bar: a stylish, oval-shaped construction of mahogany, beveled antique mirrors, and topaz-blue light boxes. It's springtime in L.A.; a time when women reach their peak of desirability. I have tuned Roger out, and am undressing a tall, undernourished-looking woman with black shiny hair and bangs, standing at the bar. Then I notice someone else. She is so blisteringly hot, that I suddenly experience a savage and primordial urge to produce a thundering legion of offspring.

She is the most perfect woman I have ever laid eyes on… from a balcony. Her shimmering, strawberry blond hair is draped lithely over the graceful curve of her shoulders. Her features are finely articulated: eyes wide set, a subtle slope to her slightly upturned nose, high cheekbones, a dappling of well placed freckles matching the color of her hair, a discernible dimple in the center of her chin. I imagine life with her by my side - the most perfect love, the most perfect union between man and woman. She is my Juliet, my Josephine, my Guinevere, my Eve.

"Excuse me," I say, interrupting Roger's absurd overestimation of himself. "There's someone here I have to meet. There… at the bar."

"I don't see her," says Roger.

"She's the one headed toward the ladies room."

"Wow. She's hot. What makes you think she wants to meet you?"

"Trust me, she does."

"What are you gonna say?"

"I don't know. I'll figure something out… when I get there."

"Good luck, man. You can do it." Roger gives me two thumbs-up as I clank down the metal staircase toward my prize.

I am inexorably drawn to this woman. Have I finally found my soul mate? It's like some inexplicable, divine force is guiding me toward her. As the gap narrows between us, I realize that the myopic vision I had from the balcony did not even do her justice. She is immeasurably more breathtaking than I imagined, and seems to possess those elusive qualities that every man desires: the fleeting innocence of youth, the silvery shade of yellow reflected in a buttercup, the scent of heather after a storm, the nectar of wild berries plucked from a vine. She is all these things to me.

I move quickly through the crowd - my strategy is to intercept her before she disappears inside the ladies room – and

I am preparing for the most seminal moment of my life. I arrive not a second too soon and position myself between her and the lavatory door.

"Excuse me," she says. Her voice has the sensual rasp of a heavy smoker.

I hadn't planned what to say, and when I open my mouth to speak, my tongue is suddenly too flaccid to form words. At that instant, fantasy and reality had collided, effectively shutting down my brain. But before a stalemate is evident, I miraculously recover, as if inspired by something divine, and utter what I believe to be, under the circumstances, the perfect pick-up line: "GOD SENT ME!"

My love glances up seductively; her eyes a tranquil Mediterranean-blue mixed with tiny flecks of gold. She is braless beneath a tight fitting halter top; perfectly suited to her feminine, pert breasts. The air is electrified, and I fantasize how, years from now, I will tell our children the story of how their mother and I first met.

"Excuse me," she repeats stridently.

"GOD SENT ME!" I repeat, feeling clever.

"I heard what you said, asshole. Now get the hell out of my way before I rip you a spare one!" Her icy words strike me like a sharp blow to the chest. I stumble backwards, and she disappears behind the ladies room door.

I am still frozen when she passes me several minutes later. I watch her slither toward the bar; prompting ogles from every man she passes. It makes me smile. The other men: they don't know her like I do. The woman is a bitch; her beauty a flimsy veneer, the empty shell of a venomous serpent.

I do not return to the balcony. I do not say "good night" to my friends, or linger to inhale the golden vapors from my fifty-dollar glass of Remy. I have an urgent need to drive fast, with the windows down.

As I turn north onto the 405 freeway, I think about my tendency to idealize the unfamiliar; it is an untenable personality flaw of unknown origin and tenacious resolve. From a distance, everyone is better than me; more intelligent, more desirable, more experienced, more capable, more worthy, more secure. My tendency to idealize extends to inanimate things, too: cameras, electronics, computer programs, cars – they all seem much better, more useful, and more beautiful (in pictures, on TV, from a distance) before I purchase them. When I do, I am almost always disappointed.

From a distance I see a woman, and imagine her to be the most stunning creature on earth, compatible with my personality in every way. Before we ever meet (if we ever meet), I am already conjuring images of two lovers on the beach; free spirits dashing along the water's edge, hands clasped, laughing. I lift her up (she is surprisingly light) and we twirl, smiling into the sun, and fall fully clothed in the water, laughing. I pull her close and we lock in a passionate kiss. Our bodies, our souls, seem to melt into one. She whispers something, her voice as smooth as Hermes silk. Her soft hair is draped across my face and smells like summer rain. (I have a good imagination.)

Sometimes the fantasy is never unmasked. It burns inside me and fuels those yet to come. The truth is only revealed with some degree of intimacy. But, by then, it is usually too late: the money has been spent, the time invested, the benefit accorded. Regrets?

PARTY LIKE IT'S 1977!

ON THE FIRST DAY OF DECEMBER, we had been in L.A. for six months. It's a bright, sunny day, like almost every day in southern California. Don is at work. Rick and I are lounging around the house talking about last week's episode of "Saturday Night Live" (we laughed so hard we choked on the pepperoni slices we were snacking on), when the phone rings. This was odd because our phone never rang. When it did, it was usually Don asking us to hack some frozen something out of his corner of the freezer which he planned to eat for dinner. This time it isn't Don. It's Wendell Weatherby. Wendell had been in several of our TV production classes in college. He was not our friend, nor was he anyone we'd ever care to call our friend; he was simply not cool. On the phone, he tells me he's in L.A. visiting friends. He wants to see us while he's in town, and asks if he can stop by the house. My first inclination is to invent some excuse as to why this is not possible. None of us has any desire to devote a perfectly good evening to Wendell. Yet, since he was thoughtful enough to call, I'd feel badly disappointing him, and I didn't want to seem unappreciative or inhospitable. So I decide, quite spontaneously, to throw a party at our house. In this way we could accommodate Wendell without committing the entire evening exclusively to him. After I hang up, I tell Rick my plan.

"What? A party? Here? Why?" he asks.

"I don't know. To celebrate: because it's winter; because the phone finally rang; because it's our six month anniversary in L.A. Who cares? We've never needed an excuse to party!"

"Who we gonna invite?" Rick asks. He had a point. Between the three of us we may have known a total of about six people, half of whom we either despised or distrusted. These were "friends" we had met at work, the Laundromat, and the local Seven-Eleven. And, of course, there was Wendell, who was suddenly looking pretty good as far as friends were concerned. Back in Boston, Wendell was just another fellow classmate to whom we gave little thought. But things were different now. Friends were pitifully scarce, and we were open to untested possibilities - even if it meant lowering our standards, or scraping the bottom of the metaphorical garbage disposal for sustenance which might otherwise have been considered sewage.

The party was set for Saturday night. We spent the entire day preparing: mopping and vacuuming the floors, stocking the bar (three quarts of Jack Daniels and a case of Coors Light), and baking the last of our Betty Crocker winnings.

At eight o'clock, people begin to arrive. Almost everyone brings something; a bag of chips, a container of dip, a six-pack of beer, a salami, a French bread, a hunk of brie. Wendell shows up clutching a brown paper bag filled with raw vegetables from the produce department at Ralph's supermarket. He has a strange, eerie grin on his face. He almost looks possessed.

"You look good," I say, like a gracious, lying host. Wendell's expression remains unchanged as I relieve him of the Ralph's bag and usher him into the living room. Don joins us, and I excuse myself to surreptitiously stash Wendell's sack of veggies behind the bar. Rick must have seen my eyes roll. He hands me an empty jam jar and pours me a river of Jack Daniels. Then Don joins us and pops open a beer. Wendell is standing alone in the center of the living room, looking very much like an ostrich in need of a sand hole.

"What's with Wendell?" I ask. "He looks weird."

"Oh," Don says. "He was telling me... something about surrendering to Jesus."

Rick chuckles. "Good ol' Wendell. He's not gonna try to convert us, is he?"

The party started out cordially enough. Everyone was drinking and eating the snacks they brought. Don discovered the bag of raw vegetables and arranged them artfully on top of the bar. Our cake remained untouched, probably because the guests assumed (albeit falsely) it was intended for dessert. About an hour into the festivities, Rick and I notice something unusual: our guests (all of them) are still wearing their winter coats. Rick, Don and I have on t-shirts and running shorts. Then, one of the guests, a native New Yorker, confides in me.

"It's winter," he says. "People here are cold."

I tell him I don't think it's cold.

"Your blood thins out after awhile," the former easterner explains. "We're freezing in here."

The thought of this depresses me. Are there no hearty people in L.A.? I notice Don, who is conspicuously absent, suddenly reappear wearing heavy sweats. Maybe it was the Jack Daniels, or maybe I was just uneasy about having my house invaded by so many strangers; but while everyone was outfitted for a night at the North Pole - and still shivering - I stood half naked among them, abundantly moist in the pits.

Nevertheless, Rick and I are determined to make our first Hollywood party a stellar success. We had never used the fireplace in the living room, and this seemed like the perfect opportunity to break it in. Problem was; we had no wood. A cursory inspection of the property revealed an abundance of palm fronds and weeds, but nothing suitable for burning. Still, we were not about to abandon our icy invitees. Rick and I always prided ourselves on our resourcefulness. We were going to build a fire, we agreed, even if it meant appropriating several nonstructural wooden beams from the attic (as a last resort, of course).

We're mulling it over in the back yard when the solution appears before us, plain as day, and dry as a bone: the log cabin.

Rick emerges from the garage clutching the fireman's hatchet. His first swing strikes with such force, the cabin topples like a house of toothpicks. Minutes later, we've got armloads of firewood to burn.

We catch up with Wendell at the kitchen sink, rinsing a knife under steaming hot water.

"What are you doing?" I ask.

"Apparently, you didn't consider all your guest's preferences when planning the refreshments," he admonishes. "There's nothing here for me to drink, so I'm making my own lemonade."

"With what?" Rick asks.

"With lemons: from your tree." Wendell points out the window.

"That's an orange tree," Rick explains.

"Clearly not," Wendell insists as he brings one to eye-level. "This is a lemon."

"It is not, you idiot." Rick does not like to be contradicted, especially when he's right - and he's usually right. He definitely was right this time. Our landlord had confirmed that the tree was orange bearing, although, to Wendell's credit, the fruit more closely resembles a lemon until it's fully ripe.

"Obviously, you don't know what you're talking about," Wendell announces with an air of superiority. I cringe and then prepare to duck and cover; Wendell was picking a fight with the wrong guy.

"What is the matter with you?" Rick spits and, to *his* credit, leaves the room without escalating the confrontation. Wendell smiles at me (a strange, otherworldly smile), and says: "Where do you keep the sugar?"

When I return to the living room, Rick is stoking a thunderous fire, but I notice a curling mass of thick, grey smoke billowing forth into the room. It seemed as though the chimney had never been cleaned. Even when I raise every operable window in the house, the added ventilation is not sufficient to dissipate the dense, hanging layer of smog shrouding the room. Surprisingly, this condition doesn't seem to be of any great consequence to any of our guests. In fact, the party is thriving; cooking (metaphorically and literally), like a house on fire. Winter coats are now littered about the room. Everyone (except Wendell) is drunk, sweating, and stripped to their undershirts. One young woman, having exceeded the amount of alcohol her petite body could tolerate, has stripped down to her bra and panties. (A short time later I'd find her first on her knees driving the porcelain bus, and then passed-out on the bathroom floor after all the other guests had left for the evening).

Copious laughter fills the living room as the smoke continues to build, pouring in from a chimney which provided no egress. Rick and I lay on the floor (where the air is still breathable), drinking, poking irons at the fire, and poking fun at everyone else. I conjecture that we have unwittingly created a mini-biosphere of summertime in downtown L.A., and making our guests feel utterly at home. Rick asks: "What's wrong with these people?" At the time I am holding a whole cauliflower in my hand - it resembles a human brain – and I spontaneously toss it into the fire, wistfully concluding, "If your brain don't work, burn it." Though I don't fathom its precise meaning, Rick immediately understands, claiming that the gesture perfectly punctuated the evening.

Don crawls over to alert us that Wendell is leaving. I stagger to my feet and discover he already has one foot out the door.

"Where are you going?" I ask, feigning disappointment.

"I'm leaving."

"Leaving, without saying 'goodbye'?"

Wendell surveys the hazy scene in the living room, shakes his head and says, "How long are you going to languish in this squalor?" his countenance registering an odd mixture of disdain and inner peace. I find myself at a precious loss for words. What did he expect me to say? One week? Six months? Thirty years? If I am truly languishing in squalor, does that make me a bad person? Before I can speak, Rick appears.

"Wendell's gotta go," I say.

"No shit," Rick replies.

"I mean… He's leaving," I assert, hoping Rick will find the appropriate words of farewell. "Oh… Thanks for the cauliflower," is all Rick can muster before turning away.

After everyone departs we canvas the house for trash, weary but content with the outcome of the evening. Rick, Don and I commend each other for throwing a great party to kick-off the second half of our first year in L.A. In the process, we realize we had learned a few things about ourselves; we learned we can orchestrate a fun social gathering whenever we desired, we're gracious hosts, we're resourceful with respect to ensuring the comfort of our guests, and we're adept at sustaining lively conversation on topics ranging from Jack Daniels to Jesus.

Our future in L.A. never looked brighter. Although we couldn't predict when real change would come, or how long we would "languish in this squalor," we were certain - at least - we'd never have to languish alone.

MOONSHADOW

I CONTINUED TO USHER at the UA Theater in Westwood; still patrolled the aisles for loudmouths and smokers; still swept errant popcorn off the floor. I was also ripping tickets at the door, and had lately been assigned to tasks requiring the collection of money. This meant manning both the box office and the refreshment stand. Once I learned the system, it wasn't long before I was treating myself to some of the perks that came with my new responsibilities.

Soda sales were tracked by the cup. At the start of each shift, a certain number of cups were pulled from storage and stacked behind the refreshment counter. Soda sales were reconciled by subtracting the number of cups remaining at the end of each shift. Provided the cup count reconciled correctly, the daily balance sheet was considered accurate. The actual soda itself was of no concern to the bottom line, and I discovered I could drink an unlimited quantity of soda as long as I provided my own container. Similarly, hot dog sales were determined by the bun. No one kept track of the wieners, and they could be consumed in conspicuous amounts without raising an eyebrow at the home office. I ate lots and lots of bare, naked hotdogs, and remained sufficiently nourished during my tenure as an usher.

Ethel Gabriel and my mother had been best friends since before I was born. She was a record producer who later became the first female Vice President of a major record label, thus Ethel was a highly respected force in the recording industry - what you might call a "heavy hitter." I was pleasantly surprised when she phoned to tell me she was in L.A. to attend the annual Grammy Awards. She had one free night and offered to take me to dinner at a restaurant of my choosing. Naturally I accepted, after which it occurred to me that she might be in a position to help jumpstart my career. Maybe she could make a few introductions for me. I had known this woman all my life. Why wouldn't she?

I chose "Moonshadow," on the Pacific Coast Highway in Malibu, as the place to meet. It's easy for an out-of-towner to find, and the food is good. I suggest we meet at seven, have drinks on the terrace overlooking the ocean, and then eat. Great.

Don had been lazing around the house all day. When I tell him about the evening I have planned, he wisely suggests I leave early and take the streets. The freeway is hard to predict at that hour - a mere fender bender could render it a veritable parking lot.

"She's an important woman," Don reminds me. "You don't want her to wait." Good advice, I thought.

I am two thirds of the way there, passing through Santa Monica, when my poor, aging Toyota backfires and dies. I was expecting this (payback for ignoring the glowing proliferation of warning lights on the sunburned dash), just not tonight. Fortunately, I am within walking distance of a payphone outside a McDonald's, and call Ethel at her hotel. When her voice comes on the line, I offer an apology along with a brief explanation (which she accepts), and she agrees to come get me. "I'll deal with my car later," I tell her.

She drives up in a red Mustang convertible with black leather interior. The top is down. "Hi, hi," she says with a lilt and a wave of her hand. I recognize this as her signature greeting; the one I've associated with Ethel ever since childhood. I leap into the passenger seat without opening the door. Ethel makes a U-turn and slips onto the entrance ramp for the Pacific Coast Highway. It's late in the day, but the sun is still high. The warm sun mixes with a cool ocean breeze, imbuing me with a feeling of infinite freedom; it is a feeling I wish could last forever. As we speed toward Malibu, the act of conversation is surrendered to the roar of the buffeting wind.

Ten minutes later we're pulling into the parking lot at Moonshadow. Since there are still plenty of empty spaces for the car, we skip the valet, park it ourselves, and head directly for the outdoor terrace.

By 6pm, the winter sun is already skirting the edge of the western horizon. Ethel and I watch from our wooden perch above the ocean as the spectacular orange ball drops slowly behind a curtain of waves. We are finishing our first round of drinks when the cocktail waitress, who had earlier introduced herself as Amy, inquires about a second round. Ethel says, "Yes, that would be lovely." I nod in accord, displaying my empty glass.

Ethel is a welcome sight. Although I hadn't seen her in years, she is a link to my past, and I feel comforted by her presence.

She is shorter and somewhat wider in girth than I remembered but, aside from that, she looks exactly the same. She has a flawless coif of silvery-white hair, a soothing, gravelly voice, and a gentle smile. Behind her blue, horn-rimmed spectacles looms the wisdom of a sage. "So, what have you been up to since you're here?" Ethel asks. I consider painting the rosiest picture imaginable because I'm certain she'll report back to my mother in New York. But, since I'm hoping for an act of charity from Ethel, I respond with a soiled laundry list of failed attempts to begin my career, concluding with a brutal description of my penurious living situation. To my surprise, the picture I paint elicits neither a sympathetic reaction nor a generous offer of help. Well, I reason, the night is still young.

Amy returns with our drinks. "Let me pay," I insist. Ethel accepts without a shred of resistance. Amy says, "I was asked to give you this." She hands me a folded cocktail napkin. Inside is the following inscription: *We think you're a fox!* The words are written in blue ink; neat, cursive handwriting, unmistakably that of a woman. I smile and show the note to Ethel.

"It looks like you have a secret admirer... or two," she says.

"Two?"

"It says, *we*," she is quick to point out. "There could possibly be *more* than two."

I'm pumped. "Who wrote this?" I ask Amy, as she hands me the check.

"I promised I wouldn't say," she replies. "They're probably watching."

Since there is no one on the terrace but the three of us, I surmise that the authors of the note must be in the lounge, on the other side of the thick, smoky-glass wall that separated us.

"They can't hear. Not if they're inside," I say, flashing a fifty dollar bill.

"Two women, at a round table near the bar," Amy says, barely moving her lips.

I slip her the cash. "Keep it," I say. It's a lot of money, but I'm feeling like the star of my own movie, and it seemed worth it. I imagine two gorgeous young ladies sipping chardonnay, wearing low cut summer dresses, and hot designer sandals. I'd saunter into the lounge and their identities would be immediately obvious. I would ask to join them, and casually order an expensive bottle of champagne.

"Can I get you anything else?" Amy asks, interrupting my private thoughts.

"We're fine," I say. "Thank you."

"Good luck," she adds, smiling as she disappears back inside.

I feel sick having parted with my fifty dollar bill, and the thought gnaws at me: that kind of money could sustain me for at least a week. To assuage my heartfelt regrets, I rationalize that sex is a form of sustenance, too. I am able to stop obsessing, but have difficulty controlling my curiosity. I simply have to see the faces of my two fans.

My struggle to see them through the glass is thwarted by my own reflection and the glare of the setting sun. Yet I feel they can see me, which makes me uneasy - self-conscious, exposed, vulnerable. It's like being on the wrong side of a two-way mirror.

"We can do dinner another time, if you'd like," Ethel says, mindful of my preoccupation. I don't want to disappoint her or appear rude, but an opportunity like this is as rare as a hot slice of New York pizza in Los Angeles.

"Are you sure?" I ask.

She smiles. "Why not see what you're getting yourself into first. I'll wait here and finish my drink. If it looks good, signal me." The familiar tone of her voice, the one I had heard throughout childhood, assures me she will be cool with whatever I decide to do.

I step into total darkness, and can tell I'm being watched; my every move is being scrutinized. As my eyes adjust to the change in light, I spot a tanned, silver-haired man wearing an Armani suit. He is perched on a barstool and checking his watch; a Rolex. An attractive brunette, who I imagine to be several years younger than he, sidles up beside him. She stands on her tiptoes and they kiss. It's a sustained, passionate kiss, indicating familiarity (a wife, a girlfriend, a lover?), and a beautiful thing to observe. I try to imagine myself in twenty years; stylish and prosperous, an alluring woman hugging my side, and a Rolex hugging my wrist. I am mired in envy. This man seemed to have it all. At the moment, I seemed to have nothing. I am nothing. Would it ever change?

Confident of my ability to see clearly now, I navigate the mélange of lounge lizards and furniture, moving deeper into the room, certain I will soon lay eyes on the two beautiful women who had cleverly summoned me on the handy cocktail napkin. I soon make eye contact with two women at a small round table near the bar. I flash the napkin, and both women nod. One had her forearm draped across an empty chair; the chair, I assume, they were saving for me. I try to invoke a clever opening line - something more appropriate and less psychotic in nature than, "God sent me" – but all I come up with is, "So, you're the guilty ones." It isn't great, but it keeps me on the playing field.

"What took so long, handsome? I'm Sharon. And this is Debbie."

Debbie says, "We think you're a fox. Have a seat."

We shake hands, and I drop into the empty seat.

"The waitress promised not to tell," says Sharon. She has long, dirty-blond hair, and, I notice, a killer body. Her face isn't bad, either.

"She didn't," I lie. "The distinctive handwriting suggested I look for two beautiful women. Obviously I was correct." (Now that's a clever line!)

Debbie looks out the window at Ethel. "Is that your mother?"

"No. We work together," I lie, again.

"What do you do?" Sharon inquires.

"I'm a director. In fact, that woman is financing my new movie." What the hell. It isn't like me to lie or even exaggerate, but under the circumstances it feels natural. "Will you excuse me a minute?" I say.

I tell Ethel that, if she really doesn't mind, I'd prefer to reschedule our dinner. She asks how I planned to get back to Santa

Monica without a car. I have no idea, but assure her I'll be fine. I kiss her on the cheek and thank her for understanding.

Before I return to the lounge, I find a payphone near the restrooms and call Don. "I'll be returning to the house with a couple of chicks. You can take the one I don't want," I tell Don.

"Are they cute?" he asks.

"Yes. Very."

"Cool. I'll straighten up so it'll look good when you get here," Don assures me, then clicks off.

I rejoin the girls, and for the next several hours it is cocktails and conversation. I learn that Sharon is a manicurist at a beauty salon in Redondo Beach. Debbie works for Con Edison. The two met in high school and have been friends ever since. Both are 28. Relative to my 22 years, they seem like older women. This turns me on. The only problem is Debbie. She's hard to look at. Her complexion is ruddy, her body rotund and doughy. (Unfortunately, there is not enough Jack Daniels in all of Malibu to change that.) But with each measurable rise in my blood-alcohol level, so increases my desire to be with Sharon. Hoping to improve my odds of getting into her pants, I flirt equally with both women while looking for opportunities to cut Debbie permanently out of the picture.

After numerous rounds of drinks, Sharon and Debbie begin slurring their words, and I suggest we call it a night.

"Wharre duu yoou wann a go?" Sharon says, before releasing a goblet-shattering belch. "I'm sooo sorry." She covers her mouth, smiling foolishly behind her long, manicured fingernails.

"My car is in Santa Monica," I tell her. "I can use a lift."

I close out the tab and help the girls to their feet. Debbie throws her arm around me - it feels more like a headlock – and we head out the door. Her breath is hot, and smells like a combination of stale tobacco and rancid meat.

In the parking lot Sharon fumbles with her keys, and drops them into a sewer drain. I spend the next ten minutes recovering them while Sharon searches for her car and Debbie naps on the pavement (in the middle of a parking spot that says, "Handicapped only"). Sharon grows hysterical, suspecting her car had been stolen. She wants to call the police. Thankfully, her car appears moments later behind a transport vehicle for the disabled - next to the spot where Debbie is napping.

I offer to drive, but Sharon insists on taking the wheel, and the three of us squeeze into the front of her Oldsmobile, with me sandwiched in the middle. The car lurches forward and Sharon turns out of the parking lot, heading south on the Pacific Coast Highway.

We immediately swerve into oncoming traffic. Horns blare. We swerve back. I notice Sharon's eyes are seriously glazed over. She isn't all there. Her face looks like a pinball machine on "tilt," and I can see she is having trouble focusing on the road. Then her eyes roll back in her head, and the car veers onto the soft shoulder, kicking up dirt and rocks. There is no retaining wall to act as a safety net; just a steep drop into the ocean. Of more immediate concern, however, is the sight of the telephone pole looming large in the windshield. A collision with the pole may have been preferable, I thought, than a splash in the ocean. The pole would cause a violent crash, but the ocean is cold and wet. To be honest, neither outcome would be acceptable: I am petrified.

"Enough," I thought, as if there is time to think. I jerk the wheel to the left. The car fishtails into the pole, pops the rear fender, and bounces back onto the highway. I shout, "Pull over!" and suddenly realize I am completely sober. Apparently, this is sobering to Sharon as well, at least to the point where she can drive a straight line, even if she is still unable to walk one. A quick check on Debbie reveals she is passed out against the passenger door. If we were to crash now, she would most likely be the lone survivor. I let her be.

Sharon and I are playing tug-of-war with the steering wheel. "I'm alright," she demands, and I eventually loosen my grip. Her eyes are suddenly much clearer, and her driving is less erratic. She keeps to the slow lane. It appears the crisis is over. Turn by turn, I direct her to the block on Ocean Avenue where I had abandoned my Toyota hours earlier. Debbie finally wakes from the dead and sits upright as Sharon pulls up to the curb. She throws the car in park, but keeps the motor idling.

"Where do you live?" Sharon asks.

I describe my house in North Hollywood (stressing the charm, not the squalor), and as I do, a scenario for the remainder of the evening develops in my mind. I imagine Don awake, reading as he awaits our arrival. Rick will already be sleeping. I introduce Debbie to Don. Sharon and I then disappear into my bedroom, alone. Perhaps we make love until sunrise, rolling passionately beneath the sheets until our last ounce of strength is exhausted.

As if she read my mind, I hear Sharon say, "Let's go."

"Okay," I say.

Debbie says: "Have you ever been with two women before?" She grins confidently at me. I'm confused. Just to be perfectly clear I say, "I have a roommate who wants to meet you."

"We don't want your roommate. We want you," Sharon says. Her eyes look funny again. This is already a far different scenario from the one I had imagined earlier. As I sit between the two girls, I know I have a decision to make. A simple "yes" or "no" would do, though I'm feeling pressure to respond in the affirmative. In order to have the girl I wanted (Sharon), it seemed I would have to tolerate the girl I didn't (Debbie) – simultaneously. Was it worth it? Was it even possible? Debbie is glaring at me in defiance, and I fear she already knows what I'm thinking. Sharon's head wobbles. I decide to approach the proposition in mathematical terms: The value of the "turn-on" minus the value of the "turn-off" equals the total value in terms of erotic (sexual) satisfaction. If Sharon is more sexy then Debbie is gross, we'll be in business. On a scale of ten, I give Sharon an eight for sexiness. I judge Debbie to be a seven on the grossness scale. I want to sleep with Sharon, and for a moment I consider a less rigid point system for Debbie, but dismiss the idea after looking at her once more, close up.

"I don't think so," I tell them. "Not tonight."

"Why not?"

"I have to be at work early," I lie, again.

"Tomorrow is Sunday."

Busted. But wait. "The movie theaters are open. The first show is at noon and I have to be there two hours in advance to set up." It's good, sound reasoning.

Debbie says, "What are you talking about? You said you were a director."

I'm suddenly hot, sweaty and speechless.

No one likes rejection, but a "no" to two women offering sex to a younger guy in the form of a threesome, even if one of the women is a pig (whether she knows it or not), is an insult to both women. Nevertheless, I respond to their offer with a resounding "no." As expected, both of them are really pissed. As if someone flipped a switch, I am suddenly the object of hatred and ridicule. They become shamelessly vitriolic, and attack me without restraint or mercy. They attack my appearance. They attack my character. They even attack my manhood. I feel helpless, outnumbered and afraid. I think about reconsidering. But after enduring a character assassination this severe, it is inconceivable that I, or any man for that matter, could have the fortitude to perform on that night, or on any other night for the next several months. Did they think treating me like scum would magically arouse me? I considered a change of heart - was it to spare them the shame of rejection, or to bring an end to their scorn? Was I being kind or weak? I think I was being kind... and weak.

Sharon is shrieking in my ear, mercilessly continuing to attack my character. But, just as her diatribe seems to reach a full crescendo, something unexpected happens: she leans over and pukes on my lap. Debbie jumps out of the car - finally! I just sit there trying to maneuver Sharon's head so the warm, alcoholic contents of her stomach are aimed more precisely toward the floor. When she finishes, I slide out and join Debbie at the curb.

"I'm really sorry," Debbie says. "I guess we had too much to drink."

(I'll say.) "No problem," I tell her. "Do you think you can get home safely?"

"I think I'm okay to drive."

I open the trunk of my car and get a small rag. It's covered with grease, and smells like gasoline, but under the circumstances the odor is refreshing. I hand it to Sharon through the driver's side window.

"Keep it," I say, magnanimously. "It was nice meeting you." Then, in a moment of weakness fueled by my hopelessly romantic imagination, I add, "Perhaps under different circumstances..." My words trail off when a slight wind stirs the putrid air inside the car. "Good night," I say, choking.

I return to the payphone outside McDonalds, and call Don. "Forget it," I say. "The chick thing is off. One of them puked on me."

"Oh, bummer," says Don, sympathetically.

As I walk back to my car, I realize it might not start. But I assure myself that the engine had probably flooded, and should be dry by now. The girls are where I had left them moments ago, still fussing by the side of the road. All I want now is to get as far away from them as possible – as soon as possible. My prayers are answered when my Toyota starts at the first turn of the ignition. Thank you, God.

Cool air encircles me as I speed through Laurel Canyon toward home. Freedom is life, I thought; as essential as clean air, as indispensable as fresh water, as vital as food. It's best to be unencumbered, if possible.

By the time I reach home, the sky is a beautiful gradation of cobalt blue and apricot. The house is quiet. My roommates are asleep. There will be a good story to tell when they're awake. But now, I need sleep. I shower and slip into bed, glad to be alone.

A PICKLE AND A NUT

AFTER MONTHS OF TRYING, I finally land a permanent job with

a production company that films television commercials. The company, located on a tree-lined, residential block in West Hollywood, is highly regarded for its big budget spots and high-end clients like Coke, McDonalds, General Motors, American Express, and General Electric. I'm hired as a Production Assistant. The position resides at the bottom of the food chain, for sure. I was expected to do whatever I was told to do, however unpleasant or menial. Mostly the tasks involved transporting equipment, props, wardrobe, and actors; picking up lunches and dry cleaning; keeping the refrigerator stocked with juice and soda; keeping the bar stocked with liquor; and sometimes running personal errands for certain members of the staff. None of this is a problem for me. I'm told to expect long workdays lasting ten hours or more. No problem. I'm required to wear a pager. No problem. I'm paid $115 per week. Problem, but since this is my first job with any real potential, I'd find a way to eat cheaper meals and have fewer of them. Anything is better than sweeping popcorn.

My first day on the job, Harvey calls me into his office. Harvey is the President of the company. He and his wife recently relocated to L.A. from New York. "I'm giving you your first assignment," he barks. I'm thinking he barks because of some Napoleon Complex. Harvey is easily five inches shorter than my five-foot-seven frame. He is portly, rotund, and balding. I estimate he's probably in his middle to late fifties. He smokes long, fat cigars, presumably to compensate for the diminutive merits of his you-know-what. "My wife is waiting outside our hotel. I need you to pick her up and bring her back here immediately," Harvey orders. I thought I detected condescension in his voice, but banished the notion, thinking I had a case of first-day jitters.

"Ever drive a Jaguar?" he asks.

"Honestly, I never have," I admit. "But I'm a good driver."

Harvey tosses me a set of keys. "It's in the lot; emerald green, with New York plates. Fill the tank while you're at it."

"Yes Sir," I reply, and Harvey hands me a company credit card and a piece of paper with an address on Robertson Boulevard.

"Do you know where Robertson is?" he asks. I tell him I do, but I am lying. In truth, this part of town is new to me. Robertson sounds vaguely familiar, but I really have no idea where it is. But I'm not stupid. I'm a college graduate. I'm confident I'll find the address once I'm behind the wheel. It's important to make a good impression on the boss. I want him to think I have all the answers. I don't want him to think he's paying me too much. I tell Harvey I'll gladly retrieve his wife, and promise to return her posthaste. This is my first chance to shine.

"Don't let me down," Harvey barks with a smile as I head out the door. He seems to like me. To be honest, I don't like being barked at. I already hate him. It doesn't matter. I've got the keys to his Jag.

I raise the windows and turn the air conditioning up full. It's before ten, and already it feels like an oven outside. I imagine it will be even hotter by noon. It's the kind of day that tests the fortitude of the local power grid, as people struggle to stay cool. It's also the kind of day that triggers health alerts, as smog levels shoot sky high, and people with breathing maladies are urged to stay indoors. It's a typical summer day in Los Angeles.

I proceed in an easterly direction, recalling (perhaps) recently passing a street sign that read "Robertson Boulevard," though I am not sure. The city blocks are rather short, with four-way stop signs at every intersection. The road dips into and out of each intersection. I surmise this is to channel flood water when it rains. I find it annoying. It is impossible to drive fast without bottoming out. I drive, stop, and dip. Drive, stop, and dip. It's like traversing an endless line of speed bumps, and after a while the effect is hypnotic. I suddenly realize I've been driving, stopping and dipping for almost thirty minutes.

The neighborhood appears to have changed. Instead of Mercedes, BMWs, and Jaguars, I am driving amid a sea of faded, off color rent-a-wrecks and flea-bitten pickup trucks. I lower my window. The air is oppressive, and smells like melted tar. I have a bad feeling that Robertson Boulevard, and the boss' wife, are probably in my rear view mirror, somewhere far away.

I tell myself, just a few more blocks; if I don't see Robertson, I'll ask someone for directions. Several blocks later, I don't see Robertson. There are no pedestrians to ask directions. I slow down. Then I begin to panic, and I speed up. The neighborhood is decrepit and unfamiliar. I don't recognize anything; not a street name, a billboard, a storefront, nothing.

I finally admit it. I'm lost. I am an idiot... why didn't I ask someone for directions fifteen minutes ago? I am a male, and most males don't ask for directions. I am a male idiot... the boss is probably wondering what happened to me. My shirt is sticky and soaked with sweat.

Relax.

There's a gas station up ahead. I drive up to one of the pumps and ask the attendant for directions.

"Can you tell me how to get to Robertson?"

The attendant looks at me quizzically. "Robertson? No. No hay Robertson," he slurs in Spanish. This is good news, and bad news. The good news is I speak a little Spanish. The bad news is he's telling me there's no such place as Robertson Boulevard. Fortunately I have been traveling on the same road since leaving West Hollywood. Therefore getting back should be easy. Unfortunately, I had left West Hollywood more than 30 minutes ago. To return after an hour, empty handed, would be disastrous.

Another car stops at the pump opposite me. The driver rolls down his window and spits tobacco juice on the hot cement. It splatters and sizzles until it completely evaporates. I feel like puking. "Robertson?" I ask the driver. I realize it sounds as if I'm begging, but I'm too distraught to care. The man shakes his head, points west, and tells me it's far.

"How far?" I ask.

"Far."

There is no time to probe. I spin the car around and bolt. I'm thinking I'm screwed - no question about it. I can hardly believe it: it's my first day on the job, I'm asked to do something simple like pick up the boss' wife, and I screw it up. It's hard to believe I graduated college with honors, and made Dean's List three years running.

I do not want my first day on the job to be my last. I point the car west and press the pedal to the metal. I pay no attention to the speed limit or the stop signs. I pray. The car bumps off the front of each intersection and flies across - literally flies, before coming down hard. I imagine one or a combination of several things happening (in no particular order): I will wreck the car; I will kill somebody; I will kill myself; I will be arrested; I will lose my job. Instead, what happens is something I didn't expect and couldn't control: I wet my pants.

I am in a pickle. I'm forty-five minutes late when I roll up to the hotel on Robertson Boulevard. The gas gauge reads empty. Harvey's wife is tapping her foot on the curb. Although I'd never met her before, I instinctively know it's her. She is smiling, but I can tell her gesture is forced. Underneath her veil of civility is an angry woman. Not that I blame her. Due to my ineptness, this poor lady was forced to wait curbside in the stifling heat and the choking smog. A task that should have taken me less than five minutes, took almost an hour. She must have called her husband several times, perhaps blaming him at first, and then believing it was not his fault; that I really was AWOL.

What must they have conjectured about my whereabouts? That I took in a movie? That I stopped for a burger? That I stole Harvey's Jaguar, and skipped town with the company MasterCard? I'm sure they didn't think I was simply lost. No idiot could get lost for that long. Besides, I claimed to know the whereabouts of Robertson Boulevard. Maybe there was no discussion. Maybe Harvey's wife was running late - putting on hot curlers, or applying fresh makeup. Maybe there was no problem at all, and I wet my pants for nothing. Why expect the worst?

I sigh, and consider gallantly opening the passenger door, but I can't risk exposing the dark, wet spot encircling the crotch of my chinos. I'm sure she is interpreting my inaction as hostile, impolite and rude, but I have no choice. I am praying the car does not reek of urine, or run out of gas. When she lets herself in (the backseat), I am relieved. She is heavily perfumed. It is not a pleasant fragrance but, given her social status, it is likely a pricy extract. I make an attempt at pleasantries. "How do you like L.A.?" I ask. "Can you believe this heat?" I ask. "That's a lovely dress you're wearing. Did you bring it from New York?" Harvey's wife is not amused. She ignores me, pretending I don't exist. I check my rearview mirror, and see her staring out the window. I realize I have made a faux pas by not apologizing the moment she got in the car. If I said something now it would be weird – I missed my opportunity – so I offer no apology or explanation. It is exceedingly clear that she is exceedingly angry. If this is her reaction, I can only conclude my boss' reaction will be of equal or greater magnitude. I am frightened, and sorely in need of a restroom.

* * *

THE LAST TIME I was in an awkward situation like this, I was fifteen. It was the first time I experimented, in a big way, with alcohol. It was a cold Saturday night in February. Cohen's parents were out of town, and he organized a small get together, with girls, at his house. For some reason, I got it in my head that I wanted to get really drunk and act silly. I waited until my mother had planted herself in front of the TV for the night, and carefully extracted a bottle of Beefeaters Gin from the liquor cabinet. I did this slowly, with surgical precision, to avoid the dreaded "clink" of bottles – a dead giveaway.

Getting the gin past my mother was easy. She was watching her favorite show, "Mission Impossible," which consistently melted her world away. She became so engrossed in the program, she often forgot there was something cooking on the stove, or baking in the oven. The consequences were usually inedible.

I slipped past her into my bathroom, and locked the door. I dumped two bottles of prescription cough medicine into the sink, rinsed them, and filled them with Gin. I returned the big bottle to the liquor cabinet, and stashed the little bottles (which weren't so little) in my coat pocket. Then, I kissed my mother goodbye, checked the kitchen to make sure nothing was burning, and headed out into the night.

Cohen's house was a ten minute walk; which was all the time I needed to swallow both bottles of Gin. It tasted like cleaning fluid. It burned my insides. But the ritual was strangely appealing, and made me feel immune to the cold. I could thumb my nose and laugh at the frigid winter air.

The details are a little sketchy, but for awhile I was the life of the party. Everyone thought I was funny and charming. It seemed I was masquerading as someone funny and charming. But it wasn't me. Nevertheless, I was happy to entertain my friends. At one point, I am lying on the sofa, on my back, when some girl decides to sit on my stomach and bounce – for ten minutes. This did not sit well with the gin in my stomach. It wanted to come out, and it did. I made it to the bathroom, no problem, but when I finished, I was ratty as a dishcloth, and smelled like a well-primed compost pile.

"I can't go home tonight," I told Cohen. "You have to let me sleep over." I was tired and dizzy and weak. It was difficult to enunciate my words.

"My parents told me I couldn't have sleepovers," he said.

"You don't understand. I can't go home," I repeated. "I'm in no condition."

"Sorry," Cohen said. "I promised them."

"Please. They'll never know. I'll sleep in the bathtub," I slurred. But Cohen refused to acquiesce. I was in a pickle. I couldn't stay and I couldn't go home. "I can't walk a straight line," I said.

"Ash will take you home in a cab," Cohen volunteered.

Ash nearly carried me to the taxi. He slid beside me in the back seat. Throughout the short ride home, it was all I could do to keep from falling asleep on his shoulder. When the blur of my house came into view, it seemed to have a slightly sobering effect. Ash told the driver to wait, hoisted me out of the cab, and dragged me across the lawn, onto the brightly lit porch. He propped me against the wall, rang the doorbell once, and vanished before my mother arrived at the door. This was awkward. I was inebriated. I smelled like a fast-food dumpster, and there was nowhere to hide. My only possible means of extrication was to up the charm, and attempt to elicit my mother's sympathy.

"What's with you, Buster?" I heard my mother say. Sometimes she called me "Buster." I could never figure out when she saw it appropriate to employ that nickname, and this time I was equally clueless.

"I got sick and threw-up," I murmured.

"Come in. Let's get you to bed."

As she guided me upstairs, my brother emerged from his bedroom. "What's wrong?" he asked. My mother answered for me. "He threw-up at Cohen's house." She touched my forehead. "He feels a little warm to me, too," Mom said. My brother eyed me suspiciously. I knew he could see through my little charade.

"Why do you suppose you threw-up?" he asked.

I told him: "I think I ate a bad cookie." Is that lame or what? It's definitely not charming. But my mother, amazingly, demanded no further explanation. She tucked me into bed, put a bucket at my bedside, and quietly backed out of my room, pulling the door shut. To be sure, the bucket came in handy throughout the night.

The next morning my brother poked his head in my room. At first I saw two brothers; identical twins, standing side-by-side. Then the images merged into one. Rex smiled at me and said, "A bad cookie?" I realized there was nowhere to hide.

* * *

BUT I AM DRIVING my boss' Jaguar, and his wife is in the back seat. She is a captive audience. I realize I may have a unique opportunity to charm her and gain her sympathy. If I win her over, perhaps she will present my case to her husband, assuage his anger, and minimize the repercussions resulting from my pathetic performance. Unfortunately, when we arrive at the office, she disappears the moment we set foot in the door.

The magnitude of Harvey's reaction is greater than his wife's. It is unlike anything I have ever seen. His head turns purple and veined. He swears and yells so ferociously, it sounds like he is speaking some foreign language. Harvey looks like a human volcano ready to erupt.

I want to save my job, but the charm and sympathy cards are no longer playable. I decide that if I have to beg, I'll beg. Turns out I have to beg. I beg Harvey not to fire me. I beg him for another chance. I beg him for my lousy $115 dollars a week, and for long hours of menial work. It is the first time in my life I have ever begged for anything. Yet, I feel I have no choice. I am begging for my life.

Harvey is reveling in his power over me. He seems to enjoy watching me squirm. I would have kissed his feet if he insisted. I'm not thinking of my pride, or my dignity. All I want is my job; that, and a dry pair of underwear, perhaps.

Harvey found it in his heart to let me keep my job. He didn't suspect that he was making a huge mistake. I was angry for the way he treated me, and I saw him for who he really was: a little man who enjoyed abusing power. My fear of Harvey was gone, replaced by hatred and a desire for revenge. I was bent on his undoing. I would find a way to expose him, and send him back to New York - with his stubby tail between his stubby little legs.

* * *

IT TOOK A FEW MONTHS to settle into my job, but I settled nicely. I had many successful pick-ups and deliveries under my belt, and soon knew every street and every shortcut from downtown L.A., to the Pacific Coast Highway, and beyond. I put extra effort into everything I did, and it paid off. I became the star employee. Everyone at the company came to respect, and admire me. I was put in charge of the casting department, and transformed an empty bungalow on the property into a video production studio. I purchased equipment and recorded auditions. The directors loved this; it meant they didn't have to sit through long, boring casting sessions watching bad actors commit acts of desperation. It was painful, even for me, to watch.

There was a job in the house for Illinois Bell, and though it was a small, local commercial, the client insisted on casting the perfect spokesman to represent the company brand. Three full days of auditions were set up with the best casting director in all of Hollywood. Her name was Connie.

On the first day of casting, thirty actors had already auditioned before lunch, and each was worse than the last. Connie never lost her composure, patiently coaching each actor with respect to motivation, body language, energy level, and inflection. But it seemed no one was listening. Nothing she said had any effect on anyone's performance. The actors were simply unable to stretch beyond their own preconceived notions of the character they were being asked to play. These are not actors, I thought. Although we still had the entire afternoon ahead of us, given the first crop of "actors," the situation looked grim. Yet, Connie was undaunted, and as we approached our lunch break, I noticed her excitement building.

"What's up?" I ask.

"Our first audition after lunch is this amazing new talent." She mentions his name.

"Never heard of him."

"I'm telling you," Connie says, "this guy is going to be big… really big."

Connie is raving about this actor, but I am having my doubts. I wonder if she is touting him because he is a friend or relative. Or maybe he is some sexy hunk, albeit untalented, who rings her bell. In Hollywood, you never know. My stomach is growling.

I'm about to bite into my sandwich when this guy bursts into the bungalow. When he does, Connie lights up like a pink Christmas tree. The guy is talking a mile a minute. Everything is a quirky, running commentary. He never stops talking. He is wired. Connie introduces me. He says something which I don't comprehend, then quickly turns away. I have never before met anyone remotely like him. I'm thinking this guy is a nut.

He and Connie jabber incessantly. I am dizzy trying to follow the conversation. It's exhausting. Finally, Connie suggests we begin the audition. I show the actor his "mark" -where to stand. It is the best place for lighting and camera. I throw the videotape machine into record. The tape rolls, and I compose my shot, framing the actor in a loose medium shot. When Connie says "action," he suddenly disappears from my viewfinder. He has leapt off his mark, and is far from the illuminated area. The guy cannot stand still. He is pure, unleashed energy, bouncing off the walls. Frenetically, he says his lines, kisses Connie on the cheek, and departs. I was unable to follow him with the camera, and only glimpses of him appear on tape. I'm dazed and confused.

"You think he's right for the part?" I ask Connie.

"Oh, he's already got the part," she says. "That's nothing. You'll be seeing a lot more of him, soon. Trust me."

Connie was right. The actor was hired as the spokesman for Illinois Bell. Six months later, I am watching TV and there he is, this time playing the part of a maniacal alien from the planet Ork, screaming "nanoo, nanoo," upside down in an armchair. I cry laughing.

* * *

A FEW MONTHS LATER I am producing a television commercial for one of the top manufacturers of performance motorcycles. We're filming running shots on a dry lake in the desert where the temperature exceeds 120 degrees in the shade. Everyone is popping salt tablets, and guzzling bottled water. Harvey has a production assistant arrange four director's chairs under a portable canopy; three for the clients from the ad agency, and one for himself. I'm upset, but not surprised, when I notice that Harvey hadn't thought to set out a chair for me. Not that I have time to relax. I'd been on my feet all day, keeping things on schedule, and the shoot was going great. Several times, the clients complimented me on the wonderful job I was doing.

At one point, Harvey leaves his chair and enters the trailer, and all three clients invite me to sit with them. We are laughing and shaking hands when Harvey returns and sees me in his chair.

"What do you think you're doing?" he says.

"I'm talking with my clients."

"Your clients? Get up," Harvey barks. "This is not your job."

"I'm the producer," I correct him. At this point, Harvey grabs me by the collar and physically lifts me out of the chair. I'm wearing a white polo shirt, and it's wet with perspiration. When Harvey tugs on it, the collar and sleeve stretch horribly out of shape. Harvey slides into the empty chair and dismisses me with a shove from the dusty sole of his shoe. "Get back to work; or you're fired," he says. Harvey had staged a demonstration of his power at my expense. But the clients were clearly embarrassed.

I couldn't have been happier. This was the moment I'd been waiting for since my first day on the job. Harvey, I thought, you just dug your own grave. You dumb, little, insensitive, son of a bitch.

A FOOT OUT THE DOOR

MY BROTHER CALLED to tell me he was coming to L.A. on business, so I booked a dinner reservation for two at the Pear Garden, a Japanese restaurant on La Cienega Boulevard. I had recently discovered sushi there, and I was anxious to introduce my brother to it. (In New York, in the late seventies, sushi was still as obscure as a nine-banded armadillo.) The Pear Garden was not one of those trendy celebrity hot spots where the paparazzi lurked – I was too naïve to know better – but it was light years more exotic than the greasy Chinese take-out joints my brother and I had grown up with in Great Neck. And before the night was over, it would be counted as one of the most memorable dining experiences of my life.

The Hostess seats us promptly at eight. I had mentioned that my brother was visiting from New York, and, although the place was practically full, we are given a large table adjacent to the sushi bar. Our Hostess serves us complimentary drinks: zombies in tall ceramic glasses resembling bamboo. We finish them quickly and order a second round. Rex and I have plenty to talk about. Since neither of us was partial to the telephone, we spoke little outside of face to face encounters, and it had been months since we'd seen each other. We talk about Mom. He tells me how she has been talking to a lawyer-friend about taking in boarders to help cover the expenses on our house. I take a big swig of my drink. I don't like the sound of strangers living my house. There are too many variables; too many opportunities for bad things to happen. My bedroom door never had a lock on it. I don't want anyone messing with my stuff. Maybe my mother really had no intention of taking in boarders. Maybe she was only making idle conversation with her friend, the lawyer.

I shrug and change the subject, diverting our attention to the highly trained sushi chefs. We watch as they slice a variety of raw fish (tuna, yellow tail, octopus, and salmon) using sharp, sword-like knives. They are highly trained artists, and work with surgical precision. The delicate slices of fish are combined with rice and seaweed, and arranged to create beautiful presentations. A finished platter is something to behold.

"We should order what the Japanese customers are having," I suggest. Rex agrees. We look around and realize we're the only people in the restaurant who *aren't* Japanese. When the waitress arrives to take our order, I point in earnest to a colorful platter being delivered to a neighboring table.

Several hours pass. Rex and I order a lot of sushi, shrimp tempura and a few double-zombies. We talk about his job as lead design engineer of high-tech communications systems. We talk about my job producing television commercials. He shows me a photograph of the foliage in New York. I study it, and feel a painful longing in my gut. I have to fight back tears, because I don't want Rex to see how much I missed New York. I don't want to appear weak. I ask Rex if I can finish his water, and when our waiter passes, I politely request a check.

Twenty minutes go by, and the check has not arrived. Our table had been cleared, long ago. Rex and I are getting restless. I don't see our waiter, so I ask the first person I see: "Check please." He nods and disappears, never to return.

It's approaching eleven o'clock, and the restaurant is nearly empty. The sushi has all been tightly wrapped in clear plastic, and the lights behind the sushi bar have been extinguished. Rex and I are getting upset. I ask someone else for our check. He nods and disappears.

At eleven-thirty, we had been waiting nearly ninety minutes for our check, and for the last half hour we were the only two customers left in the joint. Now we're undeniably angry and stressed out. But we're also at a loss for what to do. Whenever someone would pass through the dining room, however infrequently, they'd act like we were invisible. We couldn't get anyone's attention. We tried different things. We stood up. We sat down. We waved our wallets, our credit cards, and our cash. No one is acknowledging us. It's like being in some crazy episode of the Twilight Zone. Since there is no clear, appropriate response, Rex and I agree to improvise.

We push back from the table and inch tentatively toward the entrance. The closer we get to the door, the greater my urge is to bolt. I imagine Rex feels the same. Despite the rush of adrenaline, I remain calm, and for several awkward minutes we linger at the cash register. I sincerely hope someone will notice us and run over with our check, or some explanation, or apology: *"So sorry we didn't take money. Please accept humble apology,"* or *"In Japan, it is custom to avert eyes from honorable guest until shown secret signal,"* or *"We thought you work here,"* or even, *"No one tell you? Special tonight only;*

dinner flee for everyone." Something. Anything.

But no one approaches us. I look at Rex, exasperated. He simply shrugs.

"Pretty bizarre," I say.

"What do we do?"

"I say we leave," I suggest.

"You realize if we do that, you can never come back."

"I don't want to."

"Then let's get the hell out of here."

We calmly but resolutely leave… and a wave of guilt sweeps through me the instant I pass through the door. This is not how we were raised, I thought. But I also felt it was too late to turn around and go back. We were fugitives now, culprits in the act of stealing. My only defense was that of intent. Clearly this was not a premeditated act. I rationalized that we were merely guilty of stealing in the second degree, and this put me temporarily at ease.

Our pace quickens as we near my car. Soon we're speed walking. As I dig inside my pocket for the keys, I'm mentally preparing myself for a clean, swift getaway. At the same time, I'm nervous because my aging Toyota had been acting finicky, lately. It often took several turns of the ignition to start the engine, especially in the morning. But this wasn't morning, and my car had run flawlessly during the day.

We're jogging toward my car. I panic, trying to recall when I last filled the tank. Is there enough gas in the car?

Rex and I jump into my car. I turn the ignition and the needles on the dash jump to life. I adjust the rearview mirror and see a column of angry sushi chefs wielding knives. They are racing toward us. A little voice inside my head is telling me to surrender. But a much louder voice is screaming "run!"

I gun the engine and peel out, south on La Cienega, as fast as paint peels off a burning hayloft. In my rearview mirror, I see the sushi guys pile into a vintage Chevy Impala. They are quickly in pursuit. The sushi comes alive in my stomach, like a school of flying fish. It's obvious the situation has escalated beyond a simple misunderstanding. It is serious now, for real, and seemingly irreversible. I am, perforce, in a race I have to win.

"This is crazy," I yell, looking to my brother for support.

I'm headed for the Santa Monica freeway. Once there, I can cruise up the coast, and lose them in Santa Barbara, or San Francisco, or Vancouver, if necessary. Maybe, I thought, I'll get lucky, and the Impala will run out of gas before I do.

The traffic light ahead changed from green to red, and the sushi brigade is on my tail, closing the gap.

"Floor it!" I hear Rex say.

"What? Speed up?

"If you're thinking of running the light, it's probably safer to go fast."

"Hold on." I put the pedal to the metal and blow through the intersection. In my rear view mirror, I can see the Impala cautiously slow to a crawl. This put some distance between us. It also put a smile on my face. I'm starting to think I can ditch these clowns after all, and start to relax.

This is about driving prowess. If I'm just a little craftier and a little braver, then I'll prevail. I won't have to drive all the way to Canada to resolve this.

From the corner of my eye, I see a car pass on the left. It's the Impala. It passes me, pulls into my lane, slows down, and then stops. My only option, at this point, is to stop, too. When I do, the doors of the Impala swing open, and out spills what must have been the entire kitchen staff of the Pear Garden restaurant. The image reminds me of a time, years ago, when Rex and I were back at Madison Square Garden in New York, under the Big Top, astounded by the sight of circus clowns emerging in impossible numbers from inside a minuscule automobile. All their faces were hidden behind a base of impervious white greasepaint, their lips exaggerated in red, their noses concealed behind spongy red balls, and their eye sockets filled with blue. American kabuki, I thought. The spectacle was both hilarious and frightening.

The men rushing toward us now are not clowns in a circus;

they are enraged sushi chefs wielding long, sharp knives. I scream: "They're going to fillet us!"

At the moment, nothing would have pleased me more than to settle the bill (I'd even include the full, customary twenty percent service gratuity), but it was a foregone conclusion - surrendering my MasterCard was no longer an option. On second thought, these guys *were* clowns. When I asked to pay their stupid bill, they couldn't be bothered. Now, they not only wanted their money, they were apparently ready to kill for it.

My next move, though childishly obvious, came to me in a flash of inspiration. I throw the car in reverse, back up a few feet, then shift into drive and veer around them. When they realize what's happening, their expressions turn amusingly comical. I mash the accelerator to the floor, and watch in my rearview mirror as the sushi chefs scramble back into their car like a frenzied gaggle of Keystone cops.

My speedometer rises from zero to seventy-five miles per hour. Rushing past me on both sides is the neon blur of retail establishments that people patronize by day: the convenience store, the bank, the car wash, the copy shop, the bakery, the drugstore, the thrift shop. I'm approaching a row of stores where I had been that afternoon. Just twelve hours earlier I remember taking my color TV to be repaired. [There were no metered spaces on the street anywhere nearby, so I followed a sign which read, "Parking in Rear." Running behind the row of stores was a narrow strip of crumbling asphalt riddled with yawning potholes and discarded furniture. It looked more like a junkyard than a parking lot. I carefully navigated the obstacles, parked my car, and entered the repair shop through the rear door. When I left, I threw the claim check on top of the dash and exited the far side of the parking lot onto a side street.]

I glance in my rear view mirror and see the Impala approaching. Then I see the claim check for my color TV, still sitting on my dash. That's when I have another flash of inspiration, and a strategy. I will lose the Impala in the parking lot behind the repair shop. If they try to follow, they will be unprepared for the hazards that await them.

With the layout of the parking lot still fresh in my mind, I imagined how I would maneuver from one end to the other. I saw it clearly, all at once, and a few seconds later I could hear the screech of my tires as I turned sharply into the lot. The utter darkness was something I hadn't anticipated, but it didn't seem to matter. My car zipped along flawlessly. It seemed to be driving itself. Behind me I could hear the Impala bottoming out on the asphalt. There was a flash of light, and showers of sparks. When I reached the opposite end of the parking lot I braked. The Impala had stopped moving altogether. One headlight was out; the other pointed toward the sky. For a moment I was concerned that someone may have been hurt. This was not the outcome I desired. *All I wanted was to pay the check!* The weight of the entire experience suddenly hit me like a ton of wasabi, and I am overcome with indignation. I intended to do the right thing, I tried to do the right thing, and this is how I'm rewarded. There is something wrong when you can't simply enjoy a quiet dinner in a restaurant with your brother, who is visiting from out of town, without the whole night spiraling out of control. What was I *supposed* to do, anyway? After a beat, an answer was not forthcoming. Screw it, I thought, and then drove calmly away from the scene.

It was past midnight when I returned Rex to his hotel in Beverly Hills. "Want to come in for a drink?" The lounge at the Four Seasons was still serving. We sat at the bar and ordered light beer on tap. Rex complimented me on my excellent driving, and I gave him credit for teaching me how. The beer was making my head heavy. It was a full evening and we were both exhausted. Still, I wasn't ready to call it a night. We returned to small talk. I asked Rex about the weather in New York. He told me that fall was in the air, and he had recently stacked a cord of firewood in the yard. He described the fiery brilliance of the leaves, and how he had recently spent an entire afternoon photographing the foliage. I think Rex could see the sadness in my eyes, because he suddenly began to downplay the spectacle of autumn. It was true; I clearly felt a yearning in my heart, and I began thinking that maybe, someday, I could move back to New York.

BOOK FIVE

White Heat

TOP OF THE WORLD

I'M TWELVE HOURS into a sixteen hour flight from Los Angeles to the easternmost part of the Canadian Northwest Territories; an obscure part of the world known as Baffin Island. Until now, I had felt only excitement and anticipation about my journey, but now I'm beginning to comprehend the gravity of my decision to undertake it. I reach for the air-sickness bag, and place it securely in my lap. I had taken leave from my regular job in television news to be here. It seemed like the opportunity of a lifetime: I would spend two weeks in the Arctic, scouting native talent for a new Disney feature film entitled, "Never Cry Wolf." For two weeks, I would be embedded in a culture vastly different from my own. Naturally, I expected to encounter few similarities to life in L.A., but was little prepared for just how few.

* * *

Two YEARS EARLIER, shortly after my twenty-fifth birthday, I began working at Channel Eleven in L.A. as the broadcast graphics producer for the local evening newscast; a live program, airing every weeknight from ten to eleven. I was responsible for the on-air look, supplying appropriate, evocative, and exciting visuals to accompany and enhance the information reported by our studio anchorpersons. Every day, hours before the broadcast, the stories for that evening (the ones already approved by the Executive Producer), would begin piling up in my in-basket, and had a 99% chance of making it "on air." Approved stories were only "killed" to make room for late-breaking news, which took precedence over the standard "rip and read" items extracted from the news wires. Sometimes generic graphics offered sufficient visual support. Other times, something more specific had to be designed to accommodate a particular news item.

    I loved my job. It was smart, exciting, and satisfying. It offered almost unlimited opportunity for growth. It was something

I knew I could turn into a real career. I realized this from the moment the News Director hired me. Driving home on the freeway that afternoon, I remember shouting, "There is a God! There is a God!" I was so happy.

* * *

THE PLANE BOUNCED in turbulence, and my stomach filled with butterflies. I fingered the paper bag on my lap. Whatever I was thinking when I agreed to this assignment escapes me now. I turn my thoughts back to the newsroom.

* * *

IT TAKES AN ENORMOUS AMOUNT of work to put on a nightly news show. It still amazes me that a news department with a staff as small as ours can pull it off. But we do. Mostly everyone is, at some point, required to wear several different hats. I often assumed the roles of writer, assignment editor, and field producer - sometimes all on the same day. It's very hard work, but you're rewarded every night when the newscast beams live into millions of homes in the Los Angeles area. We have a devoted viewership, and we try to be responsive to the needs of the community.

Sitting at home one evening, I thought of an idea for a documentary special. I wrote it up and pitched it to my boss. "This is a great idea," he said. "I'd like to air it during March sweeps. Can you have it shot and edited in six weeks?"

The "sweeps" are critical in television. They occur four times a year, and last for a month. It's the period of time that viewer numbers are most closely tracked and scrutinized by advertisers. Broadcasters air their best programming during sweeps hoping to pull in the greatest number of viewers - ratings are analogous to revenue. By allowing me to produce a program specifically for sweeps week, my boss was not only showing me a big vote of confidence, but giving me a huge opportunity as well.

Together we invented the title, "Brother, Can You Share a Ride?" It was to be an hour-long documentary about an effort to improve traffic conditions on L.A. freeways at rush hour. The City of Los Angeles was going to use the resources of its new supercomputer to match single-occupancy commuters, creating ridesharing opportunities for the general public. If successful, the program promised to reduce traffic congestion, accidents, fuel consumption, pollution, road rage, and stress. When the Mayor's office learned of my idea for a documentary, they instantly offered their full support. Numerous top city officials agreed to on-camera interviews. They also granted us rare access to the City's highly secure command center, located a mile underground, below City Hall.

At the time, the news department was transitioning from film to videotape. Since I understood video technology, I assumed my crews did, too. But I was wrong. On more than one occasion, after a full day shooting interviews with prominent City officials, I'd inevitably discover some technical problem when I returned to the station: there was no audio, no video, or some other unrecoverable glitch. I had little choice but to go back the following day and re-shoot, which was frustrating, embarrassing, and put my deadline in a tailspin. Once, after returning to the station and seeing that all the video we had just recorded was puce in color, I threw a tantrum at the crew, and a videocassette against the wall. The tape shattered, but I felt better. Fortunately, the crew made no more technical errors after that, and I soon had all the material I needed to begin editing. The problem is, I was left with only two weeks to edit. There was no margin for error. The airdate had already been set, and the promotion department had already begun placing ads in TV Guide.

I worked around the clock for fourteen days, eating nothing but Chinese takeout and pizza. I also learned a few things, first hand, about sleep deprivation. It was a painful experience, stressful both physically and psychologically. But when my boss entered his office on the morning of my deadline, I was waiting. I held out the tape and said, "It's done."

"Brother, Can You Share a Ride?" received kudos from the station's General Manager. It also won several local awards for excellence in broadcasting. My editor handed me a copy of the tape. "You could take this to any television station in the country and get a job," he told me. As I drove home that evening after work (alone, not as part of a carpool), the videotape of my program on the passenger seat beside me, I began to fantasize about using it to get a job at one of the TV stations back home in New York.

Producing "Brother Can You Share a Ride" was tremendously satisfying, and gave me an enormous feeling of accomplishment. In theory I had created something of value. The program aired several times and received good ratings. But still I wondered to what extent it influenced traffic congestion, smog, gas consumption, and stress among L.A. commuters; though hard to measure, probably very little. Sadly, the City of Los Angeles scrapped their Commuter Computer project after just one year, for the simple reason that there were not enough willing participants to justify the expense. Apparently, Angelinos were a breed of driver who would rather spend a thousand hours sitting in traffic every year than surrender their independence. As far as I was concerned, every minute I spent sitting in traffic was pure torture, and having to rely so heavily on a car seemed a lot more like slavery than independence.

Several days after my program aired, while I was still basking in the glow of success, my phone rang. At the other end was a voice I recognized, but hadn't heard for some time. It was Bobby. Bobby had taken over as head of the commercial production company where I was working, after Harvey got fired for losing a multimillion dollar account – on account of his rudeness. Bobby told me that he had recently moved on, and was currently producing a major motion picture for the Walt Disney Company. The film was an adaptation of a book entitled, "Never Cry Wolf," written by Canadian journalist, Farley Mowat. Bobby was calling because he needed someone with knowledge of video equipment to go on location and cast several key players for the film. He needed someone to canvass a remote region of the Canadian Northwest Territories lying inside the Arctic Circle. I was thrilled that Bobby had remembered me and sought me out. Maybe this would be my big break. Maybe I would impress Bobby so much, that I would become the head of casting at Disney. Maybe my ship had finally come in.

"Our director is insisting on authenticity. He wants real Inuit to act in his picture," Bobby said. I didn't know what "Inuit" was, or were, as it were, but at that point it didn't matter. I had been in the news business for only two years, but suddenly my destiny seemed to point toward feature films.

"Count me in," I told him.

* * *

A BELL SOUNDED in the cabin of the Continental Boeing 707, and the pilot announced our final approach into Montreal. From there, I would be connecting to Nordair, flight 182, for the final leg of my journey to Frobisher Bay, Baffin Island. I removed the complimentary in-flight magazine from my seat pocket and flipped to a map of North America.

Baffin Island is located in the easternmost part of the Canadian Northwest Territories, inside the Arctic Circle. It is more than eight times the size of California and nearly six thousand miles (as the crow flies) from Los Angeles. From New York City to Frobisher Bay (at the southern tip of Baffin Island) the distance is almost 2500 miles due north. Although it was springtime, I was told to expect extreme cold temperatures, and the Disney Company advanced me a generous wardrobe allowance for cold weather gear: one thousand dollars in cash. Of course, I was required to submit receipts, and return any unused funds, but I found a way to spend it all. I bought a green, arctic-rated parka (with real fur lining in the hood), a pair of insulated "moon boots" with five-inch rubber soles, down mittens that extended almost to the elbow, plenty of thermal underwear, and several packs of freeze-dried ice cream -

the stuff developed by NASA and used by astronauts. (This item was unnecessary, but I thought it would be fun, and no one at Disney questioned the purchase.) Because I was also hauling three cases of video and lighting equipment, it was necessary to keep my wardrobe light and compact, so I managed to fit whatever I wasn't wearing into a small carry-on containing mostly clean T-shirts, underwear, and socks.

The layover in Montreal lasts about ninety minutes, in which time I purchase a small book about the Inuit of the Canadian Arctic. I want to learn as much as possible about the people with whom I'm about to spend the next several weeks. When I'm airborne again, I read about a world so far from L.A., it's hard to believe anything (other than a time machine), can take me there.

It's believed that the first humans arrived in Baffin Island nearly five thousand years ago. The island is inhabited by the Inuit, whose native language is Inuktitut, though some English and French is also spoken. Most of the area lies north of the 66th parallel (the Arctic Circle). As a result, the region experiences long nights in winter and long days in summer. I was arriving around the time of the Summer Solstice and could expect about twenty-three hours of daylight each day. The harsh climate severely limits the growth of plants and animals to sustain human life, so it remains one of the most sparsely populated areas in the world. My first stop, Frobisher Bay, located on the southernmost tip of Baffin Island, is the largest settlement in the region, with a population of 3000. Many smaller, remote settlements dot the Island, some with fewer than 20 inhabitants living in igloos. These people subsist primarily on caribou, seal, walrus, and arctic char, caught by local hunters and shared with the rest of the community. The cultural ethic of the Inuit stems from an ancient, nomadic hunting society where survival depends on collective sharing and a deep appreciation for the environment. It is said that there are no orphans among the Inuit. They believe that all objects and living things have a spirit.

My ears pop as the airplane starts its bumpy descent into Frobisher Bay. I blanch when the plane takes a sudden drop, but the other passengers remain calm, and I merely tighten my seatbelt and try to relax. I study a map of the area from the complimentary in-flight magazine. My proximity to the North Pole is so close as to be surreal, and it's strange to be so far from home - so far from anything, as I would soon discover.

It's apparent from the view out my window, or lack of one, that the pilot is attempting to land in a heavy snowstorm. I have to assume he has done this before. I cross my fingers anyway, and hope for the best. We hit the ground hard. I feel the wheels skid as the pilot applies his brakes, but the jet thankfully comes to rest at the end of the long runway. We taxi slowly through driving sheets of snow, but eventually reach the terminal, and the seatbelt sign goes dark.

Local time is 5pm and it's dark. I wonder if a storm like this is normal for this time of year. It's early spring, after all.

As the glow of the terminal becomes visible, I begin to focus on two things; collecting all my gear, and rendezvousing with a man named Bill.

CANADA BILL

Bill Wilkenson was born in Ottawa, but spent the majority of his formative years on Baffin Island with his dad. His father is a government man whose job is to preserve the life and culture of the Inuit peoples. He sees to it they receive adequate nourishment and medical attention. He routinely traverses the 2000 square mile island supervising airlifts of non-perishable supplies such as rice, canned vegetables, medication, and chemicals used for the breakdown of organic waste. The Inuit people neither require nor demand this assistance, but the Canadian Government regards the Inuit as a national treasure, whose preservation is a priority. Bill was raised among the Inuit, with Inuktitut as his second language. Though officially Canadian, in every other respect Bill is Inuit. He is also a lifeline - my guide and interpreter, while I'm in the arctic.

The airport terminal is one large room with several rows of faded-blue and yellow fiberglass chairs; a throwback to the Greyhound bus terminals of the late 60's. Fluorescent overheads hum, throwing a languid glimmer of chartreuse light against the already pale-green walls. A thick layer of cigarette smoke hangs at eye level, like low-lying fog on a moonlit night; it makes the inside of my eyelids feel like sandpaper.

An announcement crackles over a loudspeaker in the ceiling; the plane's cargo door is frozen shut, and the baggage will be delayed. In L.A. an announcement such as this would cause a serious meltdown inside the terminal; travelers would check their watches and tempers would flare, followed by verbal abuse, and finally threats against any and all uniformed employees with a pulse: "I'll have your job for this!" But here, no one flinches. No one points a finger. Instead, people react to the delay as something that's neither good nor bad. It simply is. How odd, I thought, and then realize my concept of time in this part of the world may no longer be relevant.

I hear a voice behind me say, "You might as well relax. We could be here all night." When I turn around, a pleasant looking man in his mid-thirties is smiling at me. He's wearing a white collared, short-sleeved shirt with wide brown stripes. He has a full mustache, and black, bushy eyebrows. "I'm Bill Wilkenson," he says, "and you're looking for me." We exchange a firm shake, and I'm relieved to have found him.

"How did you know?" I ask.

"Are you kidding? You stick out like a three-legged husky." When he says "out," it sounds like "oat." He asks if I'm hungry, and I tell him I'm starved. I can't remember the last time I ate.

"You also look like you could use a drink," Bill says, and he's right.

The baggage appears much sooner than I expected. I had checked eight cases of equipment in L.A., and each presented itself here, all in good condition, only covered with a harmless dusting of snow and frost.

"How about we head into town for some refreshments?" When he says "about," it sounds like "a boat." I'm in Canada, all right.

Bill helps me load my stuff in the back of his Chevy Suburban. I notice all four tires are wrapped in chains. As we drive away, the light from inside the terminal disappears quickly, dissolving into a blur of fine snow particles turned orange from the glow of our flashing hazard lights. Bill is a careful driver, but even chains on a four-wheel-drive have trouble gripping the icy road. We do, however, arrive in one piece at a place called, "The Roundabout," (pronounced, Round-a-boat).

The eatery is a single-story hexagonal construction made of plywood, and covered with a desultory coat of red paint. Each of the six sides has just one small rectangular window, too narrow and near the roof to have any practical purpose other than ventilation. The roof itself is only slightly pitched, allowing snow to pile ominously on top. Snow, by the way, is everywhere.

Bill swings open the entrance door, allowing a deep amber glow to spill into the night. A cordial wedge of light draws us inside, where we're greeted by a miasma of stale smoke and cheap bourbon. "This is it:" Bill says, "the local watering hole."

A bevy of slight and fragile women are huddled alone in the dark recesses of the room, striking matches and cupping the flames as they puff on small pipes. Though barely visible, I can see their shriveled faces, their gray streaked hair, their toothless smiles, and their languid, bloodshot eyes. It is impossible to guess their ages, but I suspect most are much younger then they appear. Their male counterparts might well be described similarly. It seems, with the men in particular, dental hygiene is non-existent here. Everyone is drinking bourbon from plastic cups, and everyone appears to be severely diminished.

"This crowd is not representative of the general Inuit population," Bill whispers apologetically. "Most Inuit are skilled hunters, fisherman, sculptors, builders, mechanics, or members of the Clergy. Almost everyone you see here has given up... given in, I should say, to drugs and alcohol."

"I thought this was the local hangout," I say, not understanding.

"It is; in Frobisher Bay. They're in a depression here. As we head farther north it all changes. You'll see," Bill promises, and his eyes suddenly brighten.

My appetite had disappeared. All I craved now was a little bourbon and a warm bed. Bill delivered the bourbon in a small plastic cup, and another, and another. Then he delivered me to a warm bed. I had known Bill for a few hours, but already decided I liked him a lot.

Bill had left his Chevy Suburban idling, and it is toasty warm inside. We drive a few miles to what will be my home for the next few days. The snow and ice and wind obliterate most of the light from Bill's headlights, but somehow he manages to find his way.

"This is it," Bill says as we arrive. "It's not the Four Seasons, but it has heat and an indoor honeybucket."

"Great," I say. "What's a 'honeybucket'?"

"The crapper."

"In a bucket?"

"Chemicals at the bottom break down the waste – help with the smell, too. It's a luxury around here," Bill informs me.

He's definitely right about one thing; it isn't the Four Seasons. "Shelter" is a better way to describe it. Illuminated by the orange light of a sodium-vapor streetlamp, the prefabricated, rectangular dwelling is made of wood, and painted mint green and yellow. It's approximately thirty feet long by twenty feet wide. The roof is flat. Two of the three windows across the front of the shelter are boarded up from the inside. Adjacent to the narrow entrance is a large water tank on a raised platform of crisscrossing two-by-fours. Pipes laden with icicles run lengthwise along the exterior before bending inside at right angles.

Bill thrusts his shoulder at the entrance, and the warped wooden door flies open. We step into a long hallway with fluorescent banks on the ceiling, and a series of doors running along the wall. One end of the hallway opens onto a kitchen. At the opposite end is a living area with a sofa, a lounge chair and a shaded floor lamp. The walls are lined with wood paneling, and the floor is one continuous piece of beige linoleum. Bill shows me to my room, and flips on the overhead.

"This is home," he says. "Hope you like it."

I want to appear stoic at first. "Works for me," I say. "It seems cozy."

Indeed, it isn't the Four Seasons, but it's clean and warm. There's a night table with a reading lamp by the bed, a small chest of drawers (in case I felt like unpacking), and enough space remaining to stow my equipment. The room even has a small window!

I neatly arrange my gear, charge the camera batteries, and flop onto the bed, exhausted. Bill looks at me quizzically. "You alright?" he asks. I admit I'm feeling somewhat like a stranger in a strange land, and suddenly very tired. It appeared he understood. Bill smiled and suggested a good night sleep as my best remedy.

LEAN CUISINE

THE SHARP RAYS of the morning sun pierce my eyelids like orange flames through wax paper. I wake up feeling alarmed and disoriented; like I'd been in deep-space hibernation for a dozen years and then abruptly awakened on a planet in some distant, uncharted universe. Rather than panic, I force myself to relax and take stock of my situation. Right, I have been sent to Baffin Island to find authentic Inuit tribes people to play leading roles in the movie, "Never Cry Wolf." Bill Wilkenson is my guide and interpreter. Today is our first day of casting. I brought equipment to videotape the auditions, and I remembered to charge the batteries before I went to bed last night. Everything is perfectly fine. What time is it???

My watch says ten. Had I remembered to set it ahead three hours? Yes, I'm certain I did. This is good. This means I didn't oversleep. I slept just enough. In fact, I feel incredibly well rested.

The plan was for me to meet Bill at the local radio station where he would be broadcasting news about our project. Several times each hour, while I slept, he made an announcement, in Inuktitut, encouraging local residents with certain physical characteristics to come to the station and audition in front of the camera. He had stressed that no experience was necessary, and stated it was an "open call," meaning people could arrive at anytime during the day without an appointment.

Bill had advised me the night before to eat a good breakfast, so I quickly dressed and made my way into the kitchen. Something was bubbling in a pot on the stove; a thick burgundy sludge, the color of Indian pudding. Next to the stove, on the linoleum floor, were a variety of fish and animal parts arranged on a square of corrugated cardboard. I knelt down to get a closer look. There's a whole fish which appears frozen, and something that looks like the leg of a deer severed below the knee. Everything else looks like a jumble entrails, slowly thawing in the relative warmth of the kitchen. Flies are buzzing around the carnage, and I reflexively swipe them away with the back of my hand.

Jollie, a portly Inuit woman who appears to be in her late fifties - but who knows, really - is the caretaker of the house. She shuffles into the kitchen, stirs the burgundy stew with a long wooden spoon, and samples the mixture. Jollie smiles, revealing streaked, crooked teeth (randomly spaced and startlingly few in number), and adds a pinch of sea salt. She looks at me and says, "Seal stew," whistling like a teapot whenever she makes the "S" sound. She dips her spoon in the stew, levels it, and guides it toward my mouth. I purse my lips. This is not my idea of a good breakfast. On the other hand, I don't want to insult Jollie by refusing to taste her cooking. Maybe if I hold my breath... I thought. But before I do, a curl of steam finds my nostrils, and I inhale my first whiff of seal stew. It isn't bad, and I begin to wonder if perhaps the stuff tastes as good as it smells. I silently berate myself for my closed mindedness - tasting the regional cuisine should all be part of the adventure - and I quickly adjust my attitude. If the Inuit can stomach it, damn it, so can I.

Suddenly full of resolve, I seize a large cereal bowl from

the cupboard and, as Jollie watches, I extemporaneously and non-verbally attempt to express my desire for more. I use hand gestures to symbolically transfer ladles of stew to my bowl. I smile broadly as I rub my stomach. I smack my lips while hovering over the bubbling pot. I dance the Charleston.

Jollie is quick to catch my drift. She takes my bowl and fills it to the brim with hot seal stew. It spontaneously expands, spills over the side and oozes between my fingers. She sticks a spoon into my bowl. It stands up, perpendicular, on its own. I marvel at this for a moment, and then begin eating.

The stew is ultra-rich, and contains chunks of something with a texture akin to liver. It tastes a lot like liver, too, but it also tastes a lot like fish, and I have difficulty separating out the dominant flavor. It isn't nearly as awful as I had imagined, but as I near the bottom of the bowl, my gag reflex unexpectedly kicks in. My body is telling me, in no uncertain terms, that I had had enough. I politely pass when Jollie offers more.

Jollie kneels beside the array of animal parts on the floor. "Char... seal... caribou... walrus," she says, pointing to each accordingly with the tip of a homemade carving knife. Everything is raw. She hands me the knife, and pantomimes a carving motion. I'm surprised: the large helping of seal stew I'd consumed just moments before seems to have stimulated my appetite to the extent that I am now feeling ravenously hungry. I dig in to the caribou first. It's sinewy and chewy, with the essence of venison. I pass on the seal; I had had enough of that. The char is delicate and incredibly fresh, like sushi. I save the walrus for last. It's a hard, blackened knuckle of meat covered by a light film of grayish mold. It smells like old blue cheese. I like blue cheese, so I cut a slice and pop it in my mouth. I am hugely disappointed. It tastes only vaguely like blue cheese - more like an old baseball forgotten in a dark, damp corner of a garage. As much as I feel like spitting, I resist for the sake of preserving the encouraging smile in Jollie's eyes. I chew for ten minutes before I am able to reduce the piece walrus meat to the size of something small enough to pass down my throat, and I swallow, chasing the putrid aftertaste with another slice of char.

After breakfast, while organizing my video gear for the day's casting session, I feel my stomach rumble. The rumbling continues, intensifies, and soon evolves into painfully severe, bent-at-the-waist cramps. That's when I make my first ever trip to a "honey bucket."

When I arrive at the radio station, Bill directs me to a windowless room to set up. A short time later, people begin to arrive at the audition. Bill and I had agreed on a system whereby Bill would conduct the interviews, while I videotaped them. He asks people to mimic a variety of facial expressions; a smile, a frown, a look of concern, fear, and endearment. I zoom in for a close-up at the appropriate moments.

All morning, the Inuit people arrive in unpredictable waves. One minute we're sitting around with our hands in our pockets, and suddenly there's a line out the door with an overwhelming number of people waiting to audition. On average, the turnout surpasses my expectations, and I'm impressed by Bill's ability to deliver the numbers.

Later in the afternoon, there's a noticeable decline in activity, and by five o'clock it's obvious that everyone who had any intention of showing up had already done so. In all, Bill interviewed sixty-five native Inuit, all of whom I had managed to capture on tape depicting a diverse range of emotions and mannerisms. We had a lot of fun; the most stressful part of my task was logging the correct spelling of everyone's names. I look at Bill who clearly looks pleased. "As they say in showbiz," I say, 'That's a wrap'." Together, Bill and I coil cables and neatly pack up the equipment. When we're finished, we make plans to meet for dinner.

The first thing I do when I return to my room is charge the batteries. Then I collapse onto my bed. I'm so tired I literally feel like I'm melting into the mattress. In less than three minutes I've drifted into an uncommonly deep sleep.

* * *

"WHERE ON EARTH AM I?" It's two hours later and I'm suddenly awake: disoriented and confused. At first I'm frightened, but the feeling soon passes and is replaced by the unexpected sensation of utter tranquility. I feel remarkably refreshed, like I've just slept for eight hours. I'm also famished. I'm considering returning to the insect infested pile of fish and hooves on the kitchen floor, when Bill appears. He's worried that Frobisher Bay may be tapped out of potential actors, but thinks he can find additional prospects in some of the more remote regions farther north. But since these places are not serviced by radio stations, he'll have to make his pitch in person. He wants to begin immediately, making it impossible for us to have dinner together. I'm thrilled he's taking this task so seriously, and make no attempt to dissuade him. He'd already arranged for my supper; while I napped, one of the hunters skinned a fresh caribou carcass and dragged it to the side of the house. "You said you loved caribou," Bill reminds me. "As long as it stays outside, it'll be good for a few days."

Bill promises to return for me after he's organized several casting sessions in advance. Then we'd make the 700 mile journey north to Igloolik, together, where a fresh crop of potential talent would be waiting. I wish Bill luck and he disappears out the door.

No sooner had Bill left, than I slip into my moon boots and venture outside. (By the way, I never said I "loved" caribou. Nevertheless, I'm hungry enough to be feeling a penchant for it now.) There's a glass thermometer anchored to the front doorframe. The Celsius scale is displayed on the left side of the glass; Fahrenheit is on the right. The mercury reads minus forty degrees. Upon closer inspection, I observe something astonishing, and it remains one of the great pieces of trivia I occasionally take out at parties when I feel like showing off: the Fahrenheit and Celsius scales intersect at forty degrees below zero. At that temperature, and only that temperature, they are exactly the same. Many outdoor thermometers bottom out at -40 C/F, so if you own one you can see for yourself. Otherwise, it's not difficult to use the conversion formula to get the result. The difficulty is trying to imagine what forty below feels like. I was there, so you'll have to take my word for it: forty below zero is *frig'in cold*.

I pull the drawstring on my fur-lined hood and step outside. The permafrost squeaks underfoot and makes me shudder. It sounds like two pieces of Styrofoam rubbing together.

When I reach the side of the dwelling, I see dinner staring back at me. The poor, adorable caribou (with the saucer- shaped, chestnut eyes), is lying on its side, and frozen stiff. It looks like the work of a highly skilled taxidermist, except that its hide is slit down the middle and peeled back, exposing the animal's bloodied ribcage. The missing hide has, no doubt, already been used to make a warm blanket or some article of clothing. But I don't wish to dwell on these harsh details. I'm hungry and weak. "Screw it," I say, and proceed to slice a sinewy sliver of meat with the long, sharp knife left lying by the animal's side. I hold my breath and bite down. It crunches a bit, but quickly softens in my mouth and is actually quite tender. I'm reminded of a very rare fillet mignon I once had at a fine restaurant in New York. I swallow the first piece or caribou, eat another, then another. It's not long before I'm feasting with delight. I eat until satiated, all the while filled with gratitude for the life that was taken so that I might survive.

Twenty minutes later, I'm overcome with an intense burst of energy. Heat seems to course through every fiber of my body. My eyesight is keener; my hearing is more acute. The muscles in my arms and legs feel poised for action. My skin tingles, and I realize my brow is dripping with sweat. I feel like I'm firing on all cylinders; strangely exhilarated. I'm being fueled by the caribou meat. It's HIGH OCTANE fuel. I tear off my coat and dash several times around the perimeter of the house. I'd never felt so alive.

Bill was right; Frobisher Bay had been tapped out. I spent the following two days at the radio station, waiting with my equipment (the batteries fully charged), but no one showed up to audition. I was getting antsy. Outside, the sky was as clear as glass, and it was far too beautiful to be cooped up in a small, windowless room. I was happy when Bill finally returned for me, as promised, and we left early the following morning for our next location. I was growing accustomed to the cold, stark majesty of this part of the world, and couldn't wait to discover what awaited us in the sparser regions to the north.

FISH OUT OF WATER, PART 1

FROM THE WINDOW of our twin-engine Otter, at five-thousand feet, I am looking down on top of the world at beautiful, stark, ice capped mountains, and silver white valleys. The scale of it takes my breath away. The sky is so blue I feel like an astronaut at the edge of earth's atmosphere. My thoughts turn to the notion of some higher being, some greater plan. This is a corner of the world that few eyes ever see except in photographs. But even the truest image could not communicate the awesome splendor of this landscape. To comprehend it, one must experience it, first hand.

Our pilot squeezes his small plane through a crevice barely wider than the wingspan, then pulls up sharply to avoid clipping the jagged edge of a mountain peak. On the other side is a pristine frozen lake, spreading out endlessly, and covered with a layer of snow that looks like marshmallow frosting on a birthday cake. "I'm going to set her down there," the pilot yells over his shoulder, fighting the relentless din of the propellers. Any type of landing at this point seemed unlikely to me, particularly because I couldn't see anything that even remotely resembled a runway. But the pilot did not seem to be joking. Then I see Bill gave him a thumbs-up. This will be interesting, for sure.

Our plane hits the ground, bouncing and rumbling along the icy lake on a wobbly pair of metal skis, and skids unevenly from side to side. For a moment, it appears we're going to collide with the mountain in front of us, but the pilot spins the controls hard to the left, the propellers roar, and the plane comes to rest in a powdery spray of ice crystals. While I unload our gear onto a sled, Bill commandeers a sparkling clean snowmobile. He attaches the sled, and, before I know it, we're off in a cloud of snow.

Crystalline spirals of blue ice dance in the wind, stinging my cheeks and forehead. Rivers of tears pour from my eyes. I had been riding on the back of Bill's snowmobile for almost an hour, and I'm wondering how much farther the machine can take us on a single tank of gas. We're headed for a sparsely populated village on the outskirts of Igloolik. There's nothing behind us, and nothing in front; only the flat, icy white permafrost surrounded by steep mountain ranges. Then, seemingly out of nowhere, a handful of igloos begin to dot the landscape. One of the igloos is in the process of being built. An Inuit man is sawing blocks of ice out of the ground, stacking them, and shaving the edges until what remains is a perfectly rounded dome. He uses several smaller blocks of ice to fashion an entrance. Bill and I watch until the man is finished, then Bill introduces me. The man's name is Emak, and he is the leader of a small Inuit tribe of hunters. He looks weathered and elderly, but he is actually vigorous and strong. He speaks no English, but seems to communicate with his eyes: they are deep, striking, spiritual eyes, humanitarian eyes; and their implication is punctuated by a warm, knowing smile. Bill tells me that the igloo is Emak's gift to me. It will be my sleeping quarters for the night. In addition, he is offering me the companionship of his niece, who will keep me warm, and attend to all of my needs. I'm surprised, and begin to protest, but Bill reminds me I am a guest in a foreign culture; refusing Emak's hospitality might insult him. "There are no orphans among the Inuit," Bill says. "Accept his offer gracefully. Smile with your eyes." I realize that this is no different than ingesting a bowl of hot seal stew. I smile. Accepting Emak's generous offer makes me feel both touched and honored. For the first time, I'm beginning to understand and appreciate the extraordinary ways of the Inuit.

The entrance to the igloo is long and narrow, designed to be negotiated on hand and knee. By his gesticulations, it is evident Emak wishes for me to inspect the result of his labors. Happy to oblige, I drop to all fours and crawl inside. What I see amazes me.

The floor is covered in a plush carpet of caribou skins, providing a dry cushion of insulation from the underlying permafrost - the layer of snow that never thaws. The biting wind outside is conspicuously absent. Soft light filters evenly through the dome overhead. The blocks of snow seem to fit together perfectly. Emak has created a work of art.

I crawl back outside, anxious to thank him. I feel like giving him a big hug. But when I emerge from the tunnel, Emak is gone. Standing in his place is his demure niece, Susan.

Susan (this is her English name), looks to be about eighteen years old. She has unique, exotic features, with dark, wide-set brown eyes. Her hair is silky and perfectly straight, the color of charcoal, and reaches down to her slender waist. "Hello," I say, awkwardly. Bill is standing behind her, smiling. "She speaks very little English, but you'll be surprised how well you'll be able to communicate with her," Bill says. He then exchanges a few words with Susan in Inuktitut. I'm glad he's around to intervene.

"Susan will be your host tonight," Bill explains. "She understands it's her responsibility to make sure you're comfortable, and that all your needs are adequately met."

I look at Susan, and say, "Thank you."

"Thank you," she replies, smiling back at me. Her English sounds better than I expected.

"Have a good night," Bill says, turning away.

"Wait!" I yell, somewhat alarmed. "That's it? You're leaving?"

Bill laughs, puts his face close to mine, and whispers, "The igloo's only big enough for the two of you. Relax. You'll be fine. It'll be a night you'll never forget."

I'm not sure whether Bill is trying to reassure me or scare the hell out of me. Either way, he has wholly succeeded in doing the latter. Bill hesitates before turning away. "I almost forgot," he says.

I'm hoping Bill is going to tell me this is all a charade; that things don't really happen like this in the arctic; that I can wake up and laugh about this bizarre dream of mine. Instead, he hands me a pint-sized, silver can. "Seal oil," he says. "It burns very slowly, so if you're careful you should have enough to last you through the night." He warns me against overuse, as too much heat could shorten the life of the igloo, i.e.; melt it. "This is the only type of roof that can leak directly into your bedroom," Bill says, and I'm thinking, "Wanna bet?" - referring to a place I know back in North Hollywood.

For the next several hours, Susan and I sit quietly inside the igloo. Communication is a struggle. I'm getting tired, and wonder about the sleeping arrangements. Then I realize I'll be lucky to sleep ten minutes; from where I sit, it looks like a freezer in need of a professional defrosting. True, it's colder outside, but it's still well below zero inside.

As the night wore on, it got even colder. I'm studying the can of seal oil. Susan smiles, nods in approval, and I place it in her outstretched hand. Within minutes, a thread of orange flame is glowing on the lip of the shiny can. I watch, mesmerized, as the sprightly flames leapfrog back and forth along the thin line. They generate a surprising amount of heat. Initially, I had wished for nothing short of a thunderous bonfire, but now I'm appreciating the peace and comfort provided by this modest flicker of light. I roll onto my back and place my hands behind my head.

Susan says, "Goodbye."

I feel my stomach tighten. This much I know: if Susan leaves me here I will die. In the morning, Bill will find me looking like a fetal-shaped ice cube and have to ship me back to the States in a padded Thermos. I'm not just scared that Susan is leaving, I'm blinded with fear. I bury my head in my coat and begin to hyperventilate.

"Don't go, please!" I plead, in a muffled, terrified voice. But apparently Susan has no intention of going anywhere. In fact, when I resurface from my coat, she has removed all her clothes; sitting beside me is a completely naked (barely legal) woman. I quickly turn away, in a reflexive demonstration of modesty, but (I am no fool) I continue to peek from the corner of my eye at her lean, tanned body. She slowly slips between two large caribou furs.

"Goodbye," she repeats, before closing her big brown eyes.
Wow... Can I wake up now?

* * *

WHILE SUSAN SLEEPS, I'm having trouble keeping warm. [Realize
that *warm* is a relative term. I'm warm, but, relatively, not warm
enough to fall asleep. In other words, I'm cold as hell. In relative
terms, it could have been worse – I suppose.] The igloo's tight
quarters virtually eliminate my ability to move around and increase
my circulation to warm up. I'm not a happy camper. I expect a
painfully long night ahead.

I crawl out of the igloo. It is *much* colder outside; and much
lonelier. The snow packed tundra stretches as far as the eye can
see. In the midnight sun, the sky is the color of faded denim; the
landscape, a sepia photograph of the lunar surface. It's awesome,
and beautiful. I feel like Robert Peary leading an expedition to the
North Pole. Some great distance away, on the horizon, I see the
silhouette of a dogsled traversing the icy plain, a lone hunter at the
rear, skillfully guiding its course. How otherworldly this place is.
Even as the polar wind swept through the ice flows and glaciers,
a deafening stillness prevailed; stillness beyond anything I have
ever known. Newspapers and television seemed irrelevant here.
If an atom bomb were to explode anywhere else on the planet,
this place would remain an oasis of calm and tranquility. The Inuit
would continue to exist as they have, perfectly self sufficient for a
thousand more years.

My teeth are chattering like a pair of dentures at the end of
a jackhammer. It's time to return to the relative warmth of the igloo.
When I crawl back inside, Susan is awake. She appears to be inspecting,
with great intensity, the leathery underside of a caribou fur.

I pull up beside her and ask, "What are you doing?" as if
expecting her to understand. Ignoring me, Susan continues to gnaw
at a grayish, oleaginous substance clinging to the back of the hide.

"Back-fat," she says finally, her accompanying smile

indicating delight. While she chews, she locates another fatty deposit and thrusts it in my direction as an offering. It looks dreadfully unappetizing, but I'm feeling hungry, and I scrape off the back-fat with my chattering front teeth. It melts precipitously in my mouth; a lump of frozen lard which tastes remarkably like spent auto lubricant. But since it's the only late-night snack available, I join Susan in her search for the prized nodules of fat. As a food source, the caribou back-fat begins to affect me about the same as raw caribou meat. I can feel my senses growing more acute. I'm suddenly warm, and break into a light sweat. Then something else happens – something I didn't expect. I get an erection.

Susan and I make passionate love until the heat from our bodies begins to compromise the integrity of our igloo. At the risk of sounding cliché, it's like a religious experience. My chest never stops pounding. Though I am fully undressed in sub-zero temperatures, my body is flush from head to toe.

As the igloo begins to melt, iced water drips onto my back. Cracks appear between the blocks of snow, letting in shafts of sunlight. Soon, I'm thinking, it'll be necessary to abandon ship. It's a clear case of too much back-fat. Next time I'll know better. But now, as I'm literally considering all sides of the situation, I suddenly lose consciousness and drift into a flaccid state of incomparable bliss.

* * *

A GENTLE RUMBLE infiltrates the thinning walls of our igloo. Soon I can hear the steady clatter of skis whooshing through snow, the lithe patter of feet, and a chorus of breathless wolves howling with abandon. As the clamor approaches, I quickly struggle to pull on my damp clothes and then crawl outside to investigate.

It's Emak. He looks regal at the helm of his sled, wearing the furry habiliments of an Inuit hunter: a hooded coat, high boots, long mittens, and leather straps securing each garment to his body. Six powerful Siberian Huskies anxiously await their master's next instruction. Every animal has its own distinct markings. Their eyes are ice-blue and fiery. It's the first time I have a chance to admire these handsome creatures up close, and I casually approach the pack, intent on touching their soft fur. "No!" Emak exclaims. Then I flash on something Bill had cautioned me about earlier: "They're more wolf than dog;" Bill said, "not pets." His words echo in my mind, and I freeze. As beautiful as they are to admire, the animals are, in fact, lupine beasts; savage, ravenous, predatory, and reputed to maul innocent Inuit children who venture too close. Only the animal's master dared get close; and even then, only with a whip made of leather firmly in hand.

****

AFTER THREE WEEKS IN THE ARCTIC, I recorded more than ninety auditions with the Inuit people. The tapes were shipped to Hollywood for review. When the film's director expressed interested in several of my "actors," Bill and I arranged conference calls with the producers. Bill acted as a go-between, translating the terms and conditions for filming to the Inuit. It was a preliminary negotiation, and the outcome surprised me at first. None of the Inuit from Baffin Island had any interest in relocating to Whitehorse, thirty-five hundred miles to the West, for six months, where principal filming would occur. The producers offered large sums of money, but this was not an effective means of persuasion. Apparently, cash was of little value to the Inuit. In fact, many considered money evil because it encouraged drinking, drug use, and gambling. It made sense: these people were almost entirely self-sufficient. What would they do with truckloads of cash? How many shiny snowmobiles does one Inuit family need?

In their desperation, the producers went even further, offering travel, accommodations, and stipends to family members so that they could accompany the actors on location, and remain throughout the duration of filming. Still, there were no takers. If the production had come to them, it may have been different. The Inuit actors might even have agreed to appear in the film for free, as a gesture of good will. But because it meant leaving their land, they seemed to want no part of it. They loved everything as it was. I couldn't blame them. I loved it, too. I was enamored - charmed by the Inuit, their beguiling spirit, and the place they called home.

One month after I returned to L.A., the production unit began assembling in Whitehorse, Alaska to begin principal photography on, "Never Cry Wolf." I wasn't invited to join them, and I was envious. Why wasn't there a place for me on the production team? What happened to Bobby? At first I thought I hadn't pushed hard enough for a job. Maybe the producers believed my abilities were strictly limited to casting – which wasn't true at all. Whatever the reason, no offers were made, and it seemed as if my association with Disney was over.

I missed the Arctic. As desperate as I was to return, the movie was being made without me, and I would remain – unhappily - in Los Angeles.

The day I returned to my job at the newsroom, I had already decided I was going to quit. Rick had moved back to Boston several months earlier, and was managing a large video production facility. Don was living happily with a girlfriend, and worked regularly as an assistant editor on various feature films. It wasn't the first time I was beginning to wonder, "When is *my* ship going to come in?" And I had the increasing sense that my ship was not going to dock in L.A. anytime soon.

My boss, the News Director was on vacation for two weeks, but I couldn't wait. I sat at one of the writer's desks and banged out a beautiful, three page treatise regarding my decision to leave on such short notice (actually no notice at all, since the News Director would not get to read it until long after I was gone). Ostensibly, it was a letter of gratitude. I thanked my boss for hiring me in the first place. I thanked him for the opportunity to produce and direct, "Brother, Can You Share a Ride?" I thanked him for his understanding; for allowing my unexpected departure without punishment or retribution (not that there was anything he could do about it anyway). I concluded by expressing my sincere wishes that hard feelings would not result from my admittedly unprofessional course of action.

I folded the letter and handed it to his secretary. She smiled brightly, as she always did, held out her palm, and asked me for my press credentials. It was far more difficult parting with these than I had anticipated. I had two of them, laminated, with lapel clips and beaded metal neck chains. One allowed me to cross any police barrier at any crime scene without a challenge. The other permitted me access to politicians, heads of state, even the President. It was cleared by the FBI. Both credentials held my photograph and thumb print. They were the coolest things I'd ever owned.

"You gotta turn 'em in if you're leaving us," said the secretary. "They need to go back to the authorities."

I knew she was right. There were no exceptions. For a minute I considered retracting my resignation, but no, I let the neck chain's metal beads slide through my fingers until they formed a spiral mound on the secretary's desk. My career as a news professional was officially over – gone. Gone, too, I realized, as I crept home on the freeway that afternoon, was my life-sustaining, weekly paycheck.

FISH OUT OF WATER, PART 2

I'M LYING IN BED, dreaming of Christmas, when I hear the muffled sound of bells jingling through my bedroom walls. Is his sleigh landing on the roof? Is he here to deliver the remote-controlled dinosaur, the microscope, the Flexible Flyer?

I sit up and pull aside the curtain. Deep snow is glistening on the ground; heavy on the tall pines. It's beautiful. The bells seem to grow louder. The sled will soon alight and briefly rumble across the shingles before slowing to a stop. Everything is ready: the tree is decorated with our homemade ornaments; there is tinsel and flashing lights; the milk and cookies are waiting by the chimney.

I try to get out of bed, but my legs won't move. I can't lift the covers. Everything feels incredibly heavy. The sleigh bells are ringing... louder... beside my bed... louder... inside the telephone.

The telephone: I try to ignore it. My clock radio says four a.m., and my phone is ringing loudly. This happens more often than I care to recall; some stoned-out, partying drunk has dialed the wrong number, again. I bury my head in the pillow. I want to get back - back to my dream - but the ringing (damn it) persists.

"What!" I yell into the receiver.

"Hello, how are you?" A soft voice says at the other end. It's a woman's voice. She speaks with a strange familiarity - but when you're drunk, everyone's your best friend. I let her know that I'm pissed.

"Listen, I don't know who you're trying to call, but it's definitely not me. Please dial more carefully next time!" I wait for a response; some kind of apology would be nice.

"It's Susan."

I don't know anyone named Susan. "Susan who?"

"I'm coming to Los Angeles."

Then it all comes screaming back: making love in the igloo, the passion and surrender, living life in the moment. I remembered, as I was leaving Baffin Island, telling Susan that I loved her. She promised to visit, but I never truly believed it would happen.

I relax, and focus on the sound of Susan's voice. She informs me (cryptically, but in a way I somehow understand), the details of her impending arrival. I don't ask questions – I'm incredulous and tired. She is in Montreal catching a direct flight to LAX. Could this really be happening? Following a brief anxiety attack, I realized a visit from Susan could be a good thing, even if it was unannounced. It would not interfere with my job – I had no job – and it would not interfere with any of my plans - I had no plans. I jotted down her flight information, and throughout the morning grew increasingly excited to see Susan.

* * *

I WAS LIVING IN A ONE BEDROOM apartment in Venice, a few blocks from the beach. The building was on a hill, which afforded me an unobstructed view of the Pacific Ocean. Each apartment in the two-story complex faced a central courtyard filled with gangly palms and fragrant orchids. Whenever I'd describe my life to friends in New York, they'd always get the mistaken impression that I had really "made it." That's one of the great things about Los Angeles: You can be broke, yet still have a beach and tropical vegetation just outside your door.

LAX was clogged with harried weekend travelers. Fortunately, I had taken local roads to get there and found a parking spot quickly, so I arrived inside the terminal with an hour to spare – giving me time for a leisurely cup of coffee and a magazine. I look up to see a group of Hare Krishna parading past me; chanting, shaking bells and banging on drums. Everyone in the vicinity watches; some smile, some glare, some give money. Despite looking terribly out of place, with their shaved noggins and brazen orange silks, the Krishna are a commonplace fixture at LAX.

Hordes of incoming travelers are peeling off the human conveyer belt: they look like groceries at a checkout counter; fruits, vegetables, frozen foods. Finally, I spot Susan amid the mélange - my little Eskimo Pie. But some things about her seem different; her skin tone is several shades deeper, her complexion slightly ruddier, and her hair is flat and shiny from the build-up of oil. She's still very attractive, I thought.

"Susan!" I wave as I speed toward the moving sidewalk. She smiles nervously, and then shrugs, as if to say: How do I get off this thing? I take her hand and walk alongside until she reaches the end, helping her maintain her balance as she steps abruptly onto solid ground.

Susan says little as I drive home. At first I think she's angry, or bored, or tired from the long plane ride. But, I had overlooked the obvious: she doesn't speak much English. To break the silence and lighten the mood, I flip on the car radio - everyone understands the language of music. I place my hand gently on Susan's thigh, she rests her head on my shoulder, and the connection we'd made in another world briefly sparks back to life.

We both smile throughout the remaining twenty minutes of the trip. She seems impressed when I show her my apartment, which doesn't surprise me; all the comforts of home, plus color television, running water, a telephone, and a healthy assortment of take-out menus. How could she *not* be impressed? But, since Susan was *my* guest now, I had to attend to her immediate needs, and find ways to keep her happy.

"Let's go to the beach!" I holler, poking my head in the bathroom as Susan stands stiffly under the shower. I thought this would be a great way to introduce her to Southern California. Who doesn't love the beach? And, since it was her idea to have sex the instant we walked through my door, (and I freely complied), I felt it only fair she oblige me with respect to our second activity.

I step into my blue Speedo, throw on an orange tank-top, and wait in the living room for Susan to appear.

"Did you bring a bathing suit?" I ask.

She seemed confused, but then replies, "Yes."

"Put-on-now," I say, deciding to use as few extraneous words as possible.

Ten minutes pass – I am pretending to straighten up the kitchen - before Susan emerges from the bedroom fully clothed, wearing white Levis, a white undershirt (the wife-beater type), and a white corduroy jacket.

"No," I declare. "We-go-beach… Ocean… Hot."

"Yes," she says again, clearly understanding my broken English. I'm suddenly remembering the words, *THAW SLOWLY* – something I had recently seen on a frozen package of filo pastry. I chose to forget the inedible Spanakopeta (Spinach Pie) which resulted from my precise following of the directions.

"Come," I say, and pull Susan out the door.

I swagger onto the blistering sand (holding my shirt, flip-flops, and two large towels), and chance to make eye-contact with a gloriously-blond goddess perched lavishly atop a rainbow-colored boogie board, and clad in a white fishnet bikini. Privately pledging temporary fidelity to my present company, I feign disinterest and continue my sandy advance, stopping to claim a relatively pristine section of beach near the water's edge. Susan trudges behind me at a distance of several yards. She still had not removed a single stitch of clothing; not even her clean, white Keds. Okay, I thought, she's in a strange, new environment, probably uncomfortable, perhaps even modest about her body - given the competition. I should cut her some slack; show some understanding. Eventually she'll appreciate, or even grow to adore, the unequivocal joy of the L.A. groove. As her host, I had vowed to make her feel at home, just as she did for me when I was a stranger in her strange land.

I smoothed out a towel on the sand, placing it at an angle that would maximize the rays of the midday sun, and provide the best view of the sparkling Pacific Ocean. With a theatrical sweep of my upturned palm, I gallantly offer the lovingly prepared accommodation to Susan. She says, "Thank you," and proceeds to lie, not lavishly like our blond neighbor, but on her stomach, face down and fully clothed in the blazing, eighty-eight degree sun.

I needed an explanation. How could a woman who is used to sleeping buck naked in a friggin' icebox, remain fully clothed while lying on a California beach in eighty-eight degree fucking heat? It's embarrassing, and I'm suddenly feeling the weight of a thousand gawking eyes upon me. I'm a sorry spectacle to behold, for sure.

I glance at the gloriously-blond goddess in the fishnet bikini, and beseech her, with an uncontrollably foolish grin, not to associate me inextricably with Susan in the event of a future chance encounter at a later date. But the blond just smiles dismissively and turns away. With that opportunity dead, I resign myself to do the right thing and concentrate on my guest, who, by the way, could conceivably succumb to the heat at any moment and suffer a mortal stroke. I place my towel next to hers, flop down, close my eyes, and meditate to the sound of the waves.

Things may have started out weird, I thought, but we

can still make it work. Then, I sense Susan getting closer. I feel her breath, and she whispers, "I want to lick you." My eyes pop open; we are nose to nose. "Would you mind if I lick you?" she asks, in commendably good English. I try hard not to grimace. I don't want to say "no" and disappoint her; she is my guest, after all. "Okay," I say, immediately wishing I hadn't. Susan springs to her feet, extending her hand. Obligingly, I seize it, and she merrily leads me away from the magnificent beach, and into my stuffy apartment where she proceeds to lock all the windows and draw all the shades. As I waited on my bed in the dark, I realized something truly frightening: I had become Susan's sex slave.

Suddenly, I have but one goal in life; to put Susan on a plane back to Canada. Not to be unkind. Susan had been so nurturing and accommodating to me when we were in the igloo together. For that reason alone, I couldn't just kick her out. So, I allowed Susan to have all of me for the next forty-eight hours. It was dark, (and I developed chafing and a mild case of acne), but when we finally parted, I emerged with my dignity intact and my conscience clear.

I watched while the Air Canada jet lifted off the runway and whisked Susan back to the land of frozen peas and carrots. I watched until the jet was a speck of sand in the northern yonder – until I realized it was a speck of sand on the face of my sunglasses. Anyway, she was gone.

* * *

IT HAD BECOME PAINFULLY CLEAR, I had had all I could take of Los Angeles. It appeared as though I would not be conquering Hollywood any time soon. But I could live with that now. I was, more than ever, in a New York state of mind.

Three weeks later I'm back at LAX, unloading several suitcases, my suitcases, from the back of a friend's white panel truck. An American Airlines jet roars low overhead. Its exhaust fumes spread like fairy dust, and the perfume draws me to a sweeping memory of one balmy summer evening, long ago. Great Neck, where I grew up, was not far from La Guardia airport, and on certain balmy summer nights, the smell of jet fuel filled the air. I could taste it; and it tasted wonderful - something between smoldering tar and warm apple pie. I still love that smell. It always brings me back.

One balmy summer night in Great Neck, when I was only 10, as the smell of jet fuel lingered deliciously in the air, a backyard party was raging in the neighborhood. The backyard belonged to Jay – it was actually his parent's backyard, but they were away for the weekend, so Jay assumed ownership by association, and decided to throw a bash, an ambitious bash. Jay was my brother's age, several years older than me, and the two of them were friends.

It was ten o'clock, the sky was dark, and a local amateur garage band was spewing sixties rock into the night, drowning out the usual happy cacophony of crickets and cicada heard at that hour. Jay's party was the hot ticket in town, and things were clearly heating up. By the time I arrived, a crowd had gathered on the front lawn. The backyard, and the real action, were surrounded by dense bushes and a chain-link fence, and could only be accessed through a single gate at the front of the house. Jay had smartly thought to engage the services of a bouncer (big guy) to control entry into the party. I didn't recognize the bouncer, but he was imposing, at least to me, and very likely played varsity football for Great Neck North. I noticed that he was a discriminating bouncer, permitting few to pass. Most kids he barred. He had just laughingly turned away my next door neighbor, Ira Goldstein, which truly was a joke because Ira was only eight years old.

Ira sulked toward me, and we both watched in silent envy as several kids went through the gate. I envisioned the backyard filled with all the cool people; sipping exotic drinks, dancing, and acting like grown-ups. Jay's party was the "in" place to be, and I desperately wanted to be part of it.

"I'm going in!" I exclaimed impulsively.

"No, you're not," Ira said. "You have to be thirteen."

I knew he was right, so I made several attempts to breach the fence (something I was usually good at), all unsuccessful. I'd undoubtedly have to find another way in.

"I saw your brother earlier," Ira said, and I suddenly remembered overhearing Rex saying something at the dinner table about a party. This must have been what my brother was talking about!

The band was playing a rocking rendition of, "(I can't get no) Satisfaction," by the Rolling Stones, unquestionably the most popular song of the summer, and I felt drawn to Jay's backyard like never before. I attempted a headlong stride past the bouncer when he wasn't looking, but his arm shot out like the tongue of a toad zapping a fly, and I was collared before I knew what hit me.

"But Sir," I choked. "My brother's in there."

"Who's your brother," said the bouncer, without loosening his grip.

"Rex Nathanson." I watched for his reaction, adding, "You must know him."

"Yeah, I think I know who that is." The bouncer loosened his grip and released me.

"Can I go in for a minute and talk to him?" I pleaded.

The bouncer shook his head. "I'll tell you what I can do," he said. "I'll get him for you. You can talk to him all you want, right here. But..."

"But... What?" I asked.

"It'll cost you," the bouncer said. "Ten bucks, up front."

I reached inside my pockets, hoping ten dollars would magically appear. The truth was I didn't have ten bucks, certainly not on me. I doubted I even had ten bucks worth of pennies at home... but it was worth a shot, I thought.

My house was one block away. If I cut through a few lawns, I could search my room for money and be back in five minutes or less. "Don't go away," I told the bouncer. "I'll be right back." I sprinted home.

"Slow down, Buster. You're gonna hurt yourself," my

mother exclaimed, as I flew past the living room (she was watching summer reruns of "The Outer Limits") and into my bedroom.

I gingerly removed my piggy bank from the shelf and admired it. I'd had that piggy bank for as long as I could remember. It wasn't the store-bought kind, no; my mother had made it in a ceramics class she had enrolled in shortly after I was born. It was a creamy white, kiln-fired pig, accented with blue ribbons. On one side, my mother had scrawled painted my name, all in lower case letters, "bradley." The piggy bank was finished in a clear glaze which had crackled over time, giving it a kind of antique patina.

Over time, I'd forgotten how many coins I'd dropped inside. The bank felt heavy, and I estimated it must have contained twenty dollars worth of pennies, at least. I raised it over my head, preparing to smash it and pilfer the coins inside, but I had to stop myself. I couldn't do it: sentimental reasons, I suppose.

I was only ten, but keen enough to realize there was more than one way to skin a piggybank. Rather than destroy it, I simply removed the rubber stopper from its belly (the one my mother had so cleverly thought to include in her design) and shook the coins out. They tapped the laminate surface of my dresser, and jingled as they accumulated into a sizeable molehill of pennies, with an occasional nickel or dime splaying into the mix. When the last coin rattled out, I smoothed the pile flat and admired what had apparently amounted to a small fortune, overwhelmed by my superior potential for amassing personal wealth. There must be at least *fifty* bucks here, I thought. But I also suspected that if I took the time to count all the coins, the party would be done before I was. Time to go.

I lumbered back to the party, the pennies weighing heavily in my pockets, and approached the bouncer.

"What do you want, kid?" he asked. I couldn't believe my ears. It was as if this guy had never seen me before in his life.

"I've got the money," I said. "Remember? You promised to get my brother for ten bucks. Remember? There's more like twenty in here." I shook my pockets, and the coins answered like chain links in wet cement.

"Oh yeah… you," said the bouncer, brightening. He held out a large jar used for party donations. "Put the dough in here, and I'll get your brother," he said. I transferred the coins. He told me to wait, and disappeared into Jay's backyard. My heart was pounding. I was so excited about joining the party, that I had suddenly developed a strong urge to pee.

The bouncer returned momentarily. "Your brother is not here," he said.

"What do you mean?"

"He left with Patty Weiner about ten minutes ago," said the bouncer.

At least my brother has good taste, I thought. Patty was my neighborhood heartthrob; I had been secretly in love with her for years.

"Can I have my money back?" I asked.

"Sorry, kid. This money is paying for the refreshments." The bouncer took a gulp from a can of beer. I could smell it on his breath.

"How about giving me a swig of that?" I asked, trying to get something for my investment.

"You must be kidding," he laughed. "Don't waste your time here. Go home."

I went home, dejected and penniless. But I decided to keep my chin up. At least, I thought, I didn't break my cherished piggybank. At least I didn't enter a party uninvited. At least I wasn't guilty of breaking and entering. But, ten was a dumb age. I desperately wanted to be thirteen; that was the age when the doors would finally open, I was sure. And I sure couldn't wait.

* * *

There was that beautiful odor of jet fuel, again. But I'm not ten or thirteen. Suddenly I'm twenty-five, dejected and penniless.

A friend of mine, the one who had driven me to LAX,

snapped a photograph. In the picture, I am at the curbside check-in, a broad smile on my face, striding toward the camera. My hair is tousled and parted in the middle. My left thumb is hooked in my back pocket. My right arm swings buoyantly at my side. In my hand, nestled between my fingers like a fine Cuban cigar, is a one-way ticket to New York. I was going home. Above my head, and slightly to the left, is a sign which reads, "American Departures." I am duly aware of how apropos this is of my life thus far. What I do not realize is how incredibly apropos it is of my life to come.

BOOK SIX

Chivalry

BABY BOOM

I'D ALWAYS BEEN a proud member of the baby boom generation. As boomers, our approach to life was radically different from that of our parents. We were nonconformists. We questioned the establishment. We believed we were put here to change the world, make it better; and we believed we could. I expected my path in life to be anything but a straight line. So when I decided to cut my losses in L.A. and return to New York, even though it meant living with my mother for awhile and starting over, I was fine with it. Besides, I was only twenty-five, and had plenty of time to get my act together. But when I arrived home, I was shocked to discover another kind of baby boom propagating in my mother's back yard. Actually, it was closer than that. To be precise, it was inside our house: in the kitchen, the living room, and my bedroom, too.

I returned home to four pregnant women, a toddler, two Iranian boys, a toy poodle, a parrot, and a boa constrictor. While I was in Hollywood, pursuing a career in showbiz, my mother had turned our home into a boarding house, a maternity ward, a preschool, a foreign consulate, an animal shelter, and a nature preserve.

My mother welcomed me with open arms, as always. She seemed happy and relieved that I was home. But the house no longer felt the same, or looked the same. The toddler had scribbled crayon all over the bathroom walls. The bathtub housed a snake in a wire cage. My room was occupied by a sixteen-year-old who was eight months pregnant. I held back tears as my mother introduced me to my new roommates. There was Tammy from Texas, Mickey from Oklahoma, Sylvia from the Bronx, and Margaret from Germany. The graffiti artist was her son, Timmy. All the girls were in various stages of pregnancy. Shahab and Ramin were Iranian expatriates, living in my mother's house while they finished high school.

Through my tears, I tried to imagine why my mother decided to transform our lovely Great Neck home into a boarding house full of needy strangers. I could think of only two possible reasons: compassion and money. Knowing my mother, compassion was probably the overriding motivation. This is who my mother was. She had trouble saying "no," even if it meant sacrificing her own needs. But my mother needed to be needed herself. So there was a clear symbiotic dynamic at work in the house. She also had little income, and needed money to cover the expenses of running the house. It made perfect sense. It also made me extremely uncomfortable. But if this was what my mother wanted, she would have my full support.

It's late. Although still on California time, I've had a lot to process this first day home. I'm mentally and physically exhausted. I drag my suitcases into the basement, and prepare a makeshift bed out of some spare pillows. My mother assures me it's only temporary. Margaret, she says, is about to "pop." This will free-up the pullout couch and the bathtub.

"The bathtub?" I say.

"The snake is hers, too," my mother explains. "His name is King."

"I don't like snakes."

"I know, darling. Give it time. This too shall pass," my mother says sweetly.

"Good night, Mom. I love you."

I'm falling: a hole in the ground, cellophane covered walls, diamond patterns, glowing green orbs, a rubber pitchfork, white fangs, a mouth, blackness. It's King. I'm falling, and I can't stop. The snake traps me in its tongue. I'm being swallowed alive. I scream, "Stop!" and am awakened by the sound of my own voice. My heart is pounding against my ribcage, and I desperately need a drink of water.

There's a light on in the kitchen. Tammy and Mickey are playing "War" with two decks of cards. It's 3am, and I am standing in the kitchen wearing a tee shirt and underpants. I feel ridiculous, but I need a glass of water.

The girl's bellies look huge under their nightgowns. They have to sit sideways at the kitchen table because their bellies are so huge. I realize I'm staring at their huge bellies, while, at the same time, the girls are staring at my crotch.

"I told you," says Mickey to Tammy, as if I weren't actually present in the room. "You owe me five big-ones."

"I don't have any money," Tammy says. Then she looks at me. "Can you lend me five bucks?" she asks.

"For what?" I ask.

Before Tammy can explain, Mickey lurches out of her seat and covers Tammy's mouth. "Don't you dare," says Mickey. Mickey slowly removes her hand. Tammy starts to speak, and is silenced once again. I need water.

"Mickey, you want your five bucks, you'd better let her speak," I say. Tammy and I look at Mickey. "Let her speak," I repeat. Reluctantly, Mickey removes her hand from Tammy's mouth.

Tammy: "We bet on your underwear. I said boxers. Mickey said you were the tighty-whitie type."

Mickey smiles, puts out her hand and says to Tammy, "You want to give me the cash now, or in the morning?"

"It practically *is* morning," I say, as I fill a glass with tap water. "I'm going to bed."

As I return to my doggie bed in the basement, I feel sick that I can no longer walk freely in my own house without the risk of humiliation. And I have nowhere else to go. I'm trapped. I can either live with it, albeit temporarily, until I find a job, or confront my mother and insist she put an end to this bizarre nightmare, immediately.

By now I'm unable to sleep, so I pick up my book, "The Dead Zone," and begin to read. I love Stephen King because I get totally immersed in his stories. I'm at a major turning point in the book, where John Smith is about to wake up from a coma, when Mickey bursts into the room. "You gotta see this," she says, and shows me an unwrapped cigarette filter.

"So?" I say.

"Hold this." She places the filter in my palm. "Now make a fist."

I don't know what she's up to, and I'm really not in the mood for her little game, but she's a guest of the house, and I do as she says. I close my hand around the cigarette filter. Mickey has a small bottle of nail polish remover. She unscrews the cap and fills it with the liquid. The acetone has a powerful odor, like smelling salts. It is not conducive to sleep.

"Is this really necessary?" I ask. Mickey ignores the question.

"Hold your fist, like this." When I hold out my fist, Mickey pours the capful of nail polish remover in the space between my thumb and forefinger. "Now shake," she says. I shake my fist up and down.

"Faster," says Mickey. I shake faster. "Faster," she says again. "That's good. Do it faster. Faster, faster, faster."

"That's it," I say angrily, coming to my senses. "I'm done."

"What?" she asks.

"I said I'm done."

"Let's see," Mickey says. She pries open my fist. In my palm is a gooey glob of sticky, white-stuff. I gag on the nasty odor. It is already apparent that this substance is impervious to plain soap and water. I want to puke.

"Looks like you just popped your cookies," Mickey says, laughing. "Better get a girlfriend, or you'll be growing hair on those palms."

I get it: very funny.

Actually, I wasn't amused. I said, "If you weren't pregnant, I'd drop kick your big ass out of this house." My reaction surprises Mickey. Her smile disappears, and she quietly walks away. I feel like a humorless dolt. Mickey is 14 and pregnant. She's only a child. I realize I'd just been horribly insensitive.

"Sorry," I say. "I haven't slept. I'm tired. It's a good joke."

"You think?"

I look at the sticky mess in my palm. "Just one thing," I ask Mickey. "Would you get me a tissue?" We both laughed, and I think we may even have bonded a little.

The house eventually got quiet, but not before the sky got

light. I couldn't sleep. I was beginning to second guess my move back to New York. Perhaps I had been too impulsive. No surprise. I existed on impulse; for some reason, it seems I always have. But, my optimism about making a life in New York was fading as quickly as the place I called "home." My heart grew heavy. I felt I was hanging by a thread. I was alone, lonely, and, after days of scrubbing, my hand still smelled like acetone and nicotine.

KETCHUP

SEVERAL MORE BOARDERS came and went. The minute a bedroom became vacant, I grabbed it. It was the bedroom at the top of the stairs – the one I'd used before my nana died – tiny but workable; and it had a door that locked.

Sitting alone in my room one afternoon, behind my locked door, feeling lonely and bored, I made a list of priorities. It was a short list, including only those things necessary for my immediate survival: open bank account, update resume, find job, buy car. I studied my objectives, then, at the top of the list I added: find girlfriend. Even though this little item was, perhaps, the key to everything else on my list, I realized I didn't have a clue where to begin.

I decide to call some friends. When I was in college I did work-study at a television production studio called ITV. The facility, located on the top floor of the School of Education, is a classroom facility designed to teach future educators how to use TV as an effective learning tool. It was the "Sesame Street" decade, and ITV was the place to be. Tom and Yale ran the operation. They were also resident professors. We worked together for several years (I stayed on to help with summer classes, too), and we became close friends. These were the guys I knew I should call. I was confident they could set me straight. They'd help me figure things out.

I dialed their office in Boston. Tom answered after two rings.

"Hey, sicko," Tom says, realizing it's me. "How's it going in N Y?"

"I need some advice," I say. "I'm lonely, and I'm horny."

"Sounds like you need more than advice."

"I'm never going to meet anyone."

"Hey; why not? You're a good looking guy."

'I'm stuck at my mother's house with no money, no car, and no friends," I admit.

"Hold on a second." I hear Tom tell Yale to pick up another extension.

"Hey, sicko," Yale says, seconds later. "Welcome home... you the head of a major network yet?"

"You're a funny guy," I tell him.

Tom says, "Yale, I think this would be a good time to do the shtick about Val."

They tell me about a student of theirs named Valerie. She's only loosely involved with someone. She's in the first semester of her senior year, and currently doing an internship, for credit, at PBS in New York City.

"She wants you to call her," says Yale.

"What? She knows who I am?" I ask.

"She saw the video you're in - the one we show in class," says Tom.

"Yeah... What did she say?"

"When the period ended, she wanted to know who the cute guy was," says Yale.

I begin to throw a million questions at them. Is she cute? *Yes, very.* Blond? *Brunette.* Is she smart? *Yes, and funny.* They also tell me she grew up on a street of row houses in Brooklyn, and that her Brooklyn accent is subtle yet evident, (and particularly apparent after a few glasses of wine).

I'm smiling and thrusting my fist in the air. Having survived L.A. for almost three long years, I was starving for anything New York: seasonal change, pizza, bagels, pastrami on rye, yellow taxis. A cute, funny brunette from Brooklyn was even better.

"Here's the kicker," Tom says, intentionally pausing for effect. "She reminds us of you."

"Ah, gee," I reply. "I'm assuming that's a good thing." Then, picking up a pen, I ask, "Can I have her friggin' number already?"

They give me her number at WNET-TV, which I transcribe onto my palm (no paper) like a tattooist creating a fine work of art.

"Good luck," says Yale.

"Sayonara sicko," says Tom.

I have never been on a blind date in my life. There's a stigma attached to blind dates, and, reportedly, they rarely turn out well. The girl is either too fat, or too skinny; she wears too much make-up, or too much cheap perfume; she conceals moth balls in her dress pockets; her teeth are either too long, or there aren't enough of them; she has a squeaky voice; she's not pretty enough, not smart enough, or not confident enough. I sigh. Blind dates never turn out well. Blind dates are for losers.

I lift the telephone receiver and start to dial. I'm so desperately nervous, my hands are shaking. I'm already imagining several possible outcomes. In one scenario, Valerie turns out to be a mousey girl with a deplorable, uptight sense of style. She is sweet, but not my type. We go for burgers, and, although I have no appetite, I eat quickly because I need to get some fresh air as soon as possible. I want the night to end. I don't want to hurt her feelings, but I know I'll never date her again.

In another scenario, Valerie turns out to be a beautiful woman, with a cool, relaxed sense of style. She is smart and sophisticated. We go for burgers, and, although I have no appetite, I eat quickly because I need to sleep with her as soon as possible. I wish the night would never end. Valerie might hurt my feelings, but I will try to date her again.

I tell myself to relax, and to have faith in Tom and Yale's good judgment. They knew me pretty well. If they didn't feel there was potential with this woman, they wouldn't have mentioned anything. But there was a problem. Valerie had an unfair advantage. She already knew what I looked like.

I stop dialing, and hang up. Something is telling me to sleep on it, give it time, don't act so impulsively. I'm horny, but not that horny. I consider my options. Basically, I realize I have no options. I pick up the phone, again, and dial Valerie's number.

A woman answers: "Hello?" It's a smooth, sexy voice. I imagine a beautiful, lascivious seductress at the other end, a younger version of Mrs. Robinson. I, of course, am Dustin Hoffman.

"Valerie?" I squeak. "You don't know me - well, that's not entirely true. You know what I look like from the videotape. Anyway, Tom and Yale suggested I call. My name is Brad, and I just moved back from California, and I was wondering how you were doing, or, I mean, how you like it here in New York, and who you know, you know, who you're friendly with, and what you do for fun around here anyway, and maybe you'd like to go out sometime - maybe coffee, maybe dinner?"

"This is Ruth... One moment, and I'll transfer you."

I am an idiot - a real idiot. Calm down. Relax. It's a good thing Ruth picked up the phone, and not Valerie. I would have blown it in the first ten seconds. I'm hyperventilating. My nerves are rattled. I don't *need* this aggravation. Besides, she'll probably tell me she's busy, or has a boyfriend, and that will be the end of that. Calm down. Relax. I'm an idiot.

"This is Valerie." Her voice is upbeat and friendly. At first, I didn't know what to say, but a relaxed conversation ensued. I breathe normally. We talk at length about college. She asks about L.A. She tells me about WNET. I decide I like this girl, and want to ask her out before we've said everything there is to say to each other. I also realize I am not good at this. The last time I asked out a girl within the continental United States, I used some ridiculous line and she told me to "Fuck off!"

I tell myself, "Don't waste Valerie's time. Play it straight, and get it over with." Fuck it... "Do you want to go out sometime?" I ask.

"Sure."

"You do?"

"Sure, why not?"

"Okay," I say, surprised. I hold the phone at arm's-length and eye it suspiciously.

"How does tomorrow night sound?" says Valerie.

Her decisiveness catches me off guard. Tomorrow night? I wasn't expecting it to be this easy, but I'm thrilled, and we make plans to have dinner the following evening.

Barely 24 hours later, I'm on the upper east side of Manhattan behind the wheel of my mother's white Cadillac, looking for a place to park. September had quickly rolled into October, and the memory of summer was fading as fast as the daylight. It was autumn's turn.

I find a spot on the street, and walk two blocks to the address Valerie had given me. The air is bracing, but it feels good. It's a night that calls for warmer coats, and deep, invigorating breaths. As I approach the apartment building, I feel a surge of exhilaration. I have a good feeling about my date with Valerie.

"I apologize," she says, as she opens the door. "My laundry is still in the dryer."

Valerie is holding an empty laundry basket and wearing a clean, white jumpsuit. She welcomes me, and when I follow her inside, I see the word "HOLLYWOOD" scrawled in big letters across her back, adorned with sequins and glitter. I surmise that she has worn this particular jumpsuit for my benefit. It's sweet of her, but I'm a little embarrassed. I'm relieved when she switches to jeans and a sweater before we go out.

We decide to go someplace casual. Valerie suggests Rascal's, on the corner of 70th and First. It sounds good, and I agree – but, frankly, I would have agreed to anything. We walk a block to First Avenue, grab a table outside, and order burgers and fries. I like a lot of ketchup, and when the food arrives I douse my burger to the extent that when I take a bite, the ketchup oozes down my arms. I feel like a fool, but Valerie just laughs and offers me her napkin. My embarrassment fades. She has thoughtfully put me at ease with my foibles.

Valerie asks for extra napkins, which the waitress promptly delivers, along with a damp hand towel. Then, the waitress says, "You two are either brother and sister, or you're in love." I remember what Tom and Yale said yesterday on the phone – *she reminds us of you* – and it makes me wonder.

"Well," I say, "we're not brother and sister," which seemed to imply I was supporting her second estimation of our relationship.

* * *

FOR OUR SECOND DATE, I drive to Valerie's parent's home in Sheepshead Bay, Brooklyn. They live in a row house, half a block from the Belt Parkway. When Valerie shows me around, I see that the rooms are tiny, but everything is neat and spotless.

We walk to the bay, where a fleet of charter fishing boats line up to receive passengers, ready to motor into the cold Atlantic to hook buckets of bluefish; *Bluuues*, they call them.

I spot a place called Joe's Clam Bar, and we duck inside. I'm a big fan of freshly shucked Cherrystones. Eating them reminds me of my father; he loved them, too. Valerie tells me she's allergic to shellfish, but would enjoy watching me eat. So, I'm at the counter, slurping raw clams by the sea, standing beside my girlfriend (?) from Brooklyn (!), who is nestled against my side. It feels so real; so far removed from the wantonness of L.A.; so full of everything I need. It is perfect.

"You're being rude," Valerie says.

"What."

"Say it."

"Say what?"

"Say what you're thinking."

"I'm not thinking anything."

"Sure you are. And you should just say it, rather than keep it to yourself."

"I'm not keeping anything to myself."

"I think you are."

"You do? Then *you* tell *me*."

"Okay… You're thinking, 'I can't believe I'm in Sheepshead Bay, eating clams at a place called Joe's, with a girl from Brooklyn.'

Am I right?"

Pretty close, I thought.

"Now *you* say it," she says.

"Okay… I can't believe I'm in Sheepshead Bay, eating clams at a place called Joe's, with…" I stop to consider the judiciousness of exposing my true feelings this early in the relationship, and then helplessly proceed to spill my guts.

"…a place called Joe's with…" I continue, "… with a charming, smart, sexy, funny, adorable, brown-eyed girl from Brooklyn, who I think I'm falling for."

I suck down the last briny clam in silence. It's a sensual, almost sexual pleasure. Outside, a cool breeze is stirring off the Bay. We walk west along the pier, and the late afternoon sun caresses Valerie's face in soft, amber light. I'm thinking how beautiful she looks, and feel a pang of anxiety, realizing our relationship has just turned a corner, making it possible for someone to get hurt. Yet somehow, on this beautiful, brisk afternoon, with the wind in my hair, the salty air in my lungs, the golden light on her face, the exuberance of youth, my heart racing, and the fishmongers howling *Bluuues* beneath the setting sun… getting hurt was the last thing I wanted to think about.

GUESS WHO'S COMING TO DINNER?

IT WAS LESS than two weeks since our first date, and I couldn't stop thinking about Valerie. I had romance on the brain, and decide to make a dinner reservation at a fancy French restaurant on Long Island. I knew the meal would cost a fortune, but I didn't care; you can't put a price on romance.

The reservation was set for seven o'clock. Valerie agreed to meet me at my mother's house in Great Neck, and I'd drive both to and from the restaurant. I expected Valerie to arrive around dinnertime, when my mother would be feeding all the pregnant girls, and anyone else living with us at the time. This wasn't ideal. I was afraid the perceived impropriety of the situation might wreak havoc on our budding relationship.

While I waited for Valerie to arrive, I sat at the dining room table with ten others. I sipped a can of Coke while everyone else helped themselves to meatloaf, string beans, and mashed potatoes. There's a lot of noise and activity in the room. Tammy is the only one not eating with gusto. She's pushing her food around with a fork.

"Tammy, I don't see you eating," my mother says.

"I'm not hungry."

"That's not the point, young lady. You're eating for two." My mother speaks to Tammy like a daughter, not like the beauty queen she was before she got knocked-up. Her dream is to win the title of Miss America. Unfortunately for her baby, she's highly motivated to be skinny. Eat! I'm thinking.

The door bell rings, and I nearly jump out of my seat. I have a lot to be nervous about. When Valerie sees what's going on in my house, she's liable to freak out. But I have no choice. I greet her at the front door and welcome her inside.

Valerie steps into the light of the foyer. She is wearing an elegant dress. I tell her she looks beautiful, and she smiles. "You, too," she says.

As we enter the dining room, I hear my mother's voice rise above the din, greeting Valerie with open arms. "Welcome, darling," she says, as if Valerie is the most important person in her life. I know she's sincere. My mother engages Valerie in friendly conversation while, at the same time, the two Iranian boys are having a heated argument in Farsi, Michelangelo (the crayon bandit) has discovered a new medium – mashed potatoes – and is crafting some abstract sculpture on the floor, and Mickey is trying to teach Sylvia how to play the spoons. Guess what? It's time to go.

I pull Valerie close. "I'll tell you who everyone is after we leave," I whisper, and I'm surprised (also relieved) that she is not as uncomfortable as I am by the circus-like atmosphere in the room. On the contrary, she seems drawn to it.

"Thanks for being so nice to my date," I whisper to

my mother.

"My pleasure, darling. She seems like a lovely person."

I nod in agreement, take hold of Valerie's arm, and we're out of there.

On the way to the restaurant, I attempt to explain everything as best as I can: My mother has a friend, a lawyer, who specializes in private adoptions. His clients are girls who have become pregnant unintentionally, and either cannot, or will not terminate their pregnancy. Usually, the girls want to keep the pregnancy a secret, so they leave town under some false pretense, and live with my mother until their baby is born and the adoption is transacted. My mother's friend also facilitates the process for the adopting parents.

"How does he find the girls?" Valerie asks.

"Ads in local newspapers."

"Who pays for everything?"

I explain that the adopting parents pay all the birthmother's expenses, including the room and board provided by my mother.

"Your mother sounds incredible." Valerie says.

"Yes, she is," I say, and huge snowflakes begin to fall outside our window.

Our dinner is magical; elegant. Three graceful, white-gloved servers attend to all our needs. They light our candles, replenish our wine, and present each dish with a flourish. At the end of each course, they scoop crumbs off our tablecloth, unobtrusively, while Valerie and I clasp hands and converse in hushed tones. It's perfect.

After dinner, I pay the bill, help Valerie on with her coat, and we step outside into a winter wonderland. The snow had been falling for several hours, and the white stuff sparkled like diamonds on the ground, the trees, and the rooftops, adding to the romance of the evening. Each snowflake was huge, and seemed to ride on a gentle current of air like milkweed in spring. I was very much in the moment. It would have been difficult to be otherwise. I watched Valerie's breath rising in the night air, and thought about how badly I wanted to kiss her. But I didn't want to appear too forward, and thought it best to hold back a little longer, perhaps until our next date. I was positively certain there would be a next date, very soon.

The streets are slippery, and I drive slowly. We drive most of the way home in silence. Classical music, playing softly on the radio, is interrupted only by the sound of windshield wipers repelling the falling snow. I concentrate on the road, gripping the wheel with both hands. I want to impress upon Valerie that I am a safe driver; perhaps she would relate this to her parents and they would appreciate me for it, further trusting their daughter to my charge.

When I stop for a red light, Valerie pries my right hand free and holds it in her lap. "You're driving well," she says with a smile. Her assurance allows me to justify the use of one hand to steer when the light turns green.

My mother and the girls are gathered in front of the TV when we return. The Iranian boys were at some dance club in New York City. As was her custom each night, my mother is stringing glass beads onto a length of slender wire. Tammy asks when she's going to teach them how to make beaded flowers. My mother is delighted and replies saying she can start them on something immediately. By their reaction, it seems the girls are eager and ready to learn. Everyone, that is, except Mickey. Mickey is staring dreamily out the window. "Who wants to go sledding?" she says. No one responds. I'm thinking about bringing Valerie to another part of the house - I needed to kiss her – and take her elbow.

"Boy, I'd just love to go sledding," Mickey says.

"You're seven months pregnant," says my mother.

"Oh hell, I don't care. I'm all fired up," says Mickey.

I was about to tell the girls, "Good night."

"I'll go with you," Valerie says.

I look at her, surprised. "You will?"

"Sure, why not?"

Mickey and Valerie bolt from the room, returning minutes

later wearing several layers of warm clothing. They were out the door before I could tell them we didn't have sleds; my mother had orchestrated a garage sale before I left for California, and our precious Flexible Flyers were snapped up for pocket change. But in Mickey's world, store bought sleds were a frivolous luxury which did little to enhance the joy of snow.

From the dining room window, I see Mickey and Valerie barreling down the snow-covered street on the lids of my mother's trash cans; admittedly, more swiftly than any Flexible Flier I have ever owned. Mickey is yelling, "Holy sheepshit!" repeatedly, at the top of her lungs. It's an unfamiliar expression, but I like it, and decide to add it to my permanent lexicon.

They tumble back inside an hour or so later, with red cheeks and sniffles and covered in snow. I help Valerie off with her boots and say, "It's late and still snowing. I'm sure we can find you a comfortable place to sleep."

She hesitates, and says, "Let me think about it."

"It's a lot safer if you stay."

"I'm not so sure."

"What do you mean?" I ask, confused.

Valerie laughs. "Well, other than your mother, I'm the only female in this house who isn't already pregnant." Now both of us are laughing out loud.

"What if I guarantee you'll leave here tomorrow in the same condition as when you first arrived?" I say, and Valerie smiles.

SHE STAYED

VALERIE WOULD STAY many times in the early part of our relationship, even as an endless stream of girls in various stages of pregnancy passed through the house. My mother ministered to the girls as if they were her own daughters; she'd lovingly make their beds, clean their messes, chauffeur them to the doctor for checkups, dole out prenatal vitamins, and cook their meals; she'd buy them a new pair of Keds, an extra sweater, a stuffed toy, or some little thing to make them feel good; she'd engage them in needlepoint and macramé; she'd teach them how to make beaded flowers. And that's not all. Oftentimes, my mother could be found racing to the hospital in the middle of the night whenever one of the girls experienced the unexpected onset of labor. If approached, she'd freely offer advice to the girls, candidly sharing her own experience for the benefit of the other's illumination. She'd hold their hands, laugh at their jokes (even if they weren't funny), and wipe away their tears. Throughout it all, I never once heard my mother complain; on the contrary, she always expressed gratitude for the opportunity she'd been given.

When the babies were born, my mother shouldered the emotional task of surrendering each newborn to the adoptive parents. "Having nurtured the birthmothers through childbirth, I didn't feel there was anyone more equipped to handle this delicate transaction," my mother had said.

Meanwhile, it was time for me to get serious about finding a job. I pulled out my Smith Corona, and typed out brilliant letters to every television news director in New York City. I enclosed letters of recommendation from colleagues in Los Angeles. I was essentially optimistic; confident that, if persistent, I would soon find gainful employment to suit my ability and personality.

Mostly, I received courteous replies from the Human Resources Departments informing me that there were no positions available for someone with my unique qualifications. The faceless epistles promised to keep my resume on file. I always suspected that their "file" was the nearest trash receptacle, but I didn't let that discourage me. I dug deeper for names of people in the inner circles of CBS, NBC, ABC, and the independent New York stations (channels 5, 9, and 11). But months of trying produced the same, predictable results: "We will keep your resume on file, and contact you should our needs change." I began to feel, literally, invisible. I'd punch the walls until my knuckles throbbed – and sometimes bled. Every morning, I'd wake up with a lump of desperation in my throat. For some reason, I couldn't get arrested in this town, and wondered if things would ever change. Then, I remembered a time when I *did* get arrested, nearly ten years earlier, when I was just thirteen.

It began as one of those glorious spring mornings - all was right with the world. Ash had called to say a bunch of kids were gathering in town, and I should meet them. It was only ten minutes from my house, on foot, and a perfect day for a walk.

As I stepped outside I saw Harold, my neighbor, sitting on his front porch eating a full sheet of Matzo. I knew this was his favorite snack, and he usually had it with butter and a sprinkling of salt. Spreading hard butter onto a brittle piece of Matzo usually causes the Matzo to crack into dozens of little pieces. But, somehow Harold, or his mother, had managed to spread butter onto the Matzo without it cracking. I pondered this achievement as I climbed the steps to Harold's front porch.

"How did you do that?" I asked, with growing interest.

"Do what?"

"Your Matzo is not all cracked up in a zillion pieces."

"It's a new thing," Harold licked his fingers. "It's called Migraine, I think." I knew better. Harold's mother was prone to debilitating headaches, and Harold was confusing margarine for migraine. I chose not to correct him.

"How does it taste?" I asked.

Harold had stuffed the entire Matzo in his mouth, and when he tried to speak, crumbs shot out. "Butter is better," he sputtered, and ran inside, presumably for another piece of Matzo, this time with butter. About ten minutes passed and still no Harold. I noticed he had left his transistor radio on one of the wrought iron chairs. I switched it on, coming into the middle of "Penny Lane," by the Beatles. Wow. Everything about that song, at that moment, seemed perfect. A sensation of euphoria washed over me. All was right with the world.

As I strolled into town, ("Penny Lane is in my ears and in my eyes, there beneath the blue suburban skies"), my feet barely touched the ground.

Soon I'm hanging out with about ten of my closest friends from Junior High: Ash, Cohen, Moose, Bozzie, Tracy, Nan, Linda, Lisa, and a few others. We're huddling on the sidewalk, buzzing about important stuff like bell bottom jeans, the Amazing Mets, and lunch at the Hamburger Express. Tracy mentions having seen the new Crosby, Stills, and Nash album at Barrows, the local music store. I desperately wanted a copy; "Suite: Judy Blue Eyes" would drift through me like a pull of pink cotton candy. The feeling was carefree; always carefree.

I can smell the aroma of fresh pizza. La Tosca is preparing to open at noon. We each check our pockets for cash. Thirty-five cents will buy a slice and a small Coke. I love being a teenager, and the independence that comes with it.

Suddenly, I feel a hand weighing heavy on my shoulder, and turn to see the glare of a policeman. He orders me to, "Get moving."

"What? Why?" I ask.

"I'm telling you to MOVE. Understand?"

"But... why?" I don't understand.

"You're loitering. We've been getting complaints from the store owners."

"I'm with my friends."

"I don't care. Get moving." The cop wasn't kidding. I'm confused. My friends are oblivious.

"Where do you want me to go?" I ask in a loud voice, hoping to get the attention of my group. But no one seems the least bit aware of my interaction with the cop. I'm feeling abandoned, and particularly puzzled as to why I'm being singled out. The cop points his nightstick in the direction leading out of town. "Move it!" he demands, and I start walking. When I look over my shoulder, the officer is following me, about ten paces back, but he soon passes on the right. I hear a friend call my name. "Where are you going?" she says, and I stop in my tracks. Where am I going?

By now, the cop is well ahead of me, and still walking. I shrug, and head back to my friends. The girls chat about shoes.

The guys talk about girls. Should we all go to the park? Has anyone tried the new elephant bells? Seen the new puzzle rings? Anyone want to get a slice?

I felt a hand on my shoulder, again. It's that same cop, glaring down at me. "I thought I told you to move!" he says. He's angry, but now so am I. I had been minding my own business. I wasn't hurting anyone. I didn't hear anyone complaining.

I firmly believe I have every right to be here, and calmly tell the officer, "I'm not going anywhere, sir. I'm staying right here with my friends." I look around for support. Oddly, none of my friends are paying attention; they're too busy chattering about clothes, and music, and pizza, and sports. I'm suddenly angry at them for their shallow behavior. I'm also nervous, because my altercation with the cop is growing more serious, and I can tell he is frustrated by my unwillingness to obey.

"Alright, you're coming with me," he says, then adroitly twists my arms behind my back, and slaps on a pair of handcuffs. I hear the "click, click, click" as he squeezes them closed, to the point where it hurts. "You're my prisoner now," he snaps.

The cop drags me by the arm, and I have no choice but to follow him. A few blocks away there's a freestanding police booth situated on the perimeter of a large parking lot shared by Leeds Pharmacy, Gertz clothing store, the A&P, and several other local retailers. I knew he was taking me there, but still didn't understand why. Perhaps, I reasoned, there was some mistake. Maybe the cop had confused my face with the picture of some dangerous fugitive hanging in the Great Neck Post Office. Whatever the reason, the cop was bending my arm unnaturally, and it hurt. My feelings were also being hurt; the cop was parading me through town, handcuffed, like some hardened criminal. I'm humiliated and embarrassed, and hung my head in shame. Had I disgraced my family, my friends?

Halfway there, I look up, and what I see lifts my spirits. It appears the entire town is following me. It looks like a parade: an organized march of solidarity. Dozens of people on both sides of the street are shouting my name, and raising clenched fists in the air. Now, it's the cop who's embarrassed - maybe even a little nervous. I imagine a riot ensuing on my behalf - people throwing rocks, overturning police cruisers, and setting the police booth ablaze. The handcuffs digging into my wrists suddenly feel like a badge of honor. Suddenly I'm feeling euphoric, again.

Everything changes when I'm summarily shoved into the little booth at the edge of the shopping center. Now I'm both prisoner and hostage. There's another cop waiting inside, and I realize I'm about to experience, firsthand, something I'd seen many times on TV: the classic good cop, bad cop interrogation. Only in this case, both cops are bad.

The cops throw all kinds of questions at me: name, age, address, phone number? Who are your friends? Why are you in town? Why didn't you obey the officer? I'm scared, and try to keep my voice from cracking as I reply to each question truthfully, and to the best of my ability. They record my answers on a pink sheet of paper. When they're through with me, the bad cop removes the handcuffs. The other bad cop holds up the pink paper and says: "This is a juvenile delinquent form. I'll keep it here on file. It will not go on your permanent record unless there's another problem. There's no need to tell your parents about this incident."

What? Did I hear him correctly, or could I possibly have imagined what this officer of the law, this defender of the peace, had just uttered? *No need to tell my parents.* Something about this seemed instinctively wrong, very wrong, and I'm outraged. "What do you mean? Of course I'm going to tell my parents!" I say. I decide these guys in blue are done playing with me. I had not broken any laws. I was innocent. I had as much right to the Great Neck sidewalks as anyone. As far as I was concerned, my gloves were off and I was ready to fight, even if it meant going to jail. My civil liberties were at stake. I glared at the two cops and they glared back. They seemed to sense I meant business.

Suddenly, a car screeches to a halt outside and I hear the sound of a heavy door slam shut. I imagine it's the paddy wagon that's about to haul me off to jail. I'm not frightened. I puff out my chest and brace myself for another round of confrontation. Just then, the door to the little police booth flies open, and my brother is standing in the doorway, silhouetted by the brilliant afternoon sun. Reinforcements!

"Rex!" I was instantly fired-up.

"Do you want to tell me what's going on?" he demands. The two cops are momentarily speechless. Only rarely have I seen Rex display such grit. "I'd like your badge numbers, please," Rex says, and he begins to jot them down. The cops have nowhere to hide.

"Who are you?" the bad cop says.

"His brother," says Rex, "and I'm taking him home. Any objections?"

No one objects, especially not me. Then Rex says, "Get in the car."

We both get in his green Firebird and drive home.

"Are you mad at me?" I ask.

"No. Ash told me what happened. It didn't sound like you did anything wrong."

"I didn't," I insisted.

When we got home, I pieced together the story for my mother as best I could. Rex encouraged her to report the cop's badge numbers. We stood by as my mother placed a stern phone call to the Chief of Police, demanding an explanation. Though my indignation demanded the cops be punished, nothing ever happened, and everyone forgot about the incident; everyone, it seems, but me. The next day, I returned to town to hang out on the sidewalk with my friends. I was making a statement and felt triumphant, although I remained somewhat cautious, looking over my shoulder from time to time. Although my permanent record was temporarily clean, my temporary trust in authority was permanently tarnished.

* * *

MAYBE I *COULD* GET ARRESTED if I stopped trying so hard, I thought.

This sounded sensible to me, and I decidedly shifted my paradigm with respect to finding a job. Amazingly, it worked. Shortly thereafter I received a phone call from an Executive Producer in charge of community service programming at WCBS-TV. His name was Michael Ortega. He was looking for someone to produce a series of half-hour shows for their Sunday morning line-up. It was odd that he called because I didn't remember mailing my resume to anyone named Ortega. I was nonetheless thrilled to get his call. We arranged to meet at his office on 57th Street the following week, and he asked that I bring a sample of my work.

Early Monday morning, I hopped a train into Manhattan. After purchasing my round-trip ticket, exactly twenty-five dollars remained in my pocket - same as my age, I thought. I grabbed a cab up to 57th Street, and, with my highly-touted, award-winning documentary tucked under my arm, I strode into the CBS building and confidently announced the purpose of my visit to the receptionist. Apparently, I was regarded as someone important who should not be kept waiting, because minutes later I was escorted into the office of the Executive Producer, who, very likely, was going to offer me an important and lucrative job. It seemed my ship had finally come in.

This is how the meeting unfolded: Mr. Ortega offers me a seat and I hand him my resume. He takes a minute to study it. As he does, I note the time – 10:15. He asks me all kinds of questions: Where did I grow up? What did I study in school? What are my interests? What did I like best about television news? Have I ever produced community service programming?

I respond knowledgably and eloquently to all his questions, then he plays my tape. While he watches the tape, I watch him. I look for a change of expression. At times, he would knit his brow and nod, as if following the logic of thought, or the careful juxtaposition of sound and image. Several times I notice an upturning in the corners of his mouth, possibly denoting approval or amusement. His eyes blinked infrequently, which I interpret as an indication of thoughtful consideration for my work. When he had seen enough, he smiles, ejects my tape, and peruses my resume again.

"Do you have a list of references?" he asks. I thought it a strange remark; I had already given him several letters of recommendation from the people I had worked with at KTTV News in Los Angeles (the News Director, the Senior Producer, and the Head Writer), all on official letterhead. When I remind him of that fact, he says, "Is there anyone else I can call? Your resume states that you've had other documentary experience." He points to a line at the bottom of my resume, one which I had seen fit to include because I had, in fact, assisted on two documentary films for PBS when I was a senior at Boston University. However, on my resume, I embellished a bit (the only time I have ever embellished anything), by stating I was an *associate producer*, a title I was never officially awarded, but one, given my level of contribution, and the extent of my commitment to both projects, I felt I deserved. I had completely lost touch with the woman I had worked for back then, but for some reason my interviewer was bent on contacting her.

"Oh, that," I say, with a wave of my hand.

"May I have her number?" he asks.

"Sure. No problem," I reply, desperate to conceal my reluctance. "But I'll have to get back to you."

"No problem," he says. "My secretary can dig it up."

Thirty seconds later, Ortega's secretary hands him a slip of paper with the telephone number of this producer in Boston.

"Do you mind if I copy the number?" I ask, suddenly feeling flush. I copy it down. Ortega stands and extends his hand, ending the interview with a firm, if clammy, shake. Except for that one little hitch at the end, the meeting went flawlessly. But I worried what might happen when Ortega made the call to Boston.

My tape, which I had tucked under my arm, crashed to the ground as soon as I entered the hallway, but no heads turned; no one seemed to notice. I picked it up and strode briskly toward the exit.

There's a payphone on the wall in the lobby, and I have an idea. I empty my pockets of change and call the producer in Boston, hoping to reach her before Ortega does. I grasp the phone nervously as it rings. I am desperate for the woman to answer. The receptionist is glaring at me, as if she knows I'm guilty of something, but I don't care, this is my career on the line.

"Hello?" I instantly recognize the producer's voice and identify myself, reminding her of our past association. She hesitates, and I get the feeling she doesn't remember me, at all. Nevertheless, I quickly explain my problem, and beseech her to corroborate my story to Ortega.

"Who is this?" she asks.

Incredibly, I had been obliterated from the producer's memory. Hard as I tried, I could not sufficiently refresh her recollection as to who I was, or what I had done for her. She hung up without saying "goodbye." I sulked away from the phone, deflated, and hailed a taxi. "Penn Station, please."

At the end of the day, I had spent twelve dollars on cab fare and another eight for the train. You have to spend money to make money, I rationalized. But it still hurt; until I get a job, twenty dollars should last me a whole week. Then, I reconsider. If Ortega hires me, the money I'd spent will be a worthwhile investment.

Whatever the reason, Ortega never called. My ship had not yet come in, and my quest for the perfect job continued.

THE NEW GIRL

A NEW GIRL had arrived at my mother's house, just days before Thanksgiving. Her name was Edna; a pleasant woman in her late twenties, from Alabama. She was overweight, so it wasn't immediately apparent that she was pregnant, even though she was well into her third trimester. She arrived with a broken ankle and wore a hard cast that extended below the knee. On Thanksgiving Day, my mother prepared a lavish meal for the girls. Valerie and I helped, and it was quite a scene because most of the girls had never experienced a Thanksgiving feast like this. We were all in high spirits, and everyone seemed to forget their problems for awhile.

The food was plentiful and delicious. Edna loved the stuffing. "I'm stuffing my face," she says, "so my boy will grow big and strong." Mickey belched so loudly it rattled the crystal chandelier. Tammy got tipsy on stolen sips of my wine. "You're a real stud-muffin," she whispered in my ear when Valerie was out of earshot. Mickey then whispers in my other ear, "You're sporting a boner for her, I can tell," without missing a beat. Mickey seemed to have transcended the formal status of "guest," considering herself "family." Despite Mickey's crude way of showing it, I regard this as a high compliment and a tribute to my mother's capacity for unconditional love and acceptance.

There were other indications of this. My mother received cards and letters from lots of girls, long after they'd returned to their respective families:

<u>Patty, 17 (Fort Smith, Missouri)</u>
Dear Ms. N,
There was a big welcome home sign and someone sent me a dozen roses. Everyone's really happy to see me. The girls who started the rumors about me in school now think they were wrong – wink, wink. I won first prize at the annual pig roast, so maybe my luck is finally changing. I really miss you. It's not the same at home. I can't goof around with mother like I did with you.

<u>Janet, 20 (Holyoke, Massachusetts)</u>
Dear Ginny,
When I returned home, my parents presented me with an adorable terrier puppy. Boy, I'll tell you, I sure went through hell, but I did a lot of thinking while I was staying with you, and believe me, I did find out who I was and where I was going. And you are a very special person because you helped me through it. Never forget that you are special to me.

<u>Lynn, 27 (Louisville, Kentucky)</u>
Dear Virginia,

I'm sorry I didn't leave you a letter when I left. I'm the type of person who doesn't like to show my emotions, besides that, I don't like to cry. But maybe it wouldn't hurt to cry. I was sad to leave, mainly because of you. You're a person who has won a place in my heart forever.

* * *

THE MORNING AFTER THANKSGIVING, everyone sleeps late, but the girls slowly appear when the smell of fresh bacon starts to permeate the house. My mother is making pancakes. She fashions one in the shape of Mickey Mouse for Timmy. The boy is usually first at the breakfast table, but today he is curiously absent. My mother investigates, and discovers that Margaret's room is empty. She, and Timmy, and all their belongings are mysteriously gone. There is no note; no trace of anything. Then, one of the girls notices something unusual in the dining room. The doors on the breakfront cabinet are wide open, and every piece of my mother's heirloom silver is gone. Everyone stares in disbelief. I see "that look" in my mother's eyes. It is a look I recognize; it is anger, and it's a side of my mother people rarely see, if ever. It surfaces when she's pushed too far; when her patience has finally run out. The fact that she displays her anger so infrequently makes it all the more terrifying. It is an anger best not directed at you.

Her eyes narrow. "That little bitch!" my mother shouts. Only once had I heard her utter the word, *bitch*. I don't recall what set her off then, but I do remember being scared. Let it out, mom, I thought. My adrenaline was pumping. The girls in the room look shocked. Mickey's jaw hangs open, frozen like an ice sculpture.

"She had better be half way back to Germany by now, if she knows what's good for her," says my mother. For several moments the house is utterly still, silence looming in darkness. Then I hear rumbling, and the floor begins to shake. It is big Edna, ambling downstairs to join us. She is waving a sheet of paper which she hands to my mother.

"What's this... a letter? Something you wrote?" my mother says. I watch as my mother reads in silence. She appears transfixed, and has seemingly dismissed the matter of her missing heirlooms, along with the anger. Her expression returns to its characteristic softness, and she smiles. Then, a single tear forms in the corner of her eye.

When she's finished, she looks at Edna. "Would you mind if I read this aloud?"

"You can read it," Edna says, "but you have to promise you'll keep it safe until the baby comes, then give it to the parents."

"I promise." My mother clears her throat, and reads:

Dear Parents,
Hello. Even though we've never met each other I feel like I know you. The reason I'm writing this letter is in reference to something we've got in common; your son. I would really be grateful, if and when you tell him, that his other parents loved him very much, and that we gave him up for adoption because we wanted him to have a good life. And I feel that he will have loving parents. I know how much you wanted him. So will you please explain to him that he's special because he not only has one set of parents who love him, but two. This letter seemed to me like I was trying to make excuses because what's a letter telling someone that you love him dated 15 or 16 years earlier, so I'm leaving the decision up to you, and I hope when he grows into a fine young man that he won't have no bitterness. All I can say now is love him and take care.
Respectfully,
Birthparents

SLAIN

DECEMBER 9ᵀᴴ, 1980. I'm at home stuffing resumes when the phone rings.

"Hello?" as is my typical, uninspired greeting.

"Did you see the cover of Newsday?" It's Eddie; a friend of my brother's, who happened to be living in our basement at the time. "John Lennon was shot last night outside the Dakota."

I hung up the phone and raced down to the kitchen; my mother always read the newspaper at breakfast, and I knew that's where I'd find it. On the front page, there's a picture of a bloody crime scene. The headline says, "John Lennon Slain." When I read this, my heart sinks, and my head starts spinning. Clutching the paper, I run back to my room, shut the door, and return to the headline. For some reason I expect to see something different, but it's the same as before: *John Lennon Slain*. Strange, but I suddenly can't recall the precise meaning of the word "slain." There was no time to consult a dictionary. I picked up the phone and called Valerie at work. Although we had only been dating a short while, she was the one person I wanted to speak with. Thankfully she answered on the first ring.

"Did you see the cover of Newsday?" I ask. "Someone shot John Lennon."

"We've been talking about it at work all morning," she says. "It's terrible."

"The Newsday headline says, 'John Lennon Slain,'" I say. "What, exactly, does 'Slain' mean? Does *slain* mean *killed* as in *dead*? Is John Lennon dead?" I can't comprehend this, and I am angry with myself.

There's a long, ambivalent silence. Finally Valerie says, "John Lennon was murdered. Don't you understand? He's dead." Valerie was well aware of my passion for the Beatles, and the profound effect they had on my life. "I'm sorry," she added.

(A freight train barreled through my door, striking me head on.)

Had I been able to respond, I might have said, "This is the greatest loss the world has ever suffered," or, "My life will never be the same," or, "What kind of sick fuck would do this?" But I couldn't speak. I couldn't think. I didn't want to think. I dropped the phone.

I cried. I beat the pillow. I wanted my anger to flow like lightening, from my fists, through the mattress, into the earth. But all I can do is bury my head and cry. The void feels too permanent, too devastating, and too familiar. Another piece of my heart had been taken; another part of my spirit had been broken. It wasn't fair. In a span of ten years, the two most important men in my life, both named John, had become echoes of the past.

UNSUITABLE

IN THE EARLY 1980's, cable television was in its infancy, but investors on Wall Street were sensing the dawn of a new growth industry. Niche programming outlets like The Food Network, A&E, and The Sundance Channel were still years away, but a media storm was gathering strength, and would prove to be a storm of revolutionary proportion.

It was the early and unprecedented growth of cable TV that led to my first job in New York, and it seemed like the perfect job; my career was finally about to take off. I was hired by one of only a handful of companies with the resources to extend the reach of cable TV to major metropolitan areas. The company already owned and operated a vast number cable franchises around the U.S., and was investing millions to expand further against what little competition existed. There was a heated race to wire the country, involving several large media corporations, and my new employer was one of them.

I was given the title of "Director of Local Programming," which sounded good to me. I was also given a decent starting salary, a nicely appointed office on the 40th floor overlooking Central Park, an expense account, health insurance, two weeks paid vacation, personalized business cards, a personal assistant, and a handful of personal days (to be used at my discretion). In short, I was given all the tools necessary to succeed on my way to the top. All I had to do was supply my own wardrobe - although I was not enthused when I learned I was required to wear a suit and tie every day. At the time, I owned just one suit, which I rarely wore. This was no accident. I didn't like suits: they were stiff and uncomfortable, they were hot, they didn't go with sneakers, they wrinkled easily, and they were costly to maintain. But I was an executive now, and felt responsible for satisfying the dress requirements of my position. So I was eager, in a reluctant sort of way, to invest in two new suits. This would give me a total of three suits to rotate throughout the week. I also purchased two crisp, white shirts. Such was my executive wardrobe. It wasn't much, but I hoped that if I accessorized myself with a variety of inexpensive ties, no one would suspect I owned anything less than a closet full of custom-tailored suits.

I was starting out brilliantly it seemed, with all the trappings of a burgeoning young executive. I had even obtained a monthly commuter ticket from the Long Island Railroad. I would begin each morning taking the bus to the train, and the train to Penn Station, just as my father had done. I would carry a briefcase and a copy of The New York Times, like every commuter wearing a suit. What an exciting time! The possibilities were endless.

My first day on the job, I sat at my desk and stared out my 40th floor window overlooking Central Park. It was a beautiful autumn day, and the foliage was bursting with color. I had yearned for this sight the entire time I was living in Los Angeles. Now it was mine again, and I was enthralled. I sat and stared until the setting sun cast an orange glow on the orange carpet of the Park. I sat and stared until the offices on my floor had emptied and the night cleaning crew had arrived. I sat and stared until the sun had disappeared and the streetlamps were burning, and I wondered, "What am I doing here?" It was a beautiful and frightening moment.

I returned the next day wearing the same suit I had worn the day before. Since I had never left my office, I doubted anyone would notice - at least my assistant didn't raise an eyebrow as I blew past her desk in the morning. Her name is Mandy; a bookish type, void of personality, and not much to look at, but it didn't matter - the intercom on my desk provided all the necessary means of communication between us.

I pick up the phone and call Valerie. At the time, she was working as a researcher for a small production company that had a show on PBS.

"How's the new job?" she asks.

"I have no idea what I'm supposed to be doing, but the view is great," I admit. "How are things in Public TV land?"

"They want me to start producing segments for the show."

"That's great," I say, feeling a tinge of envy. "Someday you might be an executive like me." I wait for her response. "Are you there?"

"Yes," she says. "Is something wrong?"

"It's stuffy in here."

"Open a window."

"I'm on the 40th floor," I tell her. "The windows don't open. Canned air; that's what we breathe in here."

There's an uncomfortable lull in the conversation and Valerie signs off. I'm glad for that. I had become lost in my own preoccupations: Valerie seemed to have a clear direction at work. I, on the other hand, felt I had none. Each day, from the moment I entered my office, I couldn't figure out what to do with myself. What is a National Director of Local Programming supposed to *do*? In all fairness to me, my cluelessness was not entirely my fault. I had never seen a job description. I don't believe one ever existed. My boss never gave me an assignment, suggested any long-term goals, or provided any clues as to my function at the company.

I began to suspect this vagueness is simply a fundamental aspect of the corporate culture. So, in an attempt to conform and appear reasonably proactive, I occasionally ventured beyond the confines of my office to the copy machine down the hall. Unfortunately, it only aggravated my sense of paranoia and self-consciousness. I would interpret the subtle glances from my coworkers to mean, "There's that new guy making copies again. He doesn't know what to do with himself."

Before long I'm in the habit of napping each morning. Immediately after arriving to work, I would lock my office door, lie on the floor, slide a roll of paper towels behind my neck, then close my eyes and plunge into a deep sleep. I don't understand this behavior of mine (I am not narcoleptic; at least, I never have been), but I don't try to fight it.

My alarm clock is buzzing. Is it morning, already? No. This is not my alarm clock. It's the intercom on my desk. "What?"

I hear a tinny voice forcing its way through the device. "There's someone here to see you." Ah yes, it's Mandy's voice.

"I have no appointments today," I say, jumping up and flipping through my leather-bound planner.

"He says he's your friend," Mandy chimes back.

"Okay, send my friend in." I say this with authority - purposefully, to command respect, the way I imagined a successful corporate executive would address a subordinate. I drop into the chair behind my desk, and my office door swings open. To my surprise, in walks Rick.

"What are you doing here?" I ask, surprised.

"I'm in New York for a meeting."

"Cool."

"I wanted to see where you worked, if you're not too busy."

"Never too busy for you," I offer, rubbing my eyes. "I was just going over some reports. It seems cable television is taking the nation by storm."

"You think?"

"I don't know," I admit. "I think so."

Rick is admiring my view of Central Park. I can tell he's impressed. "What, actually, do you do here?" he finally asks.

"Lots of stuff, I guess, executive stuff. You know... meetings, phone calls, Xeroxing."

"I'm impressed with your view."

"Yeah," I say, trying to focus.

"Hey, isn't that the suit you wore at college graduation?" Rick asks, regarding my chic, executive wardrobe.

"Yeah, but the shirt's new. The tie, too, I think." I loosen my tie and remove a fifth of Jack Daniels from my desk drawer. It's half-empty. "You want a drink?" I ask, uncapping the bottle.

Rick's face brightens before he checks his watch. "My meeting's in an hour. I should probably wait 'till it's over before I do any of that - don't you think?"

"Your call," I shrug, and pour myself a generous eye opener. Rick smiles. Knowing him, he's probably thinking I'm not cut out for this job. Knowing me, he's probably right, yet I'm suddenly on a personal mission to prove him wrong.

Well, it was only a matter of months before the demands of my morning commute began to wear on me, both mentally and physically. Waiting for the bus was torture. I waited in oppressive heat and frigid rain, in the pre-dawn darkness of winter, in snow and slush, and in wind-chill factors which dropped temperatures to well below zero. The train was no better. The seats were often all occupied, forcing me to stand, squeezed between oblivious riders with vile breath and wet umbrellas; they reeked from the stench of damp newsprint, black coffee, and malodorous aftershave. Worst of all, there were those inescapable, silent farts which inevitably emerged from some anonymous slob standing nearby, who had smugly let one loose, and was feigning innocence. It was nauseating – particularly difficult to stomach, first thing in the morning. Hard as I tried (and I did try hard), I found no pleasure in this. It was utterly sub-zero.

Once, I was waiting for the train as a steady rain fell over the tri-state area. The rain was expected to last all day (according to the Accu-weather forecast). An autumn chill was in my bones, and I was shivering. My socks were soaked. I was miserable, and desperately wanted to be somewhere else, anywhere else. I wanted to be dry and warm.

The mass of men lead lives of quiet desperation.

Thoreau's astute and depressing observation came to

mind. How true it seemed, as I studied the faces of the men and women standing on the platform that morning. How true and how sad, I thought. Everyone was trying so hard to not be unhappy. One man, in particular, seemed to epitomize the plight of all commuters. I watched as that man craned his neck and peered down the wind-swept track, presumably hoping for a glimpse of the train. He glanced at his watch, then down the empty corridor again, anticipating the train's imminent arrival. But the train did not appear. The man's New York Times was wet from the blowing rain, and was slowly disintegrating into a semi-liquid, sticky pulp. His umbrella, crowded amidst so many other umbrellas, was losing the battle for airspace above his head. A long tangle of hair, combed across his head to mask a balding crown, drooped loosely in front of his face and stuck to his forehead like a twisted strand of overdone spaghetti. He tried to blow the hair aside, (his hands were too busy grappling with his executive paraphernalia - umbrella, briefcase, newspaper, coffee), but he gave up after several attempts.

I shivered as the chilly rain penetrated my bones. I don't belong here; that's obvious. This is not the way I want to live, day after day, week after week, year after year, until I'm dead. I'm desperate not to let Thoreau's refrain become my reality. I will not be one of those people. I can't be.

Four months after I was hired as Director of Local Programming, with all the executive tools of the trade, poised for a steady climb to the top, I was called into my boss's office. When I presented myself, she wasn't smiling.

"I couldn't sleep last night," she tells me.

"I'm sorry. I know what it's like to feel exhausted."

"I was thinking about you." When she says this I am flattered and speechless, but the idea of having an affair with my boss (with this boss) was out of the question. She's too old and uptight to be of any interest to me, in the carnal sense, even if it put me on a faster track to success. I decide to play dumb. "What do you mean?" I ask.

"I was wondering what to do with you," she says softly.

"Frankly, I was wondering what to do with me too," I say, in an unexpected flash of honesty. She twists her face slightly, as though surprised by my statement.

"I turned this over in my mind many, many times," she admits. "I want to do the right thing, for both of us."

"What do you think is the right thing?" I ask.

"I think the right thing is… "

I suddenly realize I'm holding my breath, and I let out a loud sigh.

My boss continues: "I think we should just call it a day, and leave it at that. What do you think?"

I'm being asked to leave. She's firing me.

"What do you think?" she repeats.

I take a moment to consider what I think. I consider how I hate breathing canned air. I consider how I hate wearing a clean, pressed suit every day. I consider how I'm not ready to surrender my life, even if it means the security of a weekly paycheck.

I stare at my boss and think about convention. I think about freedom. I think about security. Then, I think about lunch. When I'm finished thinking, I say, graciously, "Thank you. I'll have my personal effects removed by the end of the day." As I stand to leave, I add, "Maybe you should go home and get some sleep."

"I can't," she says. "I have a late meeting. But, thank you for your concern."

"You're welcome," I say. We shake hands, and I quietly depart.

Mandy brings me an empty cardboard box. There is nothing to pack; no family photos, no plaques, no awards, no souvenirs; no mementos of any kind, just an empty bottle of Jack Daniels. As I survey my stark office for the last time, reality sets in. I have been fired from my first job as an executive. I am not proud of this, but I think I might be a little happy about it. I leave immediately, riding the elevator down from the 40th floor one last time, and call Valerie from a payphone on the street.

"Can we meet? We need to talk."

"What's wrong?" she asks, concerned.

Valerie is a woman of action. She's outside my building in fewer than ten minutes. We kiss, and she asks, "What's up?"

"Good news," I say, without wasting time.

"Don't tell me," Valerie smiles. "You got a promotion."

"I was fired," I say, then add triumphantly, "My life is my own again."

Valerie wastes no time bursting into tears. She is positively sobbing - which I can't understand, because I am positively ecstatic.

"What - are you – going to do for - work?" Valerie murmurs between gasps of air.

"I don't know. I'll find something," I say, my spirits high.

"What about money?" Valerie asks.

Valerie gets all the angles. Money, or a lack of it, was the biggest problem I now faced. I was still living at home. Both Valerie and I were hoping my executive job would be my ticket out. We had recently discussed sharing an apartment together; an idea for which my enthusiasm had been growing. Now those plans seemed (temporarily, at least) dashed. For the time being, anyway, I would be forced to rely on my mother for sustenance and shelter.

As I considered the current composition of my mother's household, a knot formed in my stomach. Edna and Sylvia remained, but Mickey and Tammy had delivered their babies. They were replaced by Betty Anne, 14, Lauren, 17, and Heather, 22. The resulting shift had relegated me from the comfort and privacy of my old room, to the pullout couch in the den. I shared a tiny bathroom next to the washer/dryer with Betty Anne and Lauren. My personal space was definitely shrinking; the house seemed to be shrinking, too, and it suddenly felt much too small.

When the taxicab dropped me outside my mother's house that night, I began to feel tightness in my chest. I knew this couldn't be a heart attack - I was only 25. No, this was a wave of mixed emotion - a potent concoction of anxiety, claustrophobia, and dread. I realized, by getting fired from my job, I had merely relinquished one form of incarceration (the staff job), for another (living at my mother's house).

I dragged my feet up the front walk like a death-row prisoner en route to the electric chair. I heard the wail of an ambulance nearby, and wished it were coming for me. Then the siren grew louder. Then it was inside my head. An instant later, the side of my house was streaked with flashes of red and white light. An ambulance skidded to a stop behind me, and my mother burst through the front door waving two paramedics inside. Disoriented, confused, my adrenaline pumping, I followed everyone into the house.

Downstairs, in the dimly lit den, a paramedic is kneeling on the floor, administering CPR to one of the girls. I take a quick accounting of everyone in the room. Betty Anne, her face white with anguish and full of tears, is clinging to my mother's side. Lauren and Heather are huddled together, sobbing hysterically. I move in for a closer look, and see Sylvia kneeling beside Edna, squeezing her limp hand. Edna's face is a deathly shade of purple. It remains that way, despite all attempts to resuscitate her.

Edna, a sweet, sensitive, unsophisticated young woman who made a mistake and tried to make it right, died of a sudden, massive heart attack while playing cards with the girls. She was wheeled out on a gurney under a clean, white sheet - a large, lifeless mass with an unborn baby inside.

Hours later, as I lay on the pullout couch in the dark, unable to sleep, my mind wandered to thoughts of Edna and the letter she had written at Thanksgiving.

My mother's house suddenly felt too big.

SOMETHING FOR POSTERITY

As THE FIRST BORN SON, my brother inherited the privilege of occupying the larger of the two bedrooms in our house. His bedroom was the only thing of his I coveted as I was growing up. Fortunately for me, he married young, and shortly afterward found an apartment of his own. I clearly remember the day he signed his lease. Before the ink was even dry, all my stuff was in my new room (his old room). I generously offered Rex a grace period, allowing several of his possessions to remain with me until he settled fully into his new home. One of those possessions was a portable video recording system. It was purchased in 1977, when video technology was still in its infancy. Sony had recently begun to market a battery-powered, portable video system. Although large and bulky by today's standards, the system was capable of recording and playing back color images with sound. It recorded on three-quarter inch video cassette tape. The equipment was complicated to operate, required a lot of light to produce a decent picture, and cost about fifteen thousand dollars. But my brother, like me, was an early adopter of new technology, and somehow convinced his future father-in-law to purchase the system, arguing that it could be used to record their upcoming wedding ceremony. On the day of Rex's marriage to Judy, I was the one operating the camera, passing it off briefly to a cousin when it came time for me to join the bridal party. I taped, and eventually edited, the celebration that followed. It may actually have been the first wedding video ever made.

* * *

IT WAS FOUR AND A HALF YEARS LATER when Edna passed away, and another shift in my mother's house took place. My brother's old room became available, and I moved right in. Valerie was on her way up from Brooklyn. She had planned to spend the weekend with me at my mother's house. We had been going steady for over a year, and although she was pressuring me to get married, particularly on holidays, I wasn't nearly ready to commit; not because I didn't love her - I was mad about her - but marriage was another matter. I needed to do some additional research, perhaps even consult a lawyer, before I signed any sort of contract affecting "the rest of my life." Unfortunately, she took it personally.

Anyway, I was straightening my room, in anticipation of Valerie's arrival, when I noticed my brother's video equipment tucked away in the back of the closet. When Valerie finally arrived, I opened a chilled bottle of Chardonnay, and soon we were tumbling on the bed, kissing and making out. That's when a light went off in my head with respect to the equipment.

"You know, we're probably going to get married someday, right?" I say.

"Oh?"

"Yes. I definitely see us growing old together." I begin to paint a colorful picture of our golden years.

"I can see us fifty years from now; grey hair, kind of fat and wrinkled."

"What? Don't say that," she scoffs. "I don't like that."

"Oh, but it's going to be wonderful, because even though we'll be old and decrepit, we'll still be very much in love."

"Can we just change the subject?" Valerie admonishes.

"You know what?" I say, refilling her glass. "I hate to think what happens when the glow of youth has faded. I feel sorry for old people."

"Me too," she admits.

"That's why it would be great if we…" I let my voice trail off, hoping my timing and delivery will pique her curiosity.

"What?"

"Never mind: It's embarrassing."

"Tell me your great idea, Honey." She gulps the remainder of her Chardonnay.

"Nah, you'll just think I'm weird or stupid."

"How do you know? Try me."

I was definitely making progress. I knew I had to go for it, now. The conditions would probably never be this right again. Okay, I thought. Why not?

"Wouldn't it be great if we videotaped ourselves, you know, having sex, for posterity's sake, to look at say, fifty years from now, on my seventy-fifth birthday?"

Valerie eyes me quizzically. I continue: "But we have to do it now while I still have hair, while we're still young, and thin, and sexy - while we still have good turgor."

"What's *turgor*?" she asks.

"The point is," I explain, "we may never have this opportunity again, ever." Valerie covers her mouth and I flinch, expecting to receive a resounding slap on the good turgor of my rosy cheek.

"I might be convinced. A drop more wine wouldn't hurt," she says, smiling.

I'm shocked, and lunge for the bottle, trembling as I fill her glass, spilling a few drops on the bedspread. "Drink up," I stammer.

I spend the next five minutes frantically adjusting lights, configuring the equipment, loading the tape, and making all the necessary connections (only once did I consult the manual). I extend the telescoping legs of the tripod, and lock the camera into place.

"Hurry up. I'm losing interest," I hear her say.

"Drink more wine!" I scream. My sense of urgency couldn't have been greater.

I feverishly untangle the long microphone cable and nose one end into the VTR, then toss the mike strategically onto the bed (in what, I estimate, will be the center of the action). Valerie is now chugging wine from the bottle. I fumble for a blank twenty-minute tape, load it into the machine and press "RECORD." The red light over the camera starts blinking.

"We're On the Air!' I cry, quickly ripping off my clothes, and tossing them carelessly on the floor. Valerie is quick to follow my lead.

It was the best sex we'd ever had. Valerie played unabashedly to the camera. I was somewhat surprised that she (or any girl, for that matter) would participate so readily in an activity such as this, and I couldn't help thinking how cool she was. While the tape rolled, we made love in every conceivable position, and even some inconceivable ones. Nothing interfered, or came between us, except the microphone - though we found imaginative ways to incorporate it into our lovemaking. As the scene unfolded, I thought about the videotape, and what a treasure it would be when we reached our golden years! This is something I would cherish forever and watch on special occasions, like my seventy-fifth birthday, fifty years from now.

We had unleashed our passion, and it was white hot. We continued until we trembled with exhaustion, depleted of all strength. When it was over, when the tape had run out, our bodies lay intertwined on the bed sheets, which had become soaked with perspiration.

Shortly afterward, Valerie is fast asleep and snoring lightly. I gather my strength, sit at the edge of the bed (still trying to catch my breath), and cover Valerie with a light blanket. I notice that the VTR had shut off automatically, so I switch it on and let the tape rewind. I'm eager to see what had been captured on tape. Referring to the equipment's quick-start diagram, I rearrange the connections for playback, switch on the TV, and push "play." The tape advances inside the cassette, and the small television speaker begins to resonate with the unmistakable sound of raw, unrestrained sex. Yeah!

Only one thing puzzled me; the screen remained dark – maybe a loose connection? I wiggle the wires, but this fails produce a picture. I play with the dials regulating brightness and contrast - still no picture. I usually have a knack when it comes to electronics, but this time I'm stumped. The troubleshooting guide offers little help. I'm sitting at the edge of the bed, staring at the camera, searching for an answer, when I see the one thing I really don't want to see: the lens cap. In my excitement and haste, I had neglected to remove it from the front of the lens. Dumb. There is no video whatsoever. All that remains for posterity is twenty minutes of XXX-rated audio.

Not that the activity was a total waste – it was tons of fun – but afterward Valerie made it unmistakably clear I had blown it. There would be no second chance to get it right. I made several attempts to change her mind, but she was unbending. What a pity our youth would not be immortalized on tape for all eternity. What a pity my seventy-fifth birthday would not include a twenty-minute stroll down memory lane with the virility and turgor of my youth immaculately preserved and untouched by the ravages of time.

* * *

SEVERAL WEEKS LATER, I was hired on short notice by a local politician to videotape a speech in which he planned to announce his official entrance in the New York Senate race. I asked him how he intended to use the video. "It's for posterity," he said. He told me it was a short speech; not more than five or six minutes. My brother agreed to let me borrow his video gear so I could earn a few bucks. I was thrilled, and fantasized about this guy winning the election. He would hire me as his media director, and a glamorous career would follow, possibly taking me all the way to the White House someday.

On the night of the shoot, I realized I could squeeze a few extra dollars out of the job if I used a previously recorded tape. So I quickly grabbed a cassette with a clean box, and headed out to the Great Neck library where the politician was scheduled to address a crowd of supporters.

The shoot went flawlessly. There was plenty of light to render good quality video. The audio was crisp and clear. I was in and out of there in a few hours. At the end of the evening, I handed the politician the tape (and a resume), and he handed me an agreed amount of cash. I wished him luck, packed up my equipment, returned to my mother's house and went to bed. I was dreaming that Valerie had given me a second chance to videotape our lovemaking when I suddenly awoke as if from a nightmare. In the dream, I came to the realization that the tape I had surrendered that evening to the politician for *his* posterity was the same tape I had previously used for mine. Although it lacked the video portion of our heated sex, the audio portion was still highly graphic and erotic, particularly if you had a decent imagination – as most politicians do.

Imagine my embarrassment when he plays the tape for his colleagues, friends, and family. It would destroy my chance of ever working for this guy again, and could possibly ruin my reputation. My head began to spin with other dreadful implications outside my own selfish interests. Had I possibly destroyed this poor man's political career? What if the tape inadvertently reached the public, sparking a scandal? I certainly hoped it would not - the guy had paid me in cash.

Fortunately, in the weeks that followed, I dutifully scanned every issue the Great Neck Record but saw no mention of a videotaped indiscretion by a politician. In fact, I never saw mention of this particular politician ever again, and assumed he opted out of running for the senate. Lost forever is that savagely erotic audio from my youth; all because I wanted to make a few extra bucks on a piece of videotape stock.

THE POLITICS OF FAITH

I AM NOT THE TYPE of person who has ever tried to convince others to adopt my belief system. In the first place, I am not truly sure what my belief system actually is: it seems to keep changing as I get older. Nevertheless, my philosophy has always been, "live and let live." It should come as no surprise, then, to learn that I am the product of a mixed marriage. My father was Jewish, and my mother, Episcopalian. Fortunately for me, my childhood encompassed the best of both worlds. We celebrated everything: Christmas, Hanukkah, Rosh Hashanah, Easter, and even Saint Patrick's Day (my mother was also part Irish).

When I was about seven or eight, my parents asked me if I wanted to start Hebrew school and become a Bar Mitzvah. Since, at that time, the town of Great Neck was largely Jewish, the majority of my friends were already enrolled – a commitment which, for many years, would occupy several afternoons every week after school; afternoons I could be frolicking in the glorious out of doors. With this in mind, I respectfully opted out of Hebrew school, and was never called to the Torah to become a Bar Mitzvah. It simply seemed like too much work for something that was only relevant to half of me. What is significant, though, is that my parents thought to ask. None of my other friends had any say in the matter - Hebrew school was simply expected of them. My parents, however, didn't force their belief systems on me, and I had no desire to choose between being Jewish and being Episcopalian. I didn't understand why I couldn't be both. Why not love everyone? Also, I felt that by choosing the religion of my father I would be rejecting my mother, and vice versa, and I refused to do that to either of them.

So I grew up embracing the ideals of two religions. I believed in Santa, and Moses, and the Easter Bunny. I enjoyed Matzo and ham sandwiches, equally. I opened presents on Hanukah and Christmas (but mostly on Christmas). One year I asked for a Jewish mezuzah to wear around my neck, and found it beautifully wrapped under the tree. Menorahs and nativity scenes were equally effective in rousing my holiday spirit. Some people – and you know who you are – said that I was… "confused." I don't think this was meant as a compliment, and yet I never believed, not even for a second, that I was confused. On the contrary, I considered myself… "enlightened."

Meanwhile, my relationship with Valerie was developing at breakneck speed. I had ceased worrying about the future, and began focusing on enjoying the time we spent together. Valerie was undoubtedly the most fun and exciting woman I had ever dated, so I suggested we take our first vacation together. I proposed Puerto Rico as a destination, pointing out that it was tropical, relatively inexpensive, and offered a variety of sights and activities. She agreed, and we were on our way.

It is our first day in Puerto Rico, and the weather is spectacular - a cloudless blue sky with a gentle tropical offshore breeze and low humidity. We decide to rent a car and explore the countryside. I have an idea. Typical of many ideas of mine, it borders on stupid and irresponsible, but since Valerie does not object, (and I trust her judgment), we sign for the rental car and drive to a local Bodega. There I purchase a three-pack of Bacardi and a bunch of plantains (a banana-like fruit, indigenous to the tropics). "Instant daiquiri!" I exclaim, glowing with pride and anticipation. "You take a bite of banana, mush it up in your mouth, and then have a swig of rum." I demonstrate, and even though the concoction is warm, it is immensely gratifying and tasty.

I drive for awhile with no particular destination in mind. All four windows are rolled down. The sultry, tropical air swirls around us as the lush scenery floats by. After driving for about an hour, we notice a sandy cove adjacent to the road. It looks like a good place to stop. I am thirsty, and the fifth of rum wedged between my legs is burning a hole in my lap.

The beach is lined with a variety of palm trees: Dwarf Palmettos, Coconut Palms, and Hat Palms. I park in the shade, cut the engine, and then Valerie and I take turns doing daiquiris. A breeze blows up the front of Valerie's shirt, exposing her bare breasts. It is highly erotic. Between drinks we kiss, and I am dizzy from the combination of sweet rum and the sweet-salty taste of her skin. Before long the rum is gone and so is the sun. Suddenly, there's a chill in the air, and Valerie wants to go back to the hotel. I want to stay a little longer. In fact, I want to stay forever. This has been a special day. I realize I could get used to this - to being with Valerie - and for the first time I am the one to raise the subject of marriage.

"I'm thinking we have potential," I suggest.

"Potential?" Valerie says, and I'm wondering if she has the vaguest idea what I'm talking about, and whether I haven't already made a fool of myself.

"As a couple," I reply, adding, "A permanent couple." Valerie can see that I'm serious, and I am. I'm looking at her with loving eyes, but I want to keep the mood light.

Knowing that I came from a mixed marriage, she asks, "How will we raise our kids?" The rum is like truth serum coursing through my body, and it doesn't occur to me to be anything but completely honest. I say, "I believe in a universal God." This, it seems, is a bad answer. Valerie is repulsed by me and my response. She insists I take her back to the hotel immediately. Nothing I say, without lying, can undo the damage. I'm certain that the night, and possibly the remainder of our vacation, is over for us. Valerie refuses to speak, and as the lights of the hotel appear in my windshield, my rental car runs out of gas. The vehicle slows and then sputters to a stop.

"I'll walk," Valerie says, opening the door.

"You can't walk! It's too far, and it's dangerous!" I try to reason with her.

"I don't care. I'm getting out, I swear," she insists.

Valerie is true to her word. She slams the door behind her, and I single-handedly spend the next hour pushing the rental car back to our hotel with one hand on the steering wheel.

This is what I mean when I say, "Religion divides." Enlightenment requires immersion into many disciplines over a lifetime, and one must never stop searching for the truth. I could never accept being told what to believe, but decided I would always keep an open mind.

SUFFOCATED

THE BREAKUP OCCURRED one year later, on a rainy night in June. We stood beneath the steamy halo of a streetlamp, framed by the soft glow of the 59th Street Bridge in the background. All I could remember were the last several holidays where the expectation of a marriage proposal was omnipresent. When a ring didn't materialize, the expectation was crushed, and the holiday changed from joyful to dreadful. It wasn't that I didn't love Valerie. I loved her very much. We had fun together. Sex was always great. But, I wondered, could I marry her when I didn't even have a job?

We had been living like nomads, constantly looking for a place to crash so we could be together, hopping from one small New York City apartment to another: her brother's, my cousin's, her brother's friend, then back to my mother's house, her parents' in Brooklyn, a two month sublet near the United Nations, a long weekend at my brother's in Queens. I never knew where my next clean pair of underwear was coming from. And I was always, always, with an overnight bag hanging from my shoulder. At first it was fun, crazy and romantic. But eventually, with no end in sight, it got old, very old. I was tired. She was, too.

"I'll probably regret this for the rest of my life," I say, believing it. A warm, diffused light is falling onto one side of Valerie's face. She looks beautiful, and I want to stop. I don't want to hurt her. I don't want to get hurt. I realize I can stop talking, now, and cancel my plan. Then everything will return to normal, and no one will get hurt. But the hurt is already there, for both of us.

A lump in my throat makes it hard to swallow. My lips are dry. I try to wet them, but there is no saliva in my mouth. *Get it over with.*

I tell her I want to move on, that it isn't working anymore, and nothing can change my mind.

I kiss her on the cheek with my dry, cracked lips, turn away, and don't look back.

I hear her sobbing as I walk down Sutton Place toward Penn Station, all the while thinking I had failed her; not because I had failed to commit, but because I had failed to be a man. (Is this what happened to a boy when a happy childhood is interrupted by the sudden death of his father?) I didn't want to blame my circumstances on my father's death. The problem was, I had no other answers. I was lost, still.

I returned to my mother's house in Great Neck, alone. The moon was full. It glowed like a giant piñata waiting to be smashed to pieces so it could spill trinkets and candy all over the earth. I felt like doing the smashing.

I tiptoed inside the house. It was very late. Thankfully, my mother was fast asleep. I didn't want to tell her how my night had ended. It was too tragic; too horrible for words. Once in bed, I tried desperately to talk myself to sleep, but sleep would not come. I opened my notebook and wrote this:

> *Your love*
> *Rains on me*
> *Like shards of glass*
> *Falling from the stars*
> *Cutting me*
> *Before I realize*
> *It isn't love at all.*

BOOK SEVEN

UNDERSTANDING

THE REST OF MY LIFE

VALERIE AND I GOT ENGAGED six months after we broke up. We were married a year later. During that time I applied to law school and received several acceptances. I enrolled in a prominent Manhattan school offering a specialization in entertainment law. We went to Paradise Island on our honeymoon, and returned to several messages on our answering machine inquiring about my availability as a producer/director. I interpreted the messages as an omen, withdrew from law school the following week, and never looked back. This was either a grave mistake, or the best thing I could have done. This was over twenty years ago, and the jury is still out (no pun intended).

    My freelance career in television admittedly did flourish for several years. I directed almost every show on the Food Network during its crucial break-out period. I had lengthy directing gigs with A&E, the History Channel, and American Movie Classics, and got to work with some of the finest actors (and human beings) around: James Earl Jones, Lauren Bacall, Janet Leigh, Peter Falk, Liza Minnelli, Peter Graves, Jack Perkins, Debbie Reynolds, Shirley Jones – the list goes on and on. I often did pro bono work for good causes. Once I directed a public service announcement for the Martin Luther King holiday and had the pleasure of filming and spending the day with Yoko Ono. But soon it became harder and harder for me to find work. I knew I was good at what I did. I had a tremendous understanding of every aspect of production; I had spent twenty years doing it. But the work receded. I didn't feel like I was building on anything. I didn't feel like I had a career. I found myself spending increasing amounts of time at home, trying to figure out what was happening, and where I may have gone wrong. Meanwhile, the world kept turning. Valerie, who also stayed in television, was in management, and on a career path which kept rising. Other directors I knew, although they sometimes found themselves out of work, continued to work on better shows, with bigger budgets. It seemed that for everyone else, one job kept leading to another. For me, everything just seemed to stop. I was left with a feeling of disenfranchisement. It was like I was standing alone in the middle of a huge, crowded playground, and everywhere I'd turn someone was telling me, "Go home. You can't play here anymore." It made no sense.

Then there was the guilt. Before I knew it, Valerie was making more money than I ever had. She ran all sorts of media companies. She flew first class, gained a favorable reputation on both coasts, collected year-end bonuses, and was usually given a corner office with its own bathroom.

Then there was the emasculation. It was futile for me to compete with my wife. She had clearly become the breadwinner in the family, and when it came to looking after our two young children, the house, the dog, and every other domestic responsibility, I was it. Usually it's the wife. Even if the wife is someone who once had a career, she is usually the one who drops everything to ensure the household runs smoothly; every day, there is so much to be done. In the affluent community where I lived, it seemed I was the only male who did not have a thriving career as a professional. I was disenfranchised. Frankly, I was lost.

I chose show business because I thought it would be fun. I reasoned that if I had to go to work every day, why not do something that's fun? If I had spent four years in medical or law school and hated it, in the end I would have been stuck. I would have been doomed to a life of misery. (How ironic that my logic would backfire on me the way it did.) But here's the thing with show business: it's a roller-coaster of ups and downs, and there's no way to control it. When you're up, you're working hard, bonding with coworkers, and making money. Then the project ends (as it inevitably does), and you're not working, you're alone, and you're without an income. I am not good with loss, but I stuck with this way of life for twenty-five years, thinking (hoping) my ship would come in at any minute.

I am not intrinsically miserable. I have always tried to do my best. I have never been afraid of hard work, or doing whatever it took to get the job done right. But, the results have been largely disappointing. Over time, the isolation of being removed from the work force wore me down. My natural response was to put my tail between my legs and do as the Universe instructed – go home. Eventually I stayed home, and misery grew like a stubborn fungus. It broke my spirit. After awhile, it became part of me - so much so, that I realized it would take a great deal of motivation and effort to purge it. I knew if I didn't, it would destroy me. I had no choice but to write this book.

I imagine we all have something we secretly want to do. It is not necessarily the thing we "should" do, the best career choice, the responsible thing, the lucrative thing, the thing our parents want us to do, or the thing that everyone else in our community is doing. We are not even sure it is something we are capable of doing; but, deep inside, we do know it is the one thing that will make us whole, and reveal our true identity. It is the greatest prize life has to offer. In my case, it was to write. I have always written stuff, from as early as I can remember. I wrote personal journals, poetry, and an occasional newspaper editorial (several of which had been published). I also wrote three screenplays: a thriller (which didn't thrill me), an action-adventure (which I never pursued), and a drama (which I never finished). I was always passionate about touching people through my writing, but something seemed to get in my way. I lacked a sense of entitlement to my passion, and I brushed it aside. I had convinced myself that the one thing in the world I really wanted was something I couldn't have, or do, or make a living from. And while for twenty-five years I suffered through the extreme highs and lows of a career in showbiz, my passion for writing gnawed at me daily.

When I was directing television, I experienced great satisfaction, especially during my years directing shows for the Food Network (I also love to cook, you see). During the occasional long stretches when the work was consistent, I was happy. But in television, change is always inevitable; management turns over, shows get cancelled, assistants get promoted. In the world of television, experience doesn't often count for much, so I couldn't even rely on my own experience to save me. The only thing I came to count on was, sooner or later - and it was usually sooner - I would be without work. It is unsettling to feel this way for too long. It makes you miserable, and eventually, misery becomes your companion. I have a running joke with my good friend Don, now a film editor who lives in Boston. I am always asking him, "When is *my* ship going to come in?" and we laugh. Our laughter is based on a principle of comedy known as "comedy through repetition." We have been laughing for many years.

It's not like the phone would never ring. Someone would occasionally recommend me for something, and I would consent to an interview.

"What's wrong?" Valerie would ask, as I returned from another disappointing meeting.

"I think I sabotaged the interview," I'd say.

"Consciously or unconsciously?" she'd ask.

"Maybe both," I'd reply.

"It seems like you're walking away," Valerie would say, analytically, the way she would so often, correctly, analyze my dreams.

"I think you're right. And, you know what? I'm tired of walking away. I want to walk TOWARD something." When I'd say this I'd realize that was exactly what I wanted, and needed, to do.

"Then write your book, and stop complaining about it," she'd demand (always the supportive one), before leaving the room abruptly, presumably to punctuate her words.

CANCER

My mother became an adult when smoking cigarettes was considered a healthy alternative to eating candy. Like so many others, she was physically addicted to nicotine, and her lungs sustained damage long before she knew she was slowly and systematically poisoning herself. Then, despite the published research, the warnings on the pack, and all the signs around her, she continued to smoke. She was in denial. She dismissed all the hype about the evils of smoking and their link to cancer.

When the phone call came from my brother informing me of the diagnosis, my initial reaction was one of anger. I was angry at my mother for refusing to heed the warnings about smoking. I was angry at her for her arrogance regarding cigarettes. I was angry at her for waiting too long to get a second opinion when her "bronchitis" didn't resolve itself. I was angry and wanted to let her know how I felt. I wanted to punish her. Fortunately, her oncologist set me straight. "This is not about punishment, or making your mother feel guilty," he told me. "It's about helping her get well." He was right. After he said this I broke into tears. When I finally calmed down, he told me that my mother's chance of survival was only thirteen percent – and I broke into tears, again.

I was not prepared for the ordeal that lay ahead. It was a cold, dark winter afternoon when Valerie and I escorted my mother to a private room in an old wing of New York Hospital. Valerie led the way, holding my mother's hand. I kept a few paces back and carried her tiny overnight bag containing simply a pair of silk pajamas and a toothbrush. My mother was cheerful, humming her way up the elevator, and commenting brightly on the spaciousness of her room. I was quiet, and cautious, and suspicious. I knew her chemo would begin soon. A cocktail of cell-destroying drugs would be pumped into her bloodstream as she slept. Three days later, we would take her back to our one bedroom apartment on Central Park West.

It wasn't long before a nurse arrived, then her doctor. On a silver tray was a large syringe filled with a white milky substance. Another large syringe lay beside that; this one filled with a yellow viscous substance. There was not much to talk about; even less that I wanted to think about. The doctor and nurse moved quickly, hooking up an IV and administering the poison that would attack the cancer. "See you on the other side, Mom," was all I remember saying, trying to show some bravado for her sake and mine. "Okay, weetheart," she said with a lilt and a chuckle. *This is my mom*, I thought. This is my mom. And I kissed her lightly on the cheek.

I cried as I drove through the park to our apartment. Valerie did everything she could to console me, but after my father died I developed a tendency to always expect the worst. This time was no different. It began as a persistent cough. Her doctor took an x-ray. The dark spot on her lung represented a bronchitis infection, he told her; with antibiotics it would clear up within a couple of days. He was wrong.

Valerie opened the sofa bed in the living room and we helped my mother under the covers. She slept, and slept, and slept. Occasionally, she would lift her head from the pillow and utter something incomprehensible.

At three in the morning, a car alarm blasted outside our window. It was still going an hour later. At four-thirty I called the police; hysterical, tired, and angry. "My mother just had chemotherapy, and a car alarm has been blaring outside my window for two hours. My mother is sick and needs rest." I described the car and its location. There was a long pause at the other end. I thought I was clear, and the desk sergeant understood. I even thought I detected a note of sympathy in his voice, even as he said there was nothing the police could do.

"Nothing?" I asked.

"Well, we can jimmy open the lock, but we're not allowed to enter the car or pop the hood," said the sergeant. "Am I being clear?" It sounded like he was implying something.

"Can *I* open the hood?" I asked.

"It's a free country," said the sergeant. "You can do whatever you like."

He instructed me to look out my window. A police cruiser was stopped beside the wailing car. An instant later it was gone. I threw on my winter coat and ran outside. Soon I was standing beside the offending car. I was not sure what to expect when I pulled on the driver's side door handle, but it opened. Presumably, the Desk Sergeant had instructed his men to jimmy the lock. I suddenly felt like part of a great conspiracy fighting against inconsiderate assholes. I reached inside and popped the hood. The alarm was deafening, but even with my head under the hood, I couldn't tell where the sound was coming from. I slid under the car. There were lots of wires and metal, but I still couldn't tell what was powering the alarm. Out of pure desperation I begin grabbing at any wire within reach, yanking it from the car. The alarm continued to wail. I looked under the hood and yanked more wires, tossing them blindly onto 82nd street in the middle of the night. I was frantic, but I didn't care. The cops were on my side. It was the most satisfying public service work I had ever done. Another bunch of wires twisted around my fingers; green, red, black, blue, yellow. I yanked hard, ripping them from their receptacles. This time the alarm stopped, and there was silence.

As I headed back to my apartment, I imagined the look on the asshole's face when he found his car in the morning, the entire electric system a mass of twisted wires in the middle of the road. For a moment I felt sorry for him. Fuck it. I was going to bed.

Both Valerie and I had work the next day. My mother assured us she would be fine, and promised to call if she needed anything. We reluctantly agreed to leave her, but decided to get home early, if possible. We did get home early, in fact, meeting at the mailbox at around three o'clock. When we entered the apartment, my mother was sitting up in bed.

"Mom," Valerie said, surprised to see her so alert. "How was your day?"

"Wonderful, darling," she said. "How was yours?"

"How are you feeling?" I added.

"I feel terrific. You know, I've been listening to the police sirens as they pass your building. Did you know they have a code - a way of communicating with each other over those things?" my mother said.

"What do you mean, mom?"

"They have these little pads on their dashboards which they scratch. Two scratches make a 'whoop, whoop.' That means, 'meet me for coffee and doughnuts.'"

"You think?" I asked, and all three of us started to laugh.

When her hair began to fall out she didn't buy a wig; she already owned two. My mother always had fine blond hair. In the late 60's she began to augment it with a synthetic "bun" that she'd pin inconspicuously to the crown of her head. A few years after my father died, her hair thinned to the point where she decided to cover it with a full-blown wig. She bought two of very high quality. When the one she was wearing began to look lifeless and weary, she would switch to her back-up wig, and toss the other in the washing machine. Her hair always looked fresh and bouncy, and most people acted very surprised if she happened to mention she wore a wig. She liked to call it her "hat." So it didn't matter that the chemo totally annihilated every hair follicle on her head. What bothered her was the rapid and total disappearance of her tiny nose hairs. She became increasingly sensitive to airborne particles, which caused her to sneeze more often than she was accustomed to.

Fortunately, after a year in and out of the hospital, the chemo eventually destroyed the cancer in her body. It would never return. Unfortunately, the chemo also fried her brain. On the night of her final chemo treatment, I sat in the dark beside her as she slept. For the first time ever, she looked small and frail. As the sound of police sirens rose from the street below, I thought about her hallucination – cops scratching out coded messages about donuts on the dashboards of their cruisers. *This is not my mother*, I thought. This is not my mother. I kissed her lightly on the cheek. The doctor said she had a thirteen percent chance of survival.

* * *

ON MAY SEVENTEENTH, 1998, Valerie and I had organized an 85th birthday party for my mother. Our dear friend Michael, who is a professional caterer, offered to take care of everything. He delivered the tables and chairs. He prepared a beautiful presentation of assorted fish, bagels, pastries, and fruit. He arranged for an omelet station. He hired attractive young women to serve and clean up. And Michael, bless his soul, arrived in his finest tuxedo, the spitting image of Humphrey Bogart - the supreme presence at *Rick's Café Americain*.

Once all the guests had arrived, (there were about fifty), I slid a half-folded piece of paper from my pocket and announced a toast. Everyone raised their glasses. Earlier, I had prepared myself for an emotional experience. Reading my speech alone in silence had made me sob. But now, in the presence of family and friends, I wanted to be cool and hold it together. This was not about me, it was about my mother, and anything short of a great performance would not do. Fortunately, as I held the page lightly between my fingers, it didn't rattle like a dry leaf in a hurricane. This was good.

I began: "Eighty-five years ago today, a star was born. And for forty-three years I have counted my blessings for the gifts you have given me, mom. Although I may not have inherited the greatest memory, certain things I do remember. First, I remember a resplendent childhood, brimming with absolute and unconditional love. It was a childhood almost too good to be true. My youth was like a dream, even though I was too young to know it at the time. But looking back, I now realize that you and dad had created the most glorious childhood for me, and I can't thank you enough. The problem is, as an adult, it's been a hard act to follow - especially after dad died. Honestly, even after 28 years, waking up in the morning has never been the same. Fortunately for me, Valerie, John, and Emily's daily love and support have been filling the gap remarkably well (and it does get a little easier every day). But in 1970, when our world suddenly collapsed, Mom, you did not collapse, despite all your pain and heartache. You kept us going and taught me that life if not always fair, but it's all we've got. And we proceeded to make the best of it. I've carried that lesson with me ever since.

"I still don't know how you managed to put me through college, (another gift which will always mean so much), but you did, and made it seem so effortless – though I know it wasn't easy for you.

"Most off all, Mom, you never forced me into anything. You never said, 'You must be a doctor, or a lawyer, or a businessman, and make a lot of money.' I suppose that, as an artist yourself, that was never your priority. Instead, you taught me patience, understanding, and independence. You always encouraged me to follow my heart, but made it painfully clear it was my job to find it – never an easy task. Maybe that was a little too idealistic for this world. But when I think of everything I now have in life, I suppose it's worked just fine. And the wonderful thing about following your heart is that you're never really sure what's just around the corner. It's frustrating, even frightening sometimes, but there's also something extraordinary about it.

"When I think of all you've done with your life, I'm always left with a feeling of amazement, wonder, and pride. It's almost as if you were born to make the world a more beautiful place, which you have, as a gifted young dancer, an accomplished singer, as one who has created beautiful works of art out of simple wire and colored glass beads, as someone who has written three books, all the while carrying yourself with grace. I'm sure the question on everyone's mind is: 'How does she do it?' I think for you it just comes naturally.

"You and I were always able to talk about anything. You made me feel comfortable. You were never out to judge me. I never had the fear of reproach. Without a father, you were the one who taught me about the birds and the bees. You never actually said anything explicit, but you were a great sounding board, and somehow I knew what the twinkle in your eye was trying to tell me. It's true, no matter what I said, you made me feel that I was safe. And I never lied to you: except three times. And I'm going to tell all now... Unknown to you, I did get my motorcycle license (with Rex as my accomplice). And remember that 'plant' you found growing in the front yard? I lied about that. It didn't belong to a friend. It was really mine. And the time I came home from Cohen's house, sick as a dog and throwing up all night? It wasn't the result of a bad Oreo cookie like I told you. It was my first time experimenting with Gin (lots of it). Everything else I ever told you was true. I swear.

"When I think of you, I think of a winner; someone who embraces all that is good and decent and beautiful in this life. You embraced my father, who was a good and decent man, and you won; you embraced an artist's passion, creating beautiful pottery and beaded flowers, and you won; you embraced all those troubled girls, total strangers: you nursed them, nurtured them, saved their lives; and you won. You embraced life, just as a deadly cancer was staring you square in the face, and you won. If ever there were a definition of a survivor, you are it.

"As your son, you have taught me so many important lessons, and enriched my life in so many ways. You've freely loved the people I've loved: my wife, my kids, my in-laws, my friends. Most of all, for better or worse, you have let me be me; which has not always been easy for me, but it's pure and genuine, and that's what my love has always been for you: pure and genuine.

"In my entire life, I have only a single regret... that I wasn't there to see you sing to Dad on the night you first met – because that's where it all began; that's when he fell in love with you. I wasn't there to see it, but I often imagine the magic of that evening, and remain always grateful that fate played its part - for my benefit, and the benefit of everyone gathered here today.

"Happy Birthday, Mom. I can never repay you for all you've given me, but I can, and will, keep telling you how much I love you. You are my inspiration. You truly have been, and will always be, my shining star."

AT RISK

SUDDENLY, I HAVE A FEELING in my gut; it is time to conclude this manuscript. Suddenly I am gripped with an unfathomable fear. It is the kind of bottomless, inescapable terror one feels when reaching the end of the line. I have pushed all my chips into the pot. I am all in. And so I am filled with dread, dizzy, like a wingless bird on a high wire. What if my work is ill received? What if the reaction is: "Who cares?" What if I discover I've just spent the last two years of my life putting it out there, and no one gets it? What then? What will be my options? Do I brush myself off and commit to another year of speculative writing on some other (less personal) topic? Do I look for a job in TV, despite the fact that the last thirty years have produced only marginal success (in my opinion)? What are my outside qualifications? Do I go back to school and learn a new skill or get a degree which may, after several years, result in only negligible financial or emotional reward? As I write this, I am glaring over the edge of a precipice, into the darkest of voids. Yet I know I must take this to its ultimate conclusion. All I should consider now is the final "period" of the last page, and nothing more. And only after the finished text has sufficiently seen the light of day should I consider my destiny. But it is way too easy to lapse into this state of "what if." This was inevitable. It is my showdown with fate; one I always knew would come, someday – the one beyond my power to avoid.

My father was not around to give me real world advice. My mother was an artist, and artists do not live in the real world. In a way, artists never grow up. They remain children, stuck in a world of fantasy and wishes. They view life as one giant, never ending playground where everything in life (love, money, health, security) takes care of itself. My mother was my role model. While there is a certain beauty to this paradigm, it offers little help in finding your way in the real world. But I don't blame anyone for my situation, except, well, maybe I blame Jeanette Lipmann, just a little.

I remember once expressing interest in becoming a doctor. Jeanette Lipmann, my mother and I were in the kitchen discussing the possibility.

"It's very hard to get into medical school right now," she explained. "Even if he has what it takes, there are so many doctors. It's difficult, extremely difficult." Jeanette said. She addressed my mother directly, as though I were not even present in the room. "Medical school is only for the brightest of the bright." She was clearly implying that I was neither smart nor hardworking. "If he insists on entering the medical profession," she continued, "then he should get his degree in pharmacology: it might get him in through the back door." While she uttered these words without malice, it was a thoughtless remark that wreaked havoc on my young psyche, and effectively kicked the legs out from under my budding self-esteem. After that, I presumed I was not good enough to get anywhere through the front door (it would always be through a dark alley and a back door), and I adopted two seriously flawed assumptions about myself; first, that I was not smart enough to be a doctor, and second, that if ever I were fortunate enough to graduate from medical school, it would be too late; by then the world would have all the doctors it needed, and I would be left holding the bag. I was convinced the person just ahead of me on the job line would be the last to get in the door.

I would have graduated medical school in 1981. Since then, I imagine not less than twenty million doctors have entered the workforce. I would have easily slipped through the door - the front door. Unfortunately, on that fateful day, that conversation affected me in such a way that any door to a career in medicine was forever slammed shut.

I entered a liberal arts program my first year in college. I was basically following my mother's career advice to find something I loved to do. It sounded so right. But, since I didn't know what I loved to do, I hoped a liberal arts education would expose me to a variety of things so that, after a few semesters, I would be drawn to something; then I could choose. Some of my friends were attending college to prepare them to enter their father's businesses. Others were on a course of pre-law or pre-med, because their fathers were doctors or lawyers.

THE SPIRITS AMONG US

The moment had finally arrived. A confluence of events made it possible for me to uncover a priceless piece of my family's history. Butterflies fluttered in my stomach; anticipation mixed with uncertainty. I removed one of the worn out, time-riddled LP's from the stack and carefully rocked it onto the stem of an old turntable. The orange "Duo phone" label read, "Santa Ana Cruise, 1947." I slid the speed lever to 78 rpm, adjusted the volume, and switched on the record player. The amp responded with a low "hum." The LP began to spin. Then, ever so carefully, I lifted the arm and set the diamond needle onto the first grove.

"How long has it been since I've done this?" I wondered aloud.

* * *

A few weeks earlier, my brother had sent me several original stock certificates he discovered while cleaning my mother's apartment. I planned to have my financial advisor sell them. I didn't expect them to be worth much. The certificates were odd lots of less than a hundred shares of several obscure companies. It was even questionable if the companies were still in existence, particularly because the certificates included 49 shares of Enron (remember Enron?).

Nevertheless, the image of Rex cleaning out my mother's cabinets reminded me of the old recordings she kept. These were original recordings my parents had made at home, long before the advent of the tape recorder, on a device called a Duo phone. It actually cut grooves into blank vinyl-coated disks at 78 rpm, creating LP records. The Duo phone was cutting edge technology at the time, and few households owned one. It seems my father was an early adopter like me. Early Adopter: from the Latin earatos opturos, meaning someone who opts to obtain all the latest electronic devices exactly two seconds after he hears about them, thereby paying full retail and inheriting all the intrinsic flaws associated with leading edge electronic devices when first introduced. Today, this would refer to gadgets and services like MP3 players, digital cameras, HDTV, cell phones, and satellite radio. Welcome to the Modern Age, where so much of what once defined a generation has been replaced; LP's with CD's, penmanship with fonts, reading with books on tape, rakes with leaf blowers, "ET" with "War of the Worlds," restraint with recklessness, house calls with waiting rooms, creation with consumption, honesty with deceit, wonderment with shock value, thoughtfulness with stupidity, collaboration with competition, and music with noise. It makes me sad. We don't even communicate by talking anymore: we send emails - which often leads to a great deal of miscommunication. Comedians have a hard time getting a laugh without infusing at least fifty percent of their act (or movie) with the words "fuck" and "pussy." Why is this so funny? Why is everyone abandoning the English language? I cannot help feeling at least somewhat accountable for all of this. But in the collective spirit of our enlightened, "Age of Aquarius" generation, I have to wonder if we were truly aware, as we moved ahead, that we were leaving the melody behind?

One of my mother's cabinets in particular, I remembered, stored recordings of her performing songs from her vaudeville act. There were also recordings of me and Rex singing Christmas and Hanukah songs when we were young; perhaps two and four, respectively. I had a vague recollection of hearing some of these recordings, but that was many years ago.

I decided I would try to preserve whatever I could by transferring the recordings to CD. The biggest hurdle would be to get my hands on a record player that could play back at 33 1/3rd, 45, and 78 rpm. I also needed a cable to connect the turntable to my computer. I hoped Rex would find the LP's, and that he would find them in good condition. I could take care of the rest.

* * *

I FIRED UP my computer and paid a visit to eBay. Within about a minute I found a record player to suit my needs. Although I could have saved twenty dollars by bidding against the current auction price of $59, I decided not to waste any time and purchased it for the "buy it now" low price of $79.

Next, I dialed my brother.

"Rex?"

I told him my plan.

"It sounds like a good idea. I'm not sure what I'll be able to find, though," he replied with some trepidation.

"Look in that cabinet where she keeps her old press clippings."

My mother had collected hundreds of magazine and newspaper clippings from her years as a vaudeville singer and dancer, including reviews, interviews, ticket stubs, photographs, head shots, and other publicity dating as far back as the 30's and 40's. Because I grew up with her scrapbooks, I always took them for granted. But they were really a fascinating chronology of my mother's show biz career. Many of the clippings had grown yellow and brittle with age. It seemed the slightest disturbance might turn them to dust. I was fairly certain my mother's old recordings could be found here.

Several days later, on Superbowl Sunday, Rex made an appearance at my house. Tucked under his arm was a dozen old LP's. My mother was on his other arm. I hugged her then helped her into the house. I hadn't seen her since the big Thanksgiving Day celebration we had here about two and a half months ago. Too long between visits, I thought. But, at 93, she doesn't get out much anymore, and neither have I since the problem with my hip began.

"Hi Mom, you look great!" I wasn't lying; she did look great. If you want to live a long life, you've got to have a good attitude. My mother is living proof. She has always had a good attitude - about everything.

"Hi, darling," she said, and added, "Ooh," as she hugged me, "it's so good to see you." Does she remember my name? Here comes Valerie and the kids. Will she remember their names? I didn't want to test it. It didn't matter. Besides, my mother is such a good person, even if she realized she didn't remember our names, she wouldn't give it away. If old age had strapped her with some dementia, her brain still had the ability to spare others from her deficiencies.

The kids hugged and pawed her. The dog howled and pawed her. Somehow, Rudy, who was two and a half, remembered my mother from the days he used to roll around on her bed as a puppy. Ironically, the dog hadn't seen her in months, but he knew exactly who she was.

We spent the afternoon having fresh bagels and coffee; Valerie valiantly working to catch my mother up on recent events. This takes tremendous patience. I have tremendous difficulty with it. My mother has been without a short term memory for many years. It would seem that losing the short term memory is something which happens gradually, over time. But, I could swear, when it happened to my mother it was like a switch. My mother now has a retention rate of about twenty seconds. Her memory seems to slip through a sieve, as though some part of her past never existed. This is why I stopped phoning her. Our conversations would go around and around. The repetition would weaken and eventually defeat me. I could no longer stay on the line. I am not that strong.

I spent the days following their visit preparing to transfer the LP's to CD's. The record player I purchased on eBay arrived in excellent condition. I also installed some software on my computer which promised to clean up unwanted clicks, pops, and hissing sounds inherent in old records. And I found the appropriate "phono to mini" cable which connected the record player to my computer.

I choose an LP at random. The moment the needle hit the groove, I heard a man's voice. It was clear and resonant. He seemed to be narrating a home movie being projected onto a screen in someone's living room. His words were deliberate, yet playful. His voice had the quality of youth. And, I detected more than a tinge of a New York accent.

"This is a commentary of our trip to South America, during the months of April and May, in 1947," the voice announced.

Who was doing this commentary? I recognized my mother's mellifluous and dulcet tones in the background. It, too, sounded young - like a little girl. I did the math, noting that in 1947 she would have been only 35-years-old.

The narration continued, "Here you see the relatives, as per usual, saying goodbye to us on the ship, and probably wishing they were going with us. Oh, what a wonderful day this was."

I strained my ears, hoping that listening more closely would help me identify this mystery voice.

"Here we are, at the saltwater pool. Virginia's got the camera, now... That's really living, though: Just sensational... Here I come with my new swimming trunks. Johnny "Weissmuller" Nathanson... This is a damn site better than selling dresses, anyway."

I took a gulp of air. My father! Is it possible? It had to be him! I hadn't heard his voice in over thirty years, and I don't remember him sounding like this. But it had to be him. I closed my eyes and there he was. Tears slid down my cheeks. I never expected this. He sounded so young. Amazingly, at the time of this recording my father was five years younger than me. I looked over at Valerie, who was with me in the room. She, too, was sobbing. Let the river run, I thought. And I did. We both did.

After recovering from the initial shock, Valerie and I talked about how priceless this recording was. Then we played it several more times. My father is speaking for nine minutes and thirty-six seconds. It is now on compact disk, and should last another hundred years. I will keep it in the drawer of my nightstand. This way it will be safe. It will be accessible so I can play it whenever I want. It will be close to me at night.

I held the CD and labeled it with a blue Sharpie: "John Herbert Nathanson, Santa Ana Cruise, 1947." I noted today's date. It was the thirty-fifth anniversary of my father's death.

MINING THE AGES

I HAVE DISCOVERED something. This is important, I feel, because there have been few times in my life - this possibly being the only one - when I have flashed on something which resonated as truly wise, as of the ages. It certainly didn't originate in my modest intellect. It ran through me like a radio wave at a time when I just happened to be listening. So here it is: The more you care for something, the more you love it. When this thought first occurred to me, it seemed quite obvious and silly. The epiphany here is that the majority of us have it backwards, and this is a mistake.

I think of it as a garden. You begin with a square of ordinary dirt. You add dry seeds or young seedlings that will perish without the proper attention. You want your garden to flourish, so you carefully plan to supply the proper food, water and sunlight. Nature is not an exact science, so along with your daily attentiveness to the needs or your emerging creation, you begin to feel empathy. And with every tiny indication of life, until the time your garden is thriving, you are feeling love, unless, that is, somewhere along the way you lose interest and turn your back on that little plot of earth, at which point love or the potential for love is lost. This concept can apply to most things; a house, a painting, a pet, a newborn baby, an ill or dying friend, even a book.

Any book, like this one, begins with an ordinary blank sheet of paper. I add ideas, which will easily perish without the proper attention. I want this book to flourish, so I carefully supply it with the proper words, punctuation, and imagery. It is the caring that generates the love. Love is the reward for caring. Unfortunately, things get confused when it is perceived the other way around. When you think of love coming first, then caring is an obligation. Obligations often cause resentment. This, in turn, poisons the love. How many countless relationships have ended due to this backwards logic? How many pets abandoned? How many gardens have turned to dust? How many books left unwritten? So here is my advice: care for something or someone as deeply as your soul will allow. Protect it, nurture it, and "water" it without thought to yourself, and a love will grow inside you; a love as complete, pure and unadulterated as the driven snow. As John Lennon once said, "In the end, the love you take is equal to the love you make."

AT LAST

Truth is such a precious commodity in life - and there is so little of it. This will probably never change. Call it an unfortunate universal truth. I hope that in reading this book you take the time to think about truth; about how much (or how little) of it there has been in your life. It's a harsh reality. Truth takes courage. Truth requires integrity. It involves putting your neck on the chopping block and sometimes getting it cut off. Truth is an act of faith. But without truth we can't have trust, or honor, or community, or friendship. Without truth, the world is an impossible place for virtuous souls to survive. It is a place of ruthless deception - a ruse. It is a place of dysfunctional, if not defunct, value systems. It is a world of fear.

My life has been closely linked to a well-known cliché. It goes like this: when you're young, you think you're going to live forever. It's been this way for fifty-two years. I've lived mostly with abandon, and without a plan. I've acted on intuition. I've not labored with most decisions, big or small. I rode the wave. My life was a story without a plot. Then, one day, I wake up and can actually see the end of the tunnel; I'm much farther on the other side of life to waste precious time. I must make decisions that will have the most positive effect on the next flash of time, the shorter one. I look at the past thirty years, the ones from age twenty to fifty, and wonder where they went, what I did. I look at pictures, telling me where I've been, and sometimes even the picture is not enough to restore the memory. But pictures don't lie. I decide to believe what I see; that this is the truth. Sometimes, connecting with old friends helps.

I've also become a classic insomniac; awake all night, catching bits of sleep in the morning. I am not on schedule with the rest of the world, or at least the greater part of it. And it's funny because in the darkest part of the night, when my head is flushed in the clash between weariness and wakefulness, I wonder: am I unable to sleep because I'm thinking of my life, or am I thinking of my life because I'm unable to sleep? Either way, it is a long and lonely night. But it's not always a bad thing. Sometimes the night reveals how we are all connected. Here's what I mean: At three a.m. one night I was flipping through the channels and tuned into the middle of a documentary about the life one of my literary heroes, Charles Bukowski, who had recently passed away after struggling from leukemia. I watched intently as the film revealed intimate details of Bukowski's life through family movie clips and interviews. One of the interviewees was an attractive woman with beautiful strawberry-blond hair cut into a shag (a style like the one Jane Fonda sported in the movie, "Klute"). She was identified as Bukowski's wife, but nothing more. This woman looked vaguely familiar to me. She continued to appear throughout the documentary until I was certain I recognized her as someone from my past, and I began to suspect that she might be Linda Beighle – however unlikely.

In the final haunting scene, the woman is sitting beside Boukowski's gravesite describing their last moment together as he lay dying. A gentle breeze is blowing back her fine hair, and she hesitates now and then, trying to hold back tears. Then, her name fades onto the bottom of the screen: Linda Beighle, Mrs. Charles Bukowski. I am able to infer this: Shortly after I had visited Linda for the last time in Redondo Beach, she met Bukowski and they were married. I never imagined Linda to be the marring type - she could not be owned – but I'm glad that she married one of my true literary heroes; it makes me feel connected to something larger than myself.

When the documentary ended, I opened my notebook to write. I often have luck when I try to write in the middle of the night. If it goes my way I can be wonderfully productive. If it doesn't, I sometimes find myself thinking: have I had enough of this place? Is it no fun anymore? And I wonder if my thoughts are real, or just the delusions of a tired mind. And so I wrestle with the past and the future until dawn.

While I was writing this book, I had a reading with a famous psychic named John Edward who claims to be in contact with people who have died. When I was a young (unofficial) member of the Occult Book Club, I was fiercely convinced of the existence of spirits. Now, I'm surprised at what a skeptic I'd become. But, during the reading I'm told that my father is present. The psychic attempts to validate this by telling me things only my father would know. He tells me that my father was in the dress business. He tells me when my father died. (Both of these facts, I'm thinking, are potentially available on the internet; although I couldn't find them the following day, even after hours of searching). He tells me my father had an ulcer. (This truth, I'm thinking, is probably not available on the internet). He says that my father wants to know about the pictures of the Siberian huskies. At first I don't know what he's talking about. Then I realize it had to do with this book, and the chapter I was currently working on. In order to jog my memory about my trip to the arctic, I had dug up a stack of photographs I had taken when I was there. Those photographs were currently on my nightstand, and on the top of the pile were five or six shots of sled-pulling huskies. How could the psychic have known something so random? For a moment, I am reduced to the child I once was, when it seemed anything was possible. And I am happy, because it means everything is good, everything happens for a reason, everything is what it's meant to be.

I ask the psychic about reincarnation, and he says: "I believe we all come back, but it can take hundreds of years."

"Can we come back as animals?" I ask, because I sometimes feel I was a dog in a past life.

"I don't believe so," responds the psychic.

"Then, is it possible I was Abe Lincoln?" I ask.

The psychic quickly returns a "No…" then hesitates, and says, finally, "Well, maybe."

Thank you, John Edward.

* * *

I JUST WENT BACK and read the first chapter of this book. It's hard to believe that two years ago, when I wrote the first line, I was trying to explain why I had felt miserable for such a long time. By the act of writing, I stumbled on the answer, and that answer is you: for what is a song without someone to hear it? What is a painting without someone to admire it? What is a rose without someone to smell it? I am still not a miserable person, never was, but more significantly, I no longer *feel* miserable.

I have experienced other profound changes, too, which are inextricably tied to the death of my father. I have spent my entire life trying to protect my mother's feelings by avoiding all confrontation, and diffusing all potential volatile situations. I would not dream of disagreeing with her, about anything, whether what to have for dinner, or who to vote for president. Who cares, anyway? What is so damn important?

Here's something else: I am always trying to anticipate the worst thing that can happen in any given situation. Among other things, this has made me an excellent driver. When I approach a green light, I look for the car which is, for whatever reason, running the red light at the intersection. When I pass another car on the left, I always accelerate quickly past their blind spot; acknowledging possibility they might switch lanes without looking and run me off the road. When I back out of a parking spot, I always do it slowly, recognizing that a child or animal may have wandered behind my car the split second I glanced away to tune the radio.

THE END

I REALIZE this story is not complete, and feel compelled to find answers to the questions I posed about my parents at the beginning of this book. I am at a disadvantage, as it is now impossible to hear stories directly from my father's lips. At least I still have my mother, and this gives me hope, despite the fact that she seemed to have begun losing her short-term memory about two years ago.

This wouldn't pose a significant problem because I was around and paying attention for most of that. But her memories from fifty, sixty, seventy, and even eighty years ago were still very much intact - the last time I checked. I have spent two years writing about my life, and the details of my mother's past belonged here.

I decided on a series of focused interviews to unearth what still remained in my mother's long-term memory. I was confident that, in a few weeks time, over the course of several lengthy sessions, I would have enough good material to enrich the first chapter of this book. I spent a week making lists of things that I was curious about. I wrote hundreds of pointed questions and ordered them to help stimulate a fluid dialogue between us, rather than a rat-a-tat-tat of random questions. I bought a good digital recorder, a microphone I could clip to her pajamas, stacks of yellow legal pads, and several boxes of black roller-ball pens. I brought a box of chocolate covered cashews; something, I remembered, she used to treat herself to when I was a boy. I had become desperate to learn everything I never knew about my mother's (and father's), past.

At the first appointment, we sat at my mother's kitchen table with steamy mugs of Lipton Tea and a dish of chocolate covered cashews. I laid out my research-gathering materials, clipped the mike to the label of her pajama top, removed a new pen from the box, switched on the recorder, and took a deep breath.

My mother wasn't looking my way. She was staring into the distance and smiling softly. This was an encouraging sign. Her mind was already fast at work, primed and ready to flood my notebooks with anecdotes and memories; to fill the beginning of this book with drama, and emotion; to fill my life with new meaning. Before even one word was uttered, I was thrilled beyond words. I scribbled the date at the top of the page and noticed my hand was trembling. This was my last chance. When my mother was gone, she would take the answers with her. What I didn't draw out of her now would be lost forever. This exercise was far more important than I had imagined, and I was trembling.

"Shall we begin?" I offered.

"Of course, darling."

I fumbled for my notes - the questions I spent weeks preparing in advance. I had compiled an assortment of my mother's keepsakes: Faded Civil War era tintypes, press clippings yellow with age, charms hanging from a bracelet, a silver money clip engraved with the initials JHN, an antique pocket watch, a greyhound racing form from Sarasota, Florida, an eclectic collection of demitasse cups, an Art Deco perfume bottle. Each item had a story to tell, concealed within a deep wellspring of a past to which I had never been privy. Each is capable of sustaining an entire novel of its own.

My mother is ninety-four. Behind her on the breakfront is a black and white photo of her, taken when she was a young vaudeville starlet. Now, by comparison, she looks so old and disconnected. But her spirit has not faded. It's the same as always.

I decide to orient my mother with a few simple questions about current events, hoping it will help ease her into the past.

"Mom, do you know what the price of gas is?"

"I haven't the faintest idea."

"Take a guess."

"I can't"

"Why not?"

"I just can't"

"You can't guess."

"No."

"Just pick a number between one and ten."

"I can't"

This is futile and frustrating. If she can't pick a random number between one and ten, how is she going to be able to describe the details of her life? It didn't seem possible. I decide to alter my approach. Maybe her long-term memory is still intact. "Do you remember what year you were born?"

"I haven't the faintest idea."

"You don't?"

"No. How old am I?"

"You're 94, Mom."

"I am? That's impossible."

"I swear. You turned 94 in May."

"I can't believe it. Really, I'm that old?"

"You're a young 94, Mom."

"How old am I?"

Maybe she was tired.

I went back a second time, months later. This time she didn't recognize me. She sat at the table and stared into space. I squirmed. Suddenly I was back in Omaha, thirty years earlier, watching her in my rearview mirror as I left for California, desperately wanting to turn back, cancel the trip, and return to the security of my mother's company. But now, as then, there was no turning back.

"Do you remember the Happy Hollow Country Club at Christmastime?" I asked.

She thought for a moment. "No. No I don't," she answered. Her voice was ethereal. It reminded me of my Aunt Irene when I last saw her in the nursing home. Is my mother going to die soon, I wondered? There was no point in continuing the interview. Answers would not be forthcoming on this day - perhaps never (I suspected never). Desperate as I was to bring my mother back, to return her to a time of remembrance, in my heart I knew the time for that had passed. I pitied myself. I pitied my children, and my children's children, and I blamed myself for dropping the ball on our living history.

* * *

It took three months before I could admit to anyone I was writing a book. Following every admission, I inevitably received the same response: "Oh, you're writing a book? What is it about?" I felt like a fool because I felt I never had an adequate answer. Now that I'm almost finished, I am somehow finally able to respond with some certainty and conviction. The book is about finding yourself. Why I was unable to articulate this until now is a mystery to me, but I'm content with it now. When I began this manuscript I was miserable. Despite the fact I had so much, I felt lost and afraid. I knew that somewhere I had lost my way. I suspected it might have happened around the time of my father's death. Miraculously, like magic, the process of writing this manuscript has helped me recover much of what I had lost. Maybe not entirely, but I can honestly say I am no longer miserable. I've come to realize that to be an artist, and in my case a writer, is not a bad thing. It can be lonely, and frightening, and filled with uncertainty, but there are many advantages; you are your own boss; you have time to cook, read, exercise, take long walks, and sleep late when you want to.

I have made peace with myself. I am a writer. I do not live a life of quiet desperation anymore. I am a writer.

My hip is almost healed. I am awake. As Valerie pours the morning coffee, she suggests we renovate our house. "We've lived here for twelve years," she says. "Don't you think the place is getting a bit tired?" She places a mug in front of me. The early sun strikes the steam, allowing me to ponder beautiful, incandescent swirls of grey. It's a crisp, spring morning. Outside, tiny birds are showing up in numbers to flitter on budding branches.

"What kind of renovation did you have in mind?" I ask. Valerie proceeds to describe her "dream house." I listen as I peel a plump navel orange and separate its sections. Valerie seems to be describing an extensive renovation; one that would require tearing down a good portion of our existing home. She is talking about raising the roof, and increasing the footprint. I realize the kitchen I am presently admiring will no longer exist. "That could cost a million dollars," I protest.

"I know," she says. Then I remind her I don't have an income. "But I do," she retorts, adding, "With two years left on my contract."

"I don't need a bigger house," I tell her. I am thinking about all the work I've already put into this one, including all the time and money I've spent on basic maintenance.

"I want something grander," Valerie says. She is very good

at saying what she wants. I am not so good, but I try to articulate what it is that I want. Then I realize I already have what I want. "I want what I have," I say.

"Well I want something grander," she repeats, adding, "I work hard."

Valerie is right. She does work hard. And she has been the breadwinner in the family for the past several years. I consider that maybe she does deserve something grander in a house. Her words ring in my head - "I work hard" – and suddenly I know we will be doing a renovation on our house: a big, gangly, ambitious renovation. I cannot deny her, and I am already thinking about architects I know. I am fully on-board with the project. I am thinking about the renovation as a metaphor for my life. The more I look at it this way, the more it works. I begin to feel a need to do this renovation. I am a writer, and my own boss. I have the time. I will work hard. I will build this dream house for my wife.

* * *

EARLY THE NEXT MORNING Valerie was already sipping her coffee and reading the Style Section of the Times when I entered the kitchen. Tucked under my arm was this manuscript. I plunked it down in front of her. "It's finished," I sighed, with mild resignation. She looked at the thick stack of pages, her eyes widening at the pure physicality of it, and smiled. Then, looking as though she were holding back tears, she told me how happy she was for me. She also said I seemed different to her this past year; less angry, more confident, sexier. She was right. I *felt* different: not necessarily sexier, but definitely less angry, more confident. I hadn't made any money to speak of, but I was feeling like a wealthy man. The Muses, the Universe, my wife, my kids, had been lavishing me with riches all along. Completing the manuscript was like receiving a year-end bonus.

"What are you going to do now?" Valerie asks.

I suddenly realized what made me different; what, for so many years, was making me feel utterly disenfranchised from the rest of the world. It is nothing more complicated than this: I was trying hard to find myself but looking in the wrong places. Whereas some people require a job (an office, an assistant, a regular schedule, paid vacations, a title, business cards, an expense account, corporate retreats, office parties, a salary, and a bonus) to feel whole, all I need (and all I want) is a book of my own; a table, a lamp, a laptop, a pen, a notebook, a legal pad, a Muse, the words, the time (lots of time), the courage (lots of courage), and, finally, the support of my family. There was only one thing I could do after finishing this book.

"What are you going to do now?" Valerie repeats.

"Start another," I say, without hesitation.

"What's it about?" she asks.

I smile, then slip into my room and gently close the door.

* * *

DID I IDEALIZE my childhood? Perhaps. And when my father was taken away, I somehow believed that the thing I wanted most was something I could never have.

I was wrong… very wrong.

Not known to millions
Anonymous
Alone
Secrets unknown
I am not known
To anyone
But myself

FOUND

For the record, I am not a miserable person. Nor did I plan, scheme, wish, or hope ever to be one in my lifetime – ever. Yet somehow, this afternoon, as I sit in my tastefully decorated living room, gazing through my bay window at the whimsical dance of falling snow, I expect to be miserable - but I'm not.

My son is in his room studying for a chemistry test. He often studies hard before an exam; something I rarely did at his age. I give him a lot of credit, and I am proud of my son. I wonder why I am no longer miserable. Curious.

My daughter ambles through the living room. She looks lovelier every day. Wearing a bright smile, she plies me sweetly with a delicious kiss before rushing upstairs to her bedroom to finish a story she's writing for English. She's a fine writer with a remarkably creative flair. I like to think she's a little like me.

My beautiful wife is still at work. She will remain there long after dinner has been prepared, the dishes have been cleared, the kids are snug in my bed for an hour or so of reading, the dog arrives, and I kick the kids out of bed. My son goes to his room. My daughter usually stays. We finally fall asleep in a generous pile of down pillows and blankets, and fur. When my wife arrives she rouses me and steers our sleeping daughter to her own bed - something she will have no recollection of in the morning. After this, my wife slips into her pajamas. She is fast asleep in less than five minutes.

At this moment in time, I am happy. I have made it through another day. Everyone I love is under one roof again, safe. But I know, after a few restless hours, I will soon be fully awake, feeling my way downstairs in the dark. I will not rummage through the refrigerator for something soothing to eat. I will not flip through a plethora of bad television programming with the sound barely audible – those days are, thankfully, over. Instead, I will open my laptop computer and begin writing. This has become my nightly ritual. It has not been this way for long – only about two years now

– but I'm sure I have already grown to love it.

The dog will join me for awhile, on the lookout for a generous handout, no doubt, (I still rarely disappoint him), but, in time, he will head back to bed, where any sane human being (or dog, for that matter) should be at three or four in the morning. I will probably join him before sunrise, and sleep for two or three hours when the house begins to stir; the kids are packed off to school, my wife leaves for work, and I am alone to live yet another day. I expect to be miserable – old habits die hard – but I am not, and I think I know why: I'm no longer miserable because I have found myself. I begin thinking of all the things I need to do with the rest of my life – because it's getting late.

Since being diagnosed with a disease called Avascular Necrosis, I have had two surgeries to repair my dying left hip. Both procedures were traumatic, but it now seems I'll be pain free and mobile, with some adjustments to my prior active lifestyle.

Some things never change. I still take Lipitor. I still remember when my primary care physician told me I would have to take Lipitor for the *rest of my life*.

"I can't take a pill everyday for the rest of my life!" I protested.

"Why?" he said, calmly. "How long are you going to live?"

Now I know what my doctor meant. The rest of my life is not a very long time. So I take my medicine, every day, as prescribed, so that I might live to do and accomplish as much as possible in the time that remains.

I am aware that I "simply CAN NOT run anymore, ever" - my surgeon has made that painfully clear – so maybe I will immerse myself in golf, instead.

I was once miserable because I was lost. Then, in an attempt to find myself, rather than stagnate around the house, steeped in self pity for a life unlived, and languishing in despair, I decided to write this book.

Writing "American Departures" was my attempt to explore and re-examine some of the most emotional and memorable moments of my life – the life of someone born in the stormy eye of the baby boom generation, where childhood came easy, and growing up was hard to do. Baby boomers share a singular window in history. Although there are some variations in our collective experience - namely, when we were dropped on the planet, whoever dropped us, and where - we are all essentially the same.

I am overjoyed that you decided to continue reading; maybe writing this wasn't so dumb after all. That you have reached the end fills me with humility and pride. I feel like I'm holding a winning lottery ticket.

Honestly, I don't know why things turned out the way they did, but I'm grateful for everything that happened. I only wish it hadn't taken so long. This book took just two years to write. The problem is it took fifty years to start. That's far too long. But it's not over yet; there's still time for more.

As I write these final words, I realize that my life thus far was summarized recently when I cracked open a fortune cookie. The message inside read, "One should never wait for their ship to come in; always swim out to meet it." When I read this I laughed and I wept. It was clear; the waiting is over, and I know what to do... Begin.

The End

ACKNOWLEGEMENTS

I could not have adequately completed this book without the invaluable aid and support of my family, friends and relations who, throughout various stages of this manuscript, generously contributed their time to read and subsequently report back with honest, thoughtful, and insightful advice: Lea Oesterricher, Sherman Nagler, Carol and Brad Cohen, David Schaer, Sidney Schaer, Melissa Borher, Paula Rudofsky, Peter Kurth, Jessica and Gary Schaer, Randi Subarsky, Harriett Diamond, Sharon & Fred Nigro, Rick DiGregorio, Don Packer, Abby Boskoff, David Moss, Rickey Ashenfarb, David Levoff, Judy and Rex Nathanson, Adrian and Aaron Schaer, Lee Hoffman, Michael Travin, Mindy Goldberg, Barry Nathanson, Gerald Berger, Michael Student, Ken Krushel, Eric Arbitblat, Bob Fleshner, Daniel and Lois Compain, Marcy Lieberman, Zina Ricci and Martin Berger.

Thanks to the folks at BookSurge who assisted me with the physical production and design of the book: Roy Francia, Julie Burnett, Aaron Voelker.

Thanks to Rudy for his daily companionship.

Valerie, John & Emily, were it not for your unconditional love and faith in me, not one word of this would have been possible. Thank you.

Made in the USA
Charleston, SC
15 September 2012